GW00363554

NA SÁIRSÉALAIGH ABÚ

125 YEARS OF
LUCAN SARSFIELDS GAA CLUB

NA SÁIRSÉALAIGH ABÚ

125 YEARS OF
LUCAN SARSFIELDS GAA CLUB

AARON DUNNE

Saltwater

Lucan Sarsfields GAA Club links an historic past and a progressive present. The players of today walk in a proud tradition … a tradition that stretches back to the infancy of the Association, and one that also provides an inspiring base on which to march forward confidently into the future.

Dublin GAA Yearbook, 1972

Front cover image: Lucan Sarsfields football team that secured the Intermediate Football League in 1904. Back cover, main image: Lucan Sarsfields hurling team, 1915.

First published 2011

Saltwater Publishing Ltd
119 Lower Baggot Street
Dublin 2, Ireland
www.saltwater.ie

British Library Cataloguing in Publication Data.
A catalogue record for this book is available from the British Library.
ISBN 978-1-908366-01-6

Typesetting and origination by Megan Sheer
Cover design by www.sinedesign.net
Images © Lucan Sarsfields GAA Club and iLivePhotos.com

Printed and bound in the UK by the MPG Books Group, Bodmin and King's Lynn.

RRP €20

CONTENTS

ACKNOWLEDGEMENTS

First and foremost, I would like to thank our hard-working book committee members who have been instrumental in taking this very special and important project from an ambitious dream to a proud reality in the space of just eight months.

It was a truly Trojan effort, and special thanks must go to Paul Stapleton, Martina McGilloway, Don Dardis and Padraig McGarrigle, who conducted many of the interviews and who were pivotal throughout the process. Thanks to Liam Mulhall, Derek Quilligan, Ronnie Smith, Garry Beegan and Stephanie Quilligan for their assistance throughout. Also thanks to Mick Mulhall, whose meticulously kept club records and minute books provided the backbone for this book, and to Seamus Clandillon who compiled so much vital information.

A big thank you also to everyone who contributed to this project in any way, and especially to those people who gave their time freely to share their memories with us. These include: Richie Crean, Jack Sheedy, Tommy Carr, Declan Carr, Kevin Synnott, Mick Molloy, Barney Bannon, Eddie Waters, Mick and Kathleen Roche, Gerry McAndrew, Shay Hurson, Tracy O'Brien, Liam Ryan, Seaghan Ó Lanagáin, Jim Quinn, Mícheál Moylan, Tommy McCormack, Paul Heneghan, Sean Nolan, Pat Mulhern, Sean Flynn, Vincent O'Connor, Noel and Betty Flynn, Bob Dardis and Aidan Dardis.

A special mention also to everyone who shared their stories, photographs and memorabilia with us along the way. Many people, including Mary Gogarty, Paddy Smith, Joe Byrne, Jimmy Doyle, Pat Keane, Alan Higgins and Jim McCarthy provided a wealth of information. A special thanks to

Mick McGrath, whose archival records on the early years of the GAA in Dublin proved invaluable. Also thanks to the *Lucan Gazette* and to iLIVEPHO-TOS.com who have kindly given us permission to use their pictures.

Most importantly however, this book would not have been possible without the hard-working club and committee members who, over the 125 years since our club's formation, have helped build what is today the largest sporting organisation in west Dublin, one of the biggest GAA clubs in the country, and a club that today enjoys some of the finest playing and social facilities in Ireland. Hopefully this book does justice to their efforts, for which we are eternally gratefully.

On a personal note, as a life-long member, it really was a tremendous honour to be asked to compile this history on behalf of the club, and I would like to thank the executive for their trust in me and for allowing me the freedom to complete this project without hindrance.

We sincerely hope you enjoy the story of our club, and hopefully the next edition of the history of Lucan Sarsfields GAA Club will contain more than one tale of county, provincial and possibly even All-Ireland senior club championship glory.

Hope springs eternal, and the future has never looked brighter.

Go raibh míle maith agaibh,

Aaron Dunne

FOREWORD

A chairde,

When a group of members started to gather material for our club history, the stories, memories and photos poured in, enough to fill a few books.

Everyone was glad when Aaron came on board to collate and edit all this material and marshal it in order for a book. He has done a great job, producing an excellent book that everyone in Lucan will enjoy reading and all club members should be proud to own.

In 1886, when the club was founded, Lucan was a small village on the outskirts of Dublin with a population of 690. Now the population has grown fifty times. From a club that once consisted of one adult football team, it now fields seventy teams (from ages six to sixty) ranging from hurling, ladies and gents football to camogie. It also hosts many social, cultural and community events and it is *ag fás fós*.

It is great that all the material has been brought together (many thanks to the hard-working Martina) and is available for everyone.

Read and enjoy.

Ar aghaidh linn, na Sáirséalaigh abú!

Don Dardis
Uachtarán
Na Sáirséalaigh Leamhcáin CLG

ONE

1886-1948
A CLUB IS BORN

The crest of Lucan Sarsfields GAA Club may state proudly that the club was first formed in 1886. That, of course, is perfectly true, but the games of the Gael themselves actually go back way further than the club's formation in the picturesque west Dublin village.

While the GAA was formally founded in Thurles on 1 November 1884, the games we know today as Gaelic football and hurling date back centuries earlier. An early version of Gaelic football, known as *caid*, is widely reported to have been played in as early as the fourteenth century, while ancient stories of Cú Chulainn date the game of hurling back to even before that. Lucan's involvement with those early versions of the Gaelic sports date back as far, it seems.

In the Lucan Sarsfields' *Irisleabhar* (yearbook) of 1973, an unnamed local historian refers to games of caid being played as far back as the fourteenth century:

> There is ample evidence that football was played in Ireland long before the coming into existence of the GAA. In 1338, in Harris's *History of Dublin*, there is a reference to the game in his account of the severe winter of that year. He mentions that the Liffey was frozen for miles, from Dec 2 to Feb 10, and the depth of the ice was so great, people were to be seen running and playing football on its frozen surface.

The GAA, as we know it today, wasn't formally founded until 1884, but clubs soon began popping up all over the country, with the first major organised event being held in Thurles on Easter Sunday in 1886, with members from the five original Dublin clubs travelling in their droves (an estimated 15,000 people made the trip to Tipp) to support the players of Faughs, Dunleary, Davitts, Bray and Metropolitans. The success of the day sparked a revolution in the GAA in Dublin.

Some months later, on 12 December 1886, at the rooms of the Regular Carpenters' Society on Aungier Street, the new clubs that had been springing up around the county came together for the first time with the formation of the Dublin County Board. Amongst those initial twenty-six Dublin club representatives was N. Hughes of Lucan Sarsfields.

Four of these first twenty-six Dublin clubs formed since the GAA's formation – Faughs, Davitts, Metropolitans and McHughs – would go on to contest the first Dublin hurling championship in March 1887, while another fifteen, including Lucan Sarsfields, would contest the football championship.

Lucan were joined at that first meeting by delegates from St Patrick's in Kilmainham, Grocers' Assistants (Young Grocers), O'Connell Branch, Metropolitan Hurling Club, Dunleary, Feagh McHugh, Bluebell, Dundrum, Shankill, C.J. Kickhams, Freeman's Journal, Parnell GFC, Geraldines of Cabinteely, Green Flags of Chapelizod, Phoenix GFC, Killiney GFC, Merrion GFC, John Mitchels, Inchicore GFC, Golden Ball, Esmonds of Bray, John Dillons of Loughlinstown, Faugh-a-Ballagh (who were represented by the colourfully named George Washington and who remain in existence today) and Michael Davitts.

The inaugural Dublin Senior Club Football Championship was to be run over six consecutive Sundays in March and April, and Lucan were drawn to face Erin's Hope, the teacher-training college which at the time was located on Marlborough Street, in the first round at Elm Park in Merrion. Thousands travelled to the ground to watch John Mitchels of Glenageary take on Geraldines, Grocers' Assistants play Killiney, Faugh-a-Ballagh clash with Feagh McHugh, and in the day's final encounter, Lucan up against Erin's Hope.

GAA president Michael Cusack's own weekly newspaper of the time, *The Celtic Times*, carried a report from the game in its 19 March 1887 edition:

> This was a contest which attracted a large amount of interest, and the play was good on both sides. Immediately as the last two teams left the field, the Sarsfields, in green and gold, and the Erin's Hopes, in orange and green, entered it. There was great difficulty in distinguishing between one team and the other, owing to the similarity in colours, but one team left off their caps to obviate the difficulty.

The match between them, however, showed how practice and training could render one club superior to another of apparently equal calibre. The students had it mostly all their own way, though the Sarsfields made a few determined raids into the enemy's country. At the call of time the score stood – For Erin's Hope, 4 goals and 11 points, to 1 point for the Sarsfields.

There was certainly no disgrace in the somewhat one-sided result; that same Erin's Hope team went on to win out that inaugural Dublin Senior Football Championship with a twenty-point hammering of Grocers' Assisants (Young Grocers) in the final. Sarsfields kept their heads up, and later that same year, in November, *The Celtic Times* once again carried a report of a Lucan game, when they took on their neighbours from Chapelizod, Green Flags:

> Two teams of the boys of the emerald bunting journeyed by steam train to Lucan last Sunday to bring off a fixture with the Sarsfields. The ground, not withstanding the rain of Saturday, was in fair condition, and a rattling game was played between both first and second XXIs.
>
> In the first teams' match, the goal got by Floody for the Green Flag was the result of a pretty piece of play; while that got by Mahon, also for the Green Flag, was smartly kicked. The ultimate result was that the sons of La Belle Izod returned home victorious in both cases, after being heartily regaled by the Sarsfields.

Things were now up and running for the GAA in Lucan. Amazingly though, Sarsfields weren't the only club representing the area. By 1888, a second Lucan club had popped up, becoming officially affiliated with the County Board. O'Donnell Aboos are believed to have been founded in the Grangecastle area (then considered Lucan) by a group of *émigré* northerners, but they did not last long and had disappeared by 1892. Other neighbouring areas began to see clubs emerging also, with Balgaddy (then considered Clondalkin), Home Rulers (Saggart), St Laurence's (Palmerstown), Round Tower Volunteers (Clondalkin) and St Finian's (Newcastle) all becoming affiliated with the board that same year.

There was also no great mystery as to the origins of the Sarsfields club name. The great Irish hero is believed to have been born in Lucan some time around 1649, and became Earl of Lucan in 1690. He was a figure famed throughout the country, particularly in Limerick, as the site of his most famous military victory over William of Orange was in Ballyneety, but the new Lucan club certainly felt they had first call on the use of his name.

GAA clubs all over the country, and indeed in every province, still bear his name, from Armagh to Galway and Kildare to Cork. The most famous amongst them, perhaps, lies in the home of GAA itself and the host club of that first major GAA gathering on Easter Sunday 1886.

Thurles Sarsfields were founded in 1885, but not, as many believe, under the name Thurles Sarsfields. No record exists of the club's initial formation, as the club's own history attests, but it is believed the club was born from the ashes of a defunct football club, Thurles St Patrick's. In the years that followed its creation, the newly formed club, as is recorded in the newspapers of the day, went under the name of, quite simply, Thurles, and in the years that followed, the club was more often known as the Thurles Blues.

The club changed its attentions solely to hurling in 1887, but it wasn't until some time later that they took the Sarsfields name officially. With no other club in the country bearing his name and claiming an older heritage than Lucan's, the oldest GAA club named after Patrick Sarsfield is the one that resides in Lucan, County Dublin.

Lucan Sarsfields, represented at the board in 1888 by James Hanna, were by this time the only club serving the Lucan village area. Considering the relatively tiny population of the town at the time, the success of putting out a twenty-one-man team in the first Dublin championship had been some achievement. It wasn't just about the games themselves however, it was a movement which was almost always political in one way or another. In 1888, for example, according to the history of the Liffey Gaels GAA Club, players from Lucan Sarsfields marched in their jerseys alongside those from Henry Grattans, Round Towers, Home Rulers, Green Flags and T.M. Healys as part of the funeral march of Wolfe Tones (Bluebell) club captain Sam Payne, who had been killed in a collision on the football field in February.

By 1890, and thanks largely to an ongoing debt problem as well as the internal wranglings within the association, the GAA was in serious decline all over the country. Although Dublin was not suffering quite as much as other areas (fifty-two clubs still being affiliated in 1890) the board would soon begin to feel the pinch. The IRB had largely infiltrated the organisation at almost every level, and as a result the GAA was being closely watched by the authorities of the day.

The Catholic Church, who opposed the dances that followed GAA games and who were vociferously against the Irish nationalist leader of the time, Charles Stewart Parnell (largely because he was Protestant), were also beginning to cause problems for the association, which is why, in 1890, Lucan Sarsfields came to the attention of the national newspapers when a priest was elected as president of the club – Canon William Donegan, who was curate in Lucan at the time.

In November 1890, the Catholic bishops finally had the ammunition they had so badly wanted against Parnell, when it emerged that the politician had been having an affair with the now infamous Kitty O'Shea. Official Church condemnation came the following June (even the GAA's first patron Archbishop Thomas Croke came out against Parnell), but at a general meeting of the GAA in the Rotunda in July, it was decided that the association would not abide by the Church's wishes and instead would fully support Parnell.

However, before the disagreement between the GAA and the Church had a chance to reach a head, Parnell passed away. His funeral took place on 17 October 1891, and the Dublin GAA came out in droves to support it. Lucan Sarsfields were among nineteen clubs and an estimated 2,000 GAA members at the funeral.

They were tricky times for the GAA, but the organisation managed to get through the political mire that existed in Ireland at the time. By 1896, thirty-four clubs had survived to remain affiliated with the Dublin County Board (Lucan represented on this occasion by a J. Harris of Mount Joseph). Things were still difficult all over, but in Lucan, Sarsfields were planning a championship run.

Despite an unofficial protest from the Parnell Volunteers Club (they disrupted the semi-final clash of Young Ireland and Geraldines by lining the pitch before the game in protest at having had a goal unfairly disallowed in an earlier round), Young Ireland would win through to provide the opposition for Lucan Sarsfields, who had earned their place in a first ever (and to this day only ever) senior championship final. Young Ireland, renowned at the time for poaching players from smaller clubs, defeated a game Lucan challenge in the October decider by 3-7 to 0-3.

There was some consolation for Lucan though. As Dublin champions, Young Ireland went on to represent Dublin in the Croke Cup, and they had the pick of the county to call upon. They selected two players from the vanquished Lucan team, J. Gannon and R. Graham, to play with them. In a delayed final against Arravale Rovers of Tipperary, which wasn't played until June 1897, they emerged 0-4 to 0-3 winners. There might not have been a county title, but Lucan now had two national medals to show for their efforts.

The same two Lucan men would go on to represent the county (wearing Young Ireland jerseys once again) in the All-Ireland final. Unfortunately, a strong Limerick team would emerge as victors, on a 1-5 to 0-7 scoreline. They were golden times for the club, though a breakthrough county title win still eluded them.

By 1904, Lucan Sarsfields were playing in the intermediate ranks, but after a few years in the doldrums (compared to their status as senior championship challengers just eight years previously at least) they secured a famous win when they defeated Benburbs to win the Intermediate Football League. An interesting aspect of this particular win – despite the fact that it represented the club's first major title – was that the success had been achieved with the aid of at least five players from Balbriggan.

In 1902, a team called Balbriggan Wanderers had won the Intermediate League, and then, for some unknown reason, the entire club went out of existence. One of the players on the Wanderers team, Paddy Richardson, worked as a fishmonger and regularly attended the Dublin fish markets. At the market, he met up with Lucan Sarsfields club secretary Mickey Ashe, and with the assistance of another fish market worker, Tom Clarke, the Balbriggan men were persuaded to throw their lot in with Lucan. The league title followed.

That same year of 1904, the club's junior hurlers secured an historic double for the club when they won the county junior league. The team brought the Michael Smith Cup home to Lucan for the first time, but, rather amazingly, it would be another seventy years before the trophy would be seen again. There were two incredible links between those two teams (of 1904 and 1974). The 1974 team included Larry Downes and Des O'Brien, who repeated the heroics of their grandfather Mick Downes, who had been on the 1904 team. Club legend and long-time president Tom Slattery was in attendance for both games. It's hard to gauge which feat had actually been the greater achievement.

Slattery would serve the club for the best part of his life, overseeing the early rise of the club as a young man, and well into old age he still often managed to cycle the length and breadth of the county to attend games. He was a driving force. As the 1973 *Irisleabhar* proceeded to add:

The 1904 football team that secured the Intermediate Football League. Back row: R. Maher, T. Byrne, P. Richardson, J. Matthews, F. Braitsford, M. Merriman, J. Brien. Middle row: J. Fagan, J. Murray, C. Brien, G. Thornberry, T. Kelly, J. McGann, J. Fitzpatrick (president), J. Keogh. Front row: T. Clarke, M. Ashe (hon. secretary), M. O'Connor, P. Murray (captain), J. Kelly, M. Downes (treasurer), R. Kane (vice-captain).

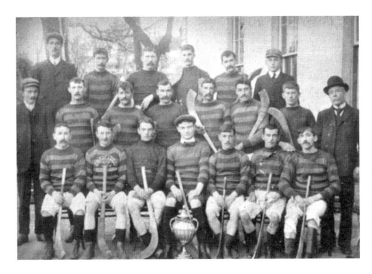

The 1904 hurling team that won the Junior Hurling League.

Lucan can claim to be one of the oldest junior hurling clubs in Dublin. Not really a hurling area, but with assistance from the local Garda stations and Air Station at Baldonnell, well poached by the old master himself, Tom Slattery, Lucan seldom, if ever, failed to turn out a team.

Another famous feat took place in 1906. The game of camogie had only been invented in 1903, but by 1906 Lucan was already celebrating success after defeating all-comers to bring the Junior League back to the club, securing a famous win in the county final in the Phoenix Park. Two years later, the club would win the Minor Camogie League. These were the first major successes for the camogie section of Lucan Sarsfields on the field, but they most certainly would not be the last.

In 1911, one of that successful Lucan senior team, Kitty Brady, would go on to represent the county in Louth against Dundalk Emers, and represent North Dublin in a Foxrock clash with Dublin South.

Meanwhile, that same year, the junior hurlers were drawn to play Crokes in the championship. Lucan did not figure in the competition, though, with newly elected Dublin County Board chairman Harry Boland (the War of Independence hero) and his club Rathmines defeating defending champions Naul in the final.

Records of the club at County Board level disappear for a time after this, but the 1973 *Irisleabhar* recalled a challenge game between long-time rivals Lucan and Leixlip on the Lock Road (the 12th Lock) in Lucan in 1914:

Lucan and Leixlip have always been the greatest of rivals. In the early 14th century they were contesting fishing rights of the Liffey in the courts of law. On a more sporting note, they were contestants in a football game played in 1914 on the Lock Road. Lucan won the contest and were captained by Tom Kelly, boilerman in the Hills at the time. In this 21-a-side game Lucan wore green and gold.

The 12th Lock was just one of several grounds the club used in the early days; there are also records of Lucan playing games in Bleach Green in Lucan Demesne (close to Weir View), in a field behind Vesey Park, on lands belonging to a Mr Hickey in Dodsboro, Mr Royce in Tandy's Lane, and Mr Kavanagh in Ballydowd, before settling into Langan's Field in Ballydowd in the early 1950s. Amazingly though, and largely coincidentally, Lucan Sarsfields would find themselves making a permanent home in the 12th Lock almost a century after first togging out there.

By the middle of the decade, the Irish political situation was reaching boiling point. As recorded in William Nolan's *The Gaelic Athletic Association in Dublin 1884-2000*:

Opposite: Lucan Sarsfields hurling team, 1915.

Left: Club legend Tom Slattery on his infamous bicycle.

The Easter Rising had enormous repercussions for the GAA in Dublin and countrywide. All games were suspended for three months and the GAA's official journal *The Gaelic Athlete* was suppressed … A Government commission established to ascertain the causes of the Easter Rising claimed that the GAA's policy of excluding military personnel was anti-British and asserted that the Irish Volunteers were practically in full control of the GAA.

In April 1918, conscription beckoned in Ireland as the battle for supremacy in the First World War reached a critical point. The GAA bitterly opposed its introduction. By July, the government had banned all public meetings that were being held without a permit, a prohibition that extended to all Gaelic games.

Shortly before the ban had been introduced, a clash had taken place between Lucan and O'Toole's players and police and military. According to Nolan's *History of the Dublin GAA*:

> On June 28 the police and military stopped a number of games in the Phoenix Park. The players from O'Toole's and Sarsfields clubs retaliated with stones and some of them were arrested and detained in the Bridewell.

Throughout the Irish War of Independence that followed, Lucan Sarsfields remained active on the field. In 1919, the club was drawn to face Sons of Erin in the Junior Football Championship and in 1920 they faced Portrane, while they also took part in tournaments in Celbridge and Leixlip, a tradition that would continue well into the 1980s. In 1920, the club even began a tournament of its own, hosting twelve teams from around the local area.

A major success had come for the club in 1919 too, when the junior hurlers won through to the league final to face St Cronan's of Bray on the hallowed soil of Jones' Road. In a thrilling game of hurling, Lucan emerged as one-point winners, with one particularly outstanding point from T. Graham (doubling a J. McConnell puck out over the bar) providing a particular highlight. It was another red-letter day for the club, but one that would be soured on the road back home to Lucan.

A mile or so into the journey home from Croke Park, the Black and Tans raided the team's tram to conduct a search, scattering playing gear all over the place. Thankfully, no one was hurt in the exchange and the Lucan team, and their supporters, safely reached west Dublin to celebrate the victory in peace.

Lucan saw silverware once again in 1921 when they secured a cup competition win. Once again, however, the political situation in the country served to spoil the party. Lucan stalwart Tom Slattery had travelled in to the Board as delegate to collect the winners' medals on behalf of the club, but shortly after the meeting commenced it was raided by the Auxiliaries and the Black and Tans. Everyone was evicted from the meeting while the Tans and Auxiliaries scattered books and documents all over the place. By the time the meeting had been reconvened, everything, including Lucan Sarsfields' winners' medals, which were suitably inscribed, had gone missing. Given the Tans' and Auxiliaries' fondness for sending home 'trophies' from Ireland in those days, it is quite likely that these same medals exist in a living room or drawer in Britain somewhere to this very day. Lucan just got on with things, however, and the following year they went on to win the same competition once again.

Lucan Sarsfields GAA, outside of mentions as an affiliate club in the County Board's records, all but disappears from significance in the 1920s. The only development that would have any bearing on the club would come in 1928, with the formation of the Cumann na mBunscol primary schools' competitions. And with the club's own minute books only reaching back as far as 1943, the first mention of the club anywhere between 1920 and the beginning of the following decade came in the form of a report from an important football league game in 1930.

A huge crowd descended on Ballydowd as Lucan took on Garda, one of the strongest teams in the county at the time, with Palmerstown referee Mr Cullen officiating. Shortly before the end of a hard-fought tussle, the game reportedly got out of hand and the referee was forced to abandon it.

The board decided to replay the game a few weeks later in Crumlin, and with a huge crowd in tow, travelling by both IOC Bus and Tower Bus Service, Lucan managed to pull off one of the biggest wins in decades,

The 1938 Junior Football League winners: J. Byrne, G. Mahoney, G. Behan, M. Meade, F. Brophy, Brady (ref), W. Heffernan, P. Dignam, T. Slattery, H. Condron, P. Condron, J. Brady, M. Crea, W. Malone. Front: M. Conway, S. McDermott, M. Tierney, T. Malone, W. Kelly, P. Slattery, F. Kavanagh, P. Nolan.

emerging 0-9 to 0-3 winners, thanks in no small part to a brilliant display at midfield from Ginger Cooper.

Following that victory, everything went quiet once again on the Lucan front, with no success to speak of. Listed as a rural senior club in the 1935 minutes of the County Board, Lucan were obviously playing at the highest standard but just failing to make the crucial breakthrough. A report from one of the players of the time, the late Jack O'Brien, in the 5 January 1975 edition of the *Lucan Newsletter* offered an insight into the state of the club at the time:

> My first game of hurling for Lucan was against a club called Droigeadoiri in March, 1936, at the ripe old age of eighteen years. Our president, Tom Slattery, was at the time, selector, manager, player, and aided by an old-time bicycle, conveyed hurlies and jerseys to the venue.
>
> Those associated with the hurling team at that time were P. and T. Graham, P. McCormack, M. Gannon, J. McConnell, all gone to their eternal reward, also Mr McCarthy of the old post office, where the club held its meetings. People say those were the good old days but I doubt this statement.

A first class hurley cost 5/-, a football 12/6, a hurling ball 3/- and jerseys 6/-. The average working man's income was approximately 30/- per week. It must have been a nightmare for any committee to run a club, the solidarity and dedication of those founders of Lucan Sarsfields must be admired and appreciated by every member of the present club. The Collins, Condrons and Malone families must be considered the oldest families associated with the club.

Not that the early '40s were any better. The 1973 *Irisleabhar* echoed the sentiment of Mr O'Brien, praising the early pioneers of west Dublin's oldest GAA club:

The leanest period came in the early 1940s, but men like Paddy Cormack, Michael Gannon, Paddy and Tom Graham, Mick Shanahan, Jack McConnell, all gone to their reward, who were ably assisted by Tom Slattery, T. Delaney, J. Kelly, J. McCarthy and J. O'Brien, by their unselfish efforts, ensured the old game was kept alive in Lucan.

The oldest surviving minutes of Lucan Sarsfields GAA Club date to July 1943, recording a meeting that took place in Gahan's Café attended by Frank Brophy (chairman), E. Moffett (secretary), Ned Commiskey (treasurer), H. Condron, T. Malone, G. Parsons, Billy Kelly, Charles Molloy, P. Slattery and Joe Dignam.

The veterans' football team of the mid-1940s, including W. Malone, K. Kane, T. Graham, T. Condron, F. Brophy, T. Horan, J. Buggle, M. Kilduff, P. Condron, J. Brophy, T. Slattery, J. Gleeson, P. Feeney, J. Dunne. Front: Poynton, M. Byrne, Major Kane, P. Buggle, J. McConnell, P. Murray.

A week later, at the club AGM, chairman F. Brophy set out the club's intentions going into the future. It was a watershed of sorts, changing the focus from the club's adult side to the rejuvenation of hurling in the club and the establishment of a minor side, as well as securing a ground of its own. The minutes read:

> The chairman explained that it was hoped to re-organise the club to include a minor team and later a hurling team. He pointed out the steps being taken to obtain a playing pitch and asked for suggestions from those present … Various suggestions were made as to getting a pitch, running weekly raffles, approaching the teachers and priest to have Gaelic games played in the school in order to re-organise the schoolboys.

At that same meeting it was decided to hold a benefit tournament that October in Mr Hickey's field in Dodsboro for one of the club's long-term servants, Tom Slattery. Teams from neighbouring clubs Erin go Bragh (Littlepace), Round Towers (Clondalkin), Leixlip and Celbridge Veterans all entered. The event was a great success, and so well known was Tom in the locality that the *Leinster Leader* newspaper reported on the event the day before, in its 16 October 1943 edition:

> An old Lucan Gael, who has finally decided to sever active association with the game, will benefit by next Sunday's attractive football bill at Dodsboro in Lucan. He is Mr Tom Slattery, for long years manager of the Lucan Sarsfields club (often unaided), and always ready to assist in the advancement of the Gaelic code.
>
> No one will deny that a benefit game is his due on the occasion of his decision to retire from active participation in GAA matters. Sunday's bill should see some good football. Sarsfields take on Erin go Bragh (a new team from Westmanstown); Round Towers (Clondalkin) meet Leixlip, and once again Lucan and Celbridge veterans will mix it to decide once and for all which is the better side.
>
> The last match should prove most exciting and the Round Towers–Leixlip affair brings old rivals together again in what should be a ding-dong struggle. The proceedings will be enlivened by the Lucan Catholic Boy Scouts' Pipe Band, and altogether a great day's sport is expected. The field of play has been kindly lent by Mr William Hickey.

Lucan football was enjoying something of a resurgence at the time, with the club's footballers having secured the Junior B League title in the 1942/43 season. The medals were presented at the club's first annual dinner dance (re-union supper) which was held in the Lucania Hall (the site of what is now the Topaz garage). The medals were presented by Ned Commiskey, club treasurer and owner of the Ball Alley Pub (where the club held many of their committee meetings at the time), and the music came from Miss Sheila Dunne's Band.

Interestingly, at a meeting in November, the club briefly considered changing colours and introducing a set of blue jerseys, the existing green and gold jerseys having been 'condemned' for their terribly worn condition. The club would play in these blue jerseys until February 1949, when they themselves had become 'dilapidated'.

There were two options for another new set: red and black or green and gold. Tony Delaney suggested he could supply fifteen green and gold jerseys with white collars for the wholesale price of £9, so it was decided to take up that option. The green would remain with the club from that point onward.

In May 1944, a Mr Patrick Blake approached the club to discuss the possibility of setting up a new GAA club in Balgaddy. Sarsfields suggested amalgamating the Balgaddy club's newly established committee, and after some discussion it was agreed to do just that. Mr Blake, accordingly, was co-opted onto the Sarsfields club committee. There were other discussions with surrounding clubs at the time, with Lucan seeking the rental of Spa Rovers Soccer Club's pitches in Ballydowd in 1944 – a request that was granted for the summer months.

In June, the club organised a tournament to raise money for the local church fund (the Lucan Branch of the Catholic Social Service Conference), with teams from Air Corps, Erin go Bragh, Green Flags of Chapelizod and Leixlip all attending. A second tournament, in aid of the local boy scouts, was organised for October, with Rathmoylan, Ardclough and Round Towers all attending. A tug-o-war was also held that day between Hill's Mills and Shackleton's Mill. They were busy times for the club, but financial issues were quickly coming to the fore.

In November of that year, the club faced another major challenge. A proposal for the formation of yet another club in the local area, St Mary's, came to Lucan's attention. It was decided to object to the proposed transfers of Michael Mahady, Liam West, Patrick Core, Patrick Slattery and Seán Graham, 'on the grounds that the Lucan Sarsfields Club experienced difficulty in fielding a team and that the transfers had not been signed by the parties involved'. A week later, the committee resolved to:

...write to the Dublin County Board protesting against the proposed affiliation of a new team from Lucan on the grounds that it would adversely affect Lucan Sarsfields as regards players and that the promoters of the new club were not sufficiently well known to justify confidence in their ability to run a team successfully.

A week later, Patrick Core's transfer to Newcastle GFC was confirmed, but the other transfers were postponed until evidence from the players concerned was heard. It is unclear as to what eventually happened, but in a rather typical twist of fate, Lucan Sarsfields' B team, or second team, would be fixed to take on Lucan St Mary's twelve months later in Ballydowd. Whatever happened, that was the last record of the fledgling St Mary's club.

By early 1945, Lucan was beginning to develop a healthy relationship with Mr Langan, owner of lands in Ballydowd behind what is now the Foxhunter Pub, with regards to the use of his field for games. Fields in the 12th Lock and the Spa Rovers soccer field in Ballydowd were all the while being used for training.

Things were going well enough on the field too, with two teams togging out and Lucan's first side playing inter league and junior championship. By 1946, however, the club was on the verge of collapse, after being hit with a series of hammer blows.

A meeting at the Grand Café in October 'was held in connection with

Lucan Sarsfields hurling team, 1947.

reports that certain players had applied for transfers to other clubs and to decide whether the club would continue in existence as a result'. Lucan weren't in a position to oppose any of the requests and so were forced to acquiesce. Some weeks later, Henry Condron lined out for the St Brigid's senior team.

In the meantime, Lucan had suddenly and unexpectedly been denied the use of Ballydowd by the landlord. The Green Flags club from Chapelizod had also been using the ground, and after Lucan approached Mr Langan to find out what was going on, the club was informed that Green Flags were now letting the grounds and that Lucan would no longer have the use of them.

These were desperate times for the club. With Ballydowd now gone, the club went in search of another field in Primrose Lane, but was denied the use of that too. Terms were finally reached with Green Flags and Mr Langan however, and although not exclusively, Lucan would at least continue to have some use of the field in Ballydowd.

By December 1947, the inevitable had occurred. Lucan Sarsfields had won their way through to a league final to face Green Flags, and, of course, the game was fixed for Ballydowd. Tensions were high going into the 7 December decider, but there would be no resolution of any sort that day. The game was abandoned 'towards the middle of the second half due to encroachment on the pitch by Green Flags supporters and threats to the referee', according to the club's minutes.

Clearly there was no love lost between the two, and the rematch took place in Crumlin three weeks later. Green Flags emerged victorious, and Lucan was denied an historic win against a team that had, by now, become their most bitter rivals. It was the latest disappointment in a seriously trying time for the club.

The hurling side of the club had been in a slump for some years too. In 1945, a separate hurling club was set up, with a host of committee members, including Tim Kennedy, M. Gannon, Paddy Cormack, Jack Kelly and the ever-present Tom Slattery, at the helm. Very limited in its success (outside of some veterans' games here and there), the club would not actually enter a hurling team again until the 1950s.

Current club president and long-serving club man Don Dardis recalls the state of affairs in the club in the late 1940s:

Towards the end of the 1940s the club was on its knees. Five or six of the junior team (the only team in the club at the time) had transferred to a neighbouring club, while the chairman and secretary had resigned due to work and domestic commitments. Some stalwarts remained, the Malones, Seán Smith, Jack Byrne, and the Nolans, amongst others, but it was fair to say the one who fought hardest to keep the club alive was Peadar Condron.

He set out to entice young players from the village and surrounding areas to play so that a team could be put out on the field rather than travelling with ten or twelve players and hoping to persuade a few others to tog out along the way. A few Garda from the local station and some lads from other counties who had come to work in Lucan also joined, so after a while a strong team was built up.

Peadar also worked hard with juvenile teams, played football and hurling, acted as selector, was delegate to the Junior Football Board, refereed matches, looked after the jerseys, marked out the pitches for games and acted as MC when singsongs started. He was the first to be awarded the Hall of Fame award [in 1994], and rightly so.

Another man who gave a lifetime of service to the club was Tom Slattery. From Tipperary originally, he played football but was mainly involved in the hurling from early in the twentieth century. He was a one-man committee from then until the 1940s acting as chairman, selector, board delegate and then president. He continued to attend games and support the club until he was nearly ninety. He would travel everywhere on his upright bike, which he also used as a prop at matches. The likes of him would be very hard to find.

Don took over as secretary and treasurer of the club in 1949, and as he recalls himself, the club was in dire straits, 'I remember at the start of the year, the club funds amounted to 8s 9d.' It was the equivalent to €0.43 nowadays. Thankfully for everyone involved, things were about to pick up.

The club marched in Dublin as part of the commemorations of the 1798 Rebellion in November 1948, and around that same time things finally turned a corner on the playing field front, with Palmerstown Gaelic Football Club, known officially as Clann Tig Guaire, agreeing to come on board in Ballydowd as co-tenants.

The teams would solidify the new relationship in December 1948 with a friendly game of football in Ballydowd (an amalgamation of the two clubs was briefly considered and opted against by Lucan in mid-1949), and from that point onwards the worst times were finally behind Lucan Sarsfields. The club would go on to take a giant leap towards the future in the months ahead.

PLAYERS OF THE ERA

Senior football championship v. Erin's Hope, March 1887: T. Kelly, A. Maxwell, T. Murphy, W. McCabe, P. Mangan, P. Flanagan, T. Lyons, M. Nolan, J. Nolan, L. Nolan, W. Cromer, P. Merriman, J. McGuire, T. Killis, J. Lawlor, P. Carroll, J. Behan, T. Hughes, N.

Hughes, C. Farrell, J. Hayes, T. Connolly.

Early club members, c. 1890: J. Fitzpatrick (president), M. Ashe (secretary), M. Downes (treasurer), J. Keogh (club captain), R. Meade (club vice-captain), J. Thornberry, P. Condron, B. Kane, J. Murray, G. Thornberry, P. Murray, M. Byrne, T. Clarke, C. Brien, T. Kelly, T. Doyle, P. Furlong, R. Maher, M. O'Connor, T. McConnell, J. Kelly.

Intermediate football league winners, 1904/05: B. Maher, T. Byrne, P. Richardson, J. Matthews, F. Braillford, M. Merriman, M. Brien, J. Fagan, J. Murray, C. Brien, G. Thornberry, T. Kelly, J. McGann, J. Fitzpatrick (president), J. Keogh, T. Clarke, M. Ashe (secretary), M. O'Connor, P. Murray (captain), J. Kelly, M. Downes (treasurer), R. Kane (vice-captain).

Junior hurling league winners, 1904/05: J. Thornberry, M. Downes (treasurer), J. Fitzpatrick (president) J. Murray, P. Murray, M. Byrne, T. Clarke, C. Brien, G. Thornberry, T. Kelly, T. Doyle, R. Meade (vice-captain), P. Furlong, R. Maher, M. Ashe (secretary), M. O'Connor, T. MacConnell, J. Keogh (Captain), J. Kelly, P. Condron, R. Kane.

Junior camogie league winners, 1906: Brigit Nugent, Annie Hughes, Kitty Brady, Dill Thornberry, Chrisie Murray, Margaret Feeney, Kate Nugent, Margaret Gannon.

Junior hurling league winners, 1919: P. Cormack, J. McConnell, T. Graham, Paddy Condron, Joe Condron, Tom Slattery, Jack Murphy, Mick Murphy, Bob Crone.

Junior football team, 1925: P. Buggle, J. Buggle, C. Collins, J. Collins, P. Feeney, Joe Buggle, John Buggle, J. McConnell, F. Hooper.

Junior football team v. Garda, 1930: Bob Farrell, Tibby Graham, Jim Buggle, Frank Buggle, Ginger Cooper, Paddy Quigley, Feathers Byrne, Chas Collins, Johnny Flanagan, Tom Forde, Mr Murphy (schoolmaster), Tom Graham, Honey Murray, Jim Murray, Jack Dignam.

Junior football league winning team, 1938: J. Byrne, G. Mahoney, G. Behan, M. Meade, F. Brophy, W. Heffernan, P. Dignam, T. Slattery, H. Condron, P. Condron, J. Brady, M. Crea, W. Malone, M. Conway, S. McDermott, M. Tierney, T. Malone, W. Kelly, P. Slattery, F. Kavanagh, P. Nolan.

Veterans' football team, mid-1940s: W. Malone, K. Kane, T. Graham, T. Condron, F. Brophy, T. Horan, J. Buggle, M. Kilduff, P. Condron, J. Brophy, T. Slattery, J. Gleeson, P. Feeney, J. Dunne, Poynton, M. Byrne, Major Kane, P. Buggle, J. McConnell, P. Murray.

Junior football team v. Rathmoylan, 1943: P. Slattery, F. Brophy, E. Moffett, T. Malone, H. Condron, J. Condron, S. Condron, G. Parsons, M. Geoghegan, S. Thornberry, L. West, Mooney, M. Meade, S. Smith, W. Kelly, J. Dignam, M. Conway, P. Sheridan, G. Sharpe.

Junior B football league winners, 1943: P. Slattery, F. Kavanagh, F. Brophy, S. Thornberry, G. Parsons, S. Condron, E. Moffett, L. West, H. Condron, G. Sharpe, T. Malone, C. Sheridan, D. Power, P. Finnegan, J. Condron, M. Mahady, T. Slattery, S. Smith, P. Nolan.

TWO

1949-1969
A VISION FOR THE FUTURE

Up until 1949, the only element of forward thinking within the club concerned the issue of where the next group of adult players were going to come from. In the last year of the decade, however, all that changed, when the club formed the first ever juvenile committee, with a vision for the future of the club, and, indeed, the entire Lucan area. It was a move that would alter the fate of a once-struggling club forever. As a club committee meeting in September 1949 recorded:

> A discussion took place on the re-organisation of the club, and a grave view was taken at the way the club was running at present. Suggestions to strengthen the club's finances and to build up stronger teams were put forward and discussed and finally it was decided that a sub-committee be set up that would meet regularly to further the interests of the club as far as possible.

Don Dardis, though still only a very young man himself at the time, was one of those selected to become part of the new committee, a group mandated with the task of securing a viable long-term future for the club in an ever-growing area. The task was daunting but the results almost immediate. Rather incredibly for the fledgling venture, success on the field wasn't long in coming. Three teams were entered in the 1950 South Dublin leagues, at under-14 football and under-15½ football and hurling, with the under-14 footballers going on to win the league.

It was an achievement that meant as much to the people of the village, it appears, as to the club and the players involved, with the medals going on display in Joe Dignam's cycle shop in the village before being presented. A band from the East Wall was hired to play at that presentation event, which would provide a huge night of celebrations for the village. The bold move towards the future was already beginning to reap rewards. Don Dardis recalls those early days in the juvenile section of the club:

We played in what was called the South County Juvenile League, and would generally set off for Clondalkin on Saturday afternoons with about twenty players, two adults and about ten bicycles. So every bicycle would carry at least two, or sometimes three, people on it.

When the match was over we would stop in Ledwidges in Clondalkin on the way home for a bottle of orange each, which was a major treat back then. After that we'd head home to Lucan, and generally we'd be singing the whole way home. Having won the league, the medals were displayed in the local shops and presented at a victory dance which generated a lot of local interest. From that point on the juvenile section really began to go from strength to strength.

At that time, adult games would have been played at the back of Langan's Pub, which is now the Foxhunter. And when the games were over we would adjourn to the bar either to celebrate victory or to drown our sorrows, and every player's performance would be analysed. Generally though, we wound up in good spirits and a bit of a singsong.

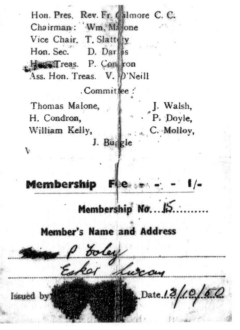

Membership card, 1950.

The success on the juvenile front continued into 1951 when the under-14 and under-15 footballers respectively won South Dublin league medals, and at this stage the club was beginning to grow faster than ever before. By the start of the 1951/52 season, Sarsfields were fielding three underage football teams and two hurling teams, progress borne out clearly in the improving fortunes of the local primary schools teams.

In 1958, St Mary's BNS stepped into the county-wide spotlight when they won both the Clonmore Cup and Millar Shield Cuman na mBunscol football titles. It was to prove a most fertile breeding ground in the years to come.

The club organised a special ceremony for the Clonmore Cup-winning under-12 team a short time later, with a report on the event even appearing in *The Irish Press* under the headline 'Medals Presented To School Team'. In the article, St Mary's principal Larry McCarthy complimented the parents for turning out the boys in such a grand manner every Saturday during the long league period, complimented the boys on being such a credit to the school, and reminded them that it was more important to play the game than to win trophies. He also thanked Lucan Sarsfields for their interest and encouragement, and hoped that the association of club and school would long continue.

A year later, the club decided to formalise that relationship. In conjunction with the principal, the first school sports day was held. The plan for the beginnings of this new and fruitful relationship was finalised at a committee meeting in May 1959, where:

> … following some discussion, it was agreed to hold a sports day, confined to parish and club members. One team each from Dodsboro, Lucan Village, Cold Blow, Esker and Ballydowd will compete at high and long jump (under 12 and under-14), girls' races (under-10 and under-14), a sack race, three-legged race and long kick and long puck competition for under-15s.

The event turned out to be a huge success, with prizes ranging from mouth organs to pencil sets. Most importantly, however, the bonds that tied club and school were now solidly in place.

Everything was moving in the right direction, and in 1961 the club enjoyed its first tangible reward at minor level, when the team won the county league. That same year the club's first ever under-21 team entered the county football league, and after a decade's work the juvenile project was really beginning to come to fruition. Lucan was beginning to produce players of a county standard too, as Billy Gogarty, P. Doyle and C. Kane attended trials for the Dublin junior football team in Swords. All thanks to the vision of a few young men back in 1949.

The official securing of the field at Ballydowd, which was finally sorted in late 1952, had also been a very important development. At the club's AGM on 10 December 1951, hopes of securing the use of Langan's Field on a more permanent basis hadn't looked all that bright, when the committee heard that it was 'decided that a big effort would have to be made to obtain a ground elsewhere'. Within six weeks, however, things began to look a little brighter, when 'a Junior Board representative contacted Mrs Langan re the pitch at Ballydowd, and her terms were £35 per year. The chairman of the Junior Board was meeting the Senior Board about taking the ground jointly, but it was probable that the Junior Board would take the ground anyway.'

The process was dragged out for a further ten months, but finally, in November 1952, it was reported to the club committee that:

> Ballydowd has been leased by the Senior Board for 10 years, and the Church committee are erecting dressing rooms and enclosing the pitch. It can now be used as a ground by the club, but the club would be expected to mark out the ground, etc., and provide officials for some of the matches there.

It was a giant leap forward for the club, and the timing couldn't have been better. While the underage project was gathering pace all through the 1950s, the club's adult section was also making serious strides of their own. The early 1950s in particular proved to be one of the most fruitful periods in the club's history. Beginning with his own introduction to the club in 1949, Tommy McCormack recalls how, before the establishment of an underage system, recruiting players had always been a somewhat opportunistic exercise:

> The first time I saw Lucan playing was in a junior football league game out in Rathfarnham against Brothers Pearse's, a club that would later go on to become known as Ballyboden St Enda's. I was getting the 25 bus from the terminus in the village, where the old public toilets used to be, opposite the Muintir na Tíre Hall. It was a Sunday afternoon and I was on my way into town heading for the Oireachtas Senior Hurling final between Galway and Wexford at Croke Park.
>
> On my way in on the bus I was sitting beside Tommy 'Chappy' Malone who was playing in that match in Rathfarnham. That was the very first time I ever met Chappy. He had his knicks and socks tied together with the boots; there was no such thing as using a bag back in those days. We got to talking

about the league match that Chappy was on his way to and he asked me if I'd like to come along out to it. So I decided to head out to Rathfarnham instead of going in to Croke Park.

I ended up togging out for the team the following Sunday in the Phoenix Park against Round Towers of Clondalkin. It was the first match I ever played in, and I think we actually won. In those days we would be up against the likes of St Brigid's in Blanchardstown and Clann Tighe Guaire of Palmerstown, who Bob Dardis would have played for once upon a time. They went out of existence some time after that, and a lot of their players ended up throwing their lot in with Lucan. We would have played against Green Flags of Chapelizod too and they were a really strong big team back in the early 1950s in particular.

I remember one particularly important fixture for us against a Guinness selection in the 1952 McEvoy Junior Cup Final. The game ended up being played four times in all. The first game was played in the Phoenix Park and ended in a draw, and the replay, which was played in Langan's in Ballydowd, finished in a draw again.

Then, amazingly, we played a third time in Clondalkin, and that ended up in a draw again. It went to a fourth game over in Guinness's home pitch in the Iveagh Grounds and that game ended up not being finished. There was an absolute mill-in. And in those days, a mill-in was a mill-in. The game was abandoned and we ended up getting suspended for a year.

Later again, on appeal to the Senior Board, the suspension was quashed altogether, though the scars remained:

A lot of the team at the time would have worked in Shackleton's Mills, Hills Mills and CPI, which all would have been very important to local employment then. We had some great teams though, with the likes of Henry Condron, Chappy Malone, Seán Smith, Peter Doyle, Finegan Smith, Peadar Condron … those lads would have been the backbone of the team at the time.

We played in a lot of junior football leagues in the early 1950s, and I remember playing in a league final against Ben Burbs from the inner city in 1953, a game we lost narrowly. We finally won a junior league final in 1956 in Islandbridge when we beat Cú Chullain's … that was the first set of medals I can honestly remember.

A special night was organised to mark that win and to present the league medals in February 1957, at the Springfield Hotel, while the club also planned to acknowledge the triumphant hurlers of that same year. No detail for the big night was left to chance by the club committee, with the number of teas to be ordered, cloakroom attendants, floor powder, door prizes, and every other minor detail ironed out well in advance. Lucan hadn't had much reason for a party up until this point, so they were damn well sure they were going to do it right.

The no-stone-left-unturned approach did the trick all the same, with the following week's committee meeting resolving that, 'the members expressed their satisfaction of this position [profit of £31], and also the manner in which the dance was run, it being felt that all that attended had enjoyed themselves'.

While the footballers had finally turned potential into medals, the hurling fraternity had been gathering steam themselves. With a core of top-quality players, the mid-fifties turned into one of the most successful eras in the history of Lucan Sarsfields. It had been decided at a November 1952 committee meeting to restart the small ball game in the club, and by the middle of the decade that finally began to bear fruit. Don Dardis recalls the spark of revolution, and the main man responsible for stoking the fires of progress in those early years:

> The senior player on the hurling team was Tommy Malone who had started playing some years earlier than the rest of the team. Tommy would have been well known around Lucan village until he died just a few years ago. If the team had been playing without much spirit at the time and they hadn't been going too well, Tommy would start a row with one of the opposition ... what Micheal O'Hehir would have described as a bit of schemozzle!
>
> All the young bloods on the Lucan team would go in to defend their father figure, and, of course, with the blood up, they would hurl an awful lot better after the row and we went on to win a lot of games. Tommy would be complaining all the time about the things he had to do to get Lucan Sarsfields playing!

Not that schemozzles were an unusual sight as far as Lucan teams were concerned in those days. So regular had they become, it seems, that they made for almost regular discussion at club committee meetings. After one particularly heated football championship game against Green Flags, an April 1952 meeting sat down to discuss what course of action to take with regard to what had happened the week before:

> It was reported that the referee's report for the match against Green Flags had been lodged, pointing out that the match had to be called off 15 minutes from

The 1952 Junior Football League winning team: W. Malone, P. Condron, M. Merriman, J.J. Condron, S. Condron, P. Slattery, J. Foley, K. Condron, J. Massey, T. Slattery, J. Core, D. O'Reilly, S. Smith, P. Craven, A. O'Toole, P. Foley, D. Hegarty, T. McCormack, L. Earls, T. Malone, P. Doyle, F. Condron, H. Condron, S. Walsh.

time, that Tommy McCormack had been ordered off the field, J. Kelly's name was taken for obscene language, that the referee was struck by a Lucan player and mobbed by the Lucan supporters.

The chairman, secretary, captain Tommy McCormack, J. Kelly, and the player in question were to attend the [County] Board on April 8 at 7p.m. Following discussion on this, it was decided that P. Condron appear as captain [in lieu of Tommy] and Jim Foley as the player named [Kelly].

It was decided to make the case firmly without creating much heat, on the following grounds ... that when Tommy McCormack had been ordered off he had only tussled with his opponent, and in the case of J. Foley that when the referee began to push Tommy McCormack off the field he lost his head and attempted to strike the referee ... that there was no mobbing by Lucan supporters as the club had not, and never had, any supporters.

At first glance, it seemed like an odd approach as appeals for leniency went and a somewhat harsh indictment of the club's own supporter base. However, the report continued:

It was also decided to point out that when the official referee failed to turn up, the club, in an effort to help the Board, agreed to a referee who claimed he was neutral, but who is a member of Green Flags.

The game started, nearly an hour late, and with Lucan leading at the time there was no need to start a row ... The referee stated that he would restart the match if the player apologised, but when the player approached to apologise the referee took off his coat to fight, and that even [in] reading the report [there] could be seen as bias against the Lucan club.

A report to the 1952 club AGM on the state of the junior football team at the time seemed to sum things up pretty succinctly:

> Don Dardis reported that during the year the club had built up the name of being one of the dirtiest teams in the Junior Leagues. Two of the worst reports ever read at the Board were against the club, and, during the year, close on a dozen members were suspended for offences on the playing field. In fact, it was only an appeal to the Senior Board that saved the club from a twelve-month suspension, but the Senior Board had issued a severe warning about the conduct of the players in future, and asked that some action would have to be taken.
>
> A full discussion followed during which the year's displays were considered, and finally, on the proposition of S. Smith, the incoming committee were instructed to take action against any player or official engaging in illegal or unsporting actions.

It wasn't all fisticuffs (though S. Smith was handed a three-year suspension in November of 1952 for an incident in that McEvoy Cup Final against Guinness), and there was some decent stuff played on the field in those days too. The newly formed hurling team would play their first game in the D league on 8 February 1953, against Maurice O'Neills [from Clonsilla], with Don Dardis, Peadar Condron, Tommy McCormack and Tommy Malone as selectors.

It would be the beginnings of an incredible few years for Lucan hurling, the first major success coming in 1956. Tommy McCormack takes up the story with his own recollections of the glory days on the hurling field that would follow:

> We had about ten fairly good players back then, along with a fair few lads who had never hurled in their lives before. I remember my first hurling

The 1954 hurling team: M. Dobbin, P. McCarthy, S. Walsh, K. Duke, P. Craven, P. Byrne, J. Byrne, S. Gorry, T. Collins, F. McNally, P. Slattery, P. Condron, P. Foley, T. Malone, T. McCormack, D. Dardis, M. Reidy, M. Condron, D. Collins.

The 1955 Junior hurling team that lost to Portrane in the Junior D League final. Back row: J. Costelloe, J. O'Brien, J. Doran, E. Waters, M. Dobbyn, J. Colldendar, P. Rabbitte, J. Dwane. Front row: P. Murphy, P. Carton, T. McCormack, D. Smyth, M. Reidy, P. Doyle.

Above: Veteran footballers, 1955: M. Lacey, P. Slattery, J. Collins, D. Byrne, E. Moffett, M. Mahady, P. Byrne. Front: J. Buggle, N. Clarke, G. Behan, Little Joe Dignam, J.J. Condron, J. O'Brien, D. Malone.

Below: Miller Shield winners, 1958: Tom Buggle, Larry Downes, T. Speight, Jimmy Dowling, Aiden Buggle, Jimmy Byrne, Tom Harris. Front: Tommy Thompson, Paddy Kelly, Ollie Malone, Richie Croake, S. Mulhall, Jonnie Byrne, Jonnie Shanaghan, Thomas Goff.

Junior Hurling League winners, 1958. Includes J. Connolly, L. Downes, B. Bannon, A. Dardis, P. Delaney, J. Kelly, D. Dardis, E. Moffett, P. Condron, P. Cassells, S. McGilloway, H. O'Neill, D. O'Brien, T. McCormack, John Collins, N. Feeney.

match for Lucan was against Maurice O'Neill's, who would have been from Clonsilla, and it was played in the Phoenix Park. Don Dardis, Eddie Waters, Mick Reidy, Chappy Malone, Dermot Smith, Peter and Paddy Byrne, Paddy Foley, Kevin Duke, and Kevin Condron would have all been playing, while Jack O'Brien, a good hurling man from Tipperary, and who would go on to become chairman a few years later, trained the team.

In 1956, we won the Junior D Hurling League and that started us on a run where we would go on to win the C, the B and then the Junior A league over the next four years. We beat Good Counsel of Drimnagh well in that Junior B final in O'Toole Park, and they would have been intermediate at the time. From there we went on to play at intermediate level and ended up in an intermediate final in Croke Park against Port and Docks. We lost that final by a couple of points though, unfortunately.

We went on to play in two Junior Championship finals in Croke Park in the early 1960s, when I was a selector, but we ended up being beaten in both of those too; the first one was to New Irelands and the second one was to Erin's Isle. But in 1962 we went on to win the Corn Céitinn. We beat Crokes, who would become Kilmacud Crokes, in the final of that after accounting for Grocers in the semi-final. That Grocers team would have had a lot of Dublin and Galway inter-county players on the team at the time.

Winning leagues in Dublin hurling at the time was far from easy though, both off the field and on it, as one of the stars of Lucan hurling in the fifties and sixties and future Hall of Fame inductee, Eddie Waters, recalls:

> I think it was around 1959 or maybe 1960 and we were going out to play a game in Ballyboughal against Fingal Rovers on a Sunday morning. Mick Dignam would have had a van at the time which was a travelling shop, and he was hired to drive out to Ballyboughal. I don't know how many were in it, but I suppose the guts of the team were in it anyway.
>
> We got as far as Swords, and at some point on the way out we came across Tom Slattery cycling on his bike. Nobody was too sure of the way to get to the pitch and the road was getting narrower and narrower and there was grass growing on a lot of it ... We ended up in a farmer's yard. We had to turn around and find our way back, but we got there eventually ... I remember we actually won that match, and that league.
>
> That time it was home and away, and when you were playing away you had your own referee. The return match was in Ballydowd and they brought their own referee. We won that match very easily, by five or six goals I think. A short time later one of the lads from the club came back from a board meeting, and the referee had put in his report for a draw. Nothing could be done about it ... It didn't affect us in the end I don't think, we won that league after anyway.
>
> I remember one particularly brutal game. We played a championship match out in Killester, in some field at the back of Killester village which I'd never heard of before, and we were up against Lusk in the first round of the Junior Championship. The grass must have been a foot high in the field ... We had a pretty good team at the time, but we were beaten on the day because Lusk had a pretty good side too.
>
> But I remember Tommy Malone and Peadar Condron were playing, and Tommy had no proper socks on him at all only ankle socks. After the game he had some amount of welts and bruises all around his legs and shins. Peadar was playing in the half-back line and I don't know how he survived with the amount of belts he got across the legs in that game too ... Somehow they survived it though ... We were beaten that day, and we were out, and that was it.

It was a golden age for Lucan Sarsfields, as the club continued to prosper and grow. The kids were coming through the ranks, the hurlers and footballers were bringing medals home, and in the late 1950s Lucan secured a famous minor football championship win over St Vincent's. Mick Molloy recalls kicking a late equaliser that day in a victory that boosted everyone within the club, and how the driving forces behind the club had helped build the team to a point where they could challenge:

> In the fifties we were playing juvenile hurling and football with the club, and the best memories I have of those days were the mentors we had, namely Billy Kelly, Don Dardis, Tom Higgins and Peadar Condron. The encouragement we got from those people was wonderful, especially Don and Billy, who would travel to away matches on bicycles and sometimes would be carrying two of us on their bikes with them.
>
> Later on in the '50s then I remember playing the mighty St Vincent's in a minor championship semi-final. Joe Collins would have been over the team. It was a very wet day and the game was played in Ballyfermot or Islandbridge, I can't remember which.
>
> Coming to the end of the game, we were a point down and we got a fifty. Joe Collins asked me would I take it as our normal free taker was injured. The ball seemed to weigh a ton – it would have been one of those old leather balls. The breeze was with us anyway and I placed the ball down.
>
> It went over and a draw looked likely at that stage, but I think it was John Collins who kicked the winner for us. I remember the great Des Foley played midfield against us that day actually. I can't even remember who we played in the final, but we didn't win it, I know that much.

Amidst all the encouraging goings on in the boys' end of things, the camogie section had also been completely reinvigorated. The sport was rekindled in 1961 with a series of challenge games, and in 1962 Sarsfields were back competing in the league. An aspect of the club that had been crucial to it since the turn of the twentieth century was finally back where it belonged, out on the playing field in the green of Lucan Sarsfields.

In late 1961, a letter was circulated around the local area giving an appraisal of the state of the club, and announcing the fact that the rejuvenation of the camogie section was indeed in the works. It also offered an insight into the growing population in the area around that time and the club's desire to benefit from it. It was very much a 'this is who we are, this is what we do, this is what we're going to do, so come join us' exercise. And it worked a treat:

> The club was formed shortly after the foundation of the GAA itself and has since successfully fielded hurling and football teams at juvenile, minor and

Club trip to Glendalough, 1960: Mary Gogarty, Mrs Feeney, May Collins, Paddy Collins, Mary Buggle, Dinny Malone, Eamonn Moffett, Peadar Condron, Jack Collins Snr, Nora Gogarty, Don Dardis.

Above left: Camogie team, 1964: Mary Feeney, Pat Kelly, Tom Slattery, Ann Foley, Alice Rodgers, Róisín Dardis, Lily Condron, Bernie Dooley, Ann Leech, Helen Kiernan, Marian Murphy. Front: Marian Langan, Mary O'Brien, Patricia O'Brien, Peggy Kemp, Nuala Behan, Mary Buggle.

Above right: Minor hurlers, 1961.

junior level. While the club has had the support of local families such as the Condrons, Malones, Kanes, etc., it has always had a welcome to hand for persons from any part of Ireland who come to reside in the area and over the years the club teams have been a good cross section of local and other players.

So it is today with new residents who are interested in Gaelic games already members of the club and helping out on the playing field and in committee. By the way, the club has also catered for the girls and very successful camogie teams have fielded out over the years. In fact, the present committee would like to hear from anyone in the Parish who could help to get the camogie section active again.

We are particularly well served at National School level just now and the dedicated teachers deserve our highest praise for the way they look after the younger generation. In so far as the provision of playing fields, they are a most pressing need. The Dublin Co. Council are supposed to be active in the matter, but we are co-operating with the AFC [athletics] clubs in keeping pressure on the authorities to place an area at our disposal which could be developed for the community as a recreational area, and leisure centre.

The future holds great promise for those of us interested in the games of the Gael and it is our earnest wish that new residents who share the same interest would come along and join us in making all our dreams come true. Indeed, what better way for a new member of the community to integrate and become part of the scene. We have had many successes in the past and with all interested residents co-operating we should see those repeated in the future.

The camogie section was beginning to take shape by late November 1961. The decision had been made by the club to actively pursue the rejuvenation of the ancient ladies' game, not just as a matter of prudence, but as a matter of responsibility to the entire association. It wasn't long in coming together.

According to an article in the 2007 club reunion programme, 'In 1960-61 a group of girls went to Parnell Park to support the Lucan Sarsfields hurling team and there was a suggestion to organise camogie within the club. The committee was approached and they agreed to give full support. Joe Collins (Collins Butchers) found out all the details regarding affiliation and registration.'

The camogie pioneers found full, and indeed highly enthusiastic, support from the club, as recorded in the minutes of a November committee meeting, where:

Joe Collins said that he had been asked by interested parties if we could help to form a camogie team in the district. D. Dardis said that, as a GAA club, we were duty bound to assist in fostering Gaelic games and said we should meet and help these girls to form their own committee. J. Higgins said he would try and get some of the Dublin County team to help with ideas and suggested that Joe Collins and himself should attend at the hall for preliminary talks.

At the end of December 1961, and with the club having paid the necessary £2 affiliation fee, the first practice took place. It was not long before the team was reminded of the club's long and eventful history at the sport, as the 2007 reunion booklet continued:

> They then went shopping for their camogie gear; they bought white material with black and green stripes for their long sleeved blouses and bought navy gym frocks. At that time camogie gear was very different to nowadays and the girls had to wear black stockings and big navy knickers as not an inch of flesh was to be seen (tights were not available at the time).
>
> When they received the official rule book there was a photo of women from Lucan Sarsfields playing camogie in the Phoenix Park (with long skirts to their ankles). They had won the first Camogie Championship final in 1904, with Mary Gogarty's (*née* Feeney) aunt on that winning team. [The article was mistaken though; the trophy won by Lucan in the early years had actually been the 1906 Junior Camogie League.]
>
> The team was too late to enter the league that season but played plenty of challenge matches. They went on to play in Junior B League and championship [1963] and did reasonably well. The next season (1964) [after having been regraded against their wishes] they won both the Junior A league and championship and were promoted to Inter B and once again won both league and championship (1965). Mr Joe Collins, Tom Slattery and the late Jack O'Brien were of immense help to the camogie section during these years.

That same year, 1961, had been a big one for the club when it came to progress on the playing field. A number of players were put forward for Dublin trials at minor level: J. Connolly, P. Delaney, D. Molloy, H. O'Neill, K. Callaghan and V. Redmond in football, and P. Delaney, T. Harris, L. Downes and V. Redmond in hurling.

Connolly, the stand-out player, would go on to win a Leinster Championship medal with the county in football that July (the first in the club's history), while Delaney was selected on the hurling panel. After much discussion, the club committee resolved to reward the endeavours of the successful candidates with 'a set of stockings'.

The club was going from strength to strength at the time, the school sports days continuing to prosper, a veterans' game being played for the first time against Round Towers of Clondalkin as part of the 1961 event, and the prospect of putting together a tug-o-war team for the first time was also being discussed.

Meanwhile, a strong showing in the semi-final of the Miller Shield warranted an article in the *Evening Herald*, 12 February 1961, under the headline 'Exciting Finish As Lucan Draw'. The report read:

> With seven minutes left to play in the semi-final of the Miller Shield competition at Islandbridge on Sunday last it looked odds-on an Eoghan Ruadh victory. However, a splendidly taken free which ended with the ball flashing past Eoghan Ruadh goalkeeper, Greene, to the net, brought forth a wonderful Lucan Sarsfields rally and in a thrilling finish they forced a merited draw – 2-6 each.
>
> Although a soft pitch made it difficult for good hurling, both teams kept the ball on the move to such an extent that the game was contested at a lively pace throughout, and as a result always held interest. The main difference between these two sides, however, lay in attack, for while the Eoghan Ruadh brigade of Lambe, Reynolds and Co. worked with great purpose, the Lucan Sarsfields full-forward line failed miserably to turn excellent chances to account.
>
> Outstanding for Eoghan Ruadh were goalkeeper Greene, Bolton and Reynolds, while prominent in this department for Lucan were McCormack, Waters and Delaney. As regards the centre-field positions, honours were about shared with O'Brien (Lucan) and Kane (Eoghan Ruadh) each in turn doing excellent work.

Those present at the club committee meeting which followed a few days later had evidently been privy to the *Herald*'s somewhat scolding words:

> Regarding the draw from the previous week against Eoghan Ruadh, the chairman [W. Kelly] said he wished to offer his congratulations to the hurlers on a fine display. He urged the selection committee not to be too conservative, and to move the odd man about if he was not playing well in his original position.

Whether that advice was eventually heeded or not, Lucan would go on to lose the replay.

Another important development was the minor football breakthrough which had come in March 1961, after which the chairman said he 'wished to congratulate the Minor Football team on their winning of the Division 2 section B for the first time'. They had ensured a place in the overall final in Islandbridge a few months later where they would go on to take home the county crown. Despite the club's objections, they were to be promoted to Division 1 for the following season.

Meanwhile, the under-21 footballers were getting set to make their debut in June. A challenge game against nearby Air Corps was organised in May, before the team finally took the field for the first time, away to Whitehall. It wasn't the dream debut the club had hoped for, but to finally have a team in the grade marked a massive progression from the foundation of the juvenile committee back in 1949.

However, the old disciplinary problems that the club had tried to stamp out some years earlier raised their head again in November 1961, during a Conlon Cup clash with Ballyfermot. At a club committee in the aftermath:

> Don Dardis said that he wished to raise the matter of the incident at Ballydowd on Sunday last, which included a selector striking an opposing player, barracking of the referee, and verbal attacks on our players by our own members after the game. He said that if we were now getting to the position where we could not take a defeat then we should consider resigning from all competition.
>
> P. Condron concurred and said that the referee had mentioned that he had occasion to stop the game three or four times because of encroachment by Lucan supporters. W. Griffin thought that, as long as games were played, there would be at intervals incidents like those that were witnessed last Sunday.

It appeared that the whole unsavoury incident had come about as a result of the players not following instructions from the sideline – a seemingly not-uncommon occurrence at the time:

> T. Higgins said that he had told the players on a couple of occasions to go for points, and said that some of the players brought on some of the arguments them-selves by their reluctance to do as they were told by their mentors. However, he said that it would be a good idea if, from next Sunday on, the available selectors keep in a group and make any changes necessary through the captain, and at the end of the game that nobody but the players to go into the dressing rooms.
>
> The chairman said that he had to restrain a person from striking one or two of our players after the game and he said that the young players needed encouragement, not bad criticism. After further discussion it was agreed that

the selector concerned in the case should be censured as to his conduct and warned about future conduct.

The blood, it seems, was very much up at this meeting. However, the warring factions were brought together within minutes, when the next topic of discussion reached the floor: the GAA's ban on foreign sports. No matter how bad things got in-house, there was always the suspicion of 'outsiders' and foreign sports to bring the group back together as a single cohesive unit. The minutes of that particular meeting almost certainly did not record everything that was said, but they do offer a very valuable insight into the mindsets of those present – especially when it came to the GAA's ban on its members playing soccer or rugby, which was still in place at the time. Some more progressive elements wanted to see the ban lifted, a motion having been brought forward by the Civil Service club to that effect:

> P. Condron then raised the matter of the motion for convention by Civil Service FC on the ban. E. Moffett, who likened this to the Irish case at the UN to consider the question of China, said that, in his view, the proposer of the motion, J. Woulfe, was not consistent, and that furthermore he knew of him to have Rugby interests at the time. He [E. Moffett] personally felt that the ban was a good rule for the GAA.

It seems the same attitude prevailed nationwide among the GAA fraternity; the ban wasn't finally lifted until 1971.

Early 1962 also marked the beginning of real ambition on the football field. A first-round win over St Patrick's in Santry had put the Junior football team into the second round of the championship, and hopes were high that this could finally be the year the club would take that giant leap forward at county level.

As a result of that new-found ambition, a decision to make that step to the next level was given some form when:

> Don Dardis raised the question of proper coaching and training for the Junior football team, especially now that we were down to the last 16 of the championship. After a long discussion on the pros and cons, and availability of suitable people, it was decided to approach Mr M. Mahady to see if he would undertake the task.
>
> If so, suitable payment would be offered. It was felt that an outsider would have better effect on the members and that they would take better to any coaching given by such a person.

The championship would prove a step too far for the team that year, but they would go on to win the 1961/62 league.

In the early part of the year it had been decided not to continue with an under-16½ team, after the club had failed to fulfil a fixture against Eoghan Ruadh. Instead it was resolved to enter an under-15 team, 'to keep the interest of boys when leaving school and maintain a necessary link in the step to under-16½'.

After a rough start to the season, and a series of narrow defeats, they finally won their first game against Kilmacud in November. The most important thing had been the high level of attendance at each game. There was certainly hope for the future.

The team started the 1963 season well, with wins over Clan na nGael in Ballydowd and what was described as their 'best win of the season' against Rialto Gaels in March. They were trucking along quite nicely, while the minor footballers were also making progress, with turnouts growing by the week, even if results had not begun to turn their way. The junior footballers, meanwhile, made an early exit from the championship after losing by a point to Fingal Ravens in St Margaret's.

Elsewhere, the hurlers were beginning to gather pace. In April, the juniors got their season off to a flying start with an excellent championship win over Air Corps. They would go on to beat St Kevin's in the league the following week, but the most encouraging aspect of early 1963 on the hurling front was the emergence of the under-15 hurlers, who had twenty-seven players in attendance at their first game.

They would walk over Good Counsel on that first Sunday and lose to Inchicore Hibernians in their second game, but they had more than twenty-five players at that second game too. Much time at committee meetings in those days was spent discussing the hiring of cars to get players to games, but the under-15s had so many players that for local games in Clondalkin or the Phoenix Park they would 'proceed on bicycle'.

The team would go on to a have a very successful season in the South County Dublin League. The only reason their efforts did not result in silverware, it appears, was the commonplace practice amongst other clubs of playing over-age players. It was encouraging stuff overall, but it was at a time when the rest of the club's teams began to really struggle.

In early May, the Junior As had been hammered by Guinness in the league, and the Junior Cs had been forced to give Clondalkin's Round Towers a walkover due to insufficient numbers. That same weekend, the minor footballers only had five players show up. At the next committee meeting the

Corn Céitinn winners, 1962.

decision was taken to withdraw the entire team from the league, a development that did not bode well for the future.

Lucan was growing exponentially at the time though, so it was hoped the lull would not last long, and in June 1963 it was agreed to, 'organise the distribution of a circular to solicit support for the club in a more substantial manner'. About 600 copies of the letter were to be distributed around the local area in October, just a week before the club's AGM. This was the birth of what, in 1967, would go on to become the *Lucan Newsletter*, and it summed up the club's progress pretty well up until that point, if a little inaccurate on the historical side:

To bring you into the picture about our general organisation we would like to put the following facts to you. The club was founded in 1890 [sic] and has continued to field hurling and football teams in Dublin competitions without break. In addition, a camogie team for the young girls had also been affiliated with the Dublin Board and in fact won the Dublin league as early as 1904. The camogie section was reformed recently and last year was promoted to Junior A League by the Co. Board.

The junior football and hurling teams have also had many good successes and indeed, in recent years, our junior football team won out the Junior B

League 1960/61. The junior hurlers had an early success this century when winning out the 1904/05 Dublin Junior League, and recent years saw them winning out the Junior C League, Junior B League 1961/62, and Special Hurling Competition, 1961.

About 1957 we increased our activities in the juvenile and minor fields and had the satisfaction of seeing our teams compete in a primary school Millar Shield final, as well as winning the Clonmore Cup in 1961. Our minor football team won the B League Dublin Board competition outright in 1961/62.

At present we have an under-14 football team, under-15 football and hurling teams, a minor football and minor hurling team, two junior football teams, a junior hurling team and a junior camogie team, which makes a grand total of nine…

Our club is well organised, and we feel, is making a useful contribution to the social life of the area. Many of our members are closely associated with other committees in the area, and work for improvement generally in the district e.g. New School Building Fund Committee, Muintir na Tíre, etc. We are anxious to provide better opportunities for the youth of the district to enjoy athletic endeavour and indeed to foster local goodwill and pride. We would be delighted for your co-operation in achieving these aims.

Whatever the reason, the 1962 Corn Céitinn had run on into 1963, and Lucan was set to play the semi-final in November against Good Counsel in Parnell Park. Bad weather would lead to the cancellation of that game, but, bizarrely, the team would go on to play the following week against St Vincent's in the 1963 version of the competition, being fairly well beaten. All was not well in the camp at the time, with a December committee meeting recording:

> Junior Hurlers beaten. Fair turn out. The Chairman appealed to all players to refrain from attacking selectors who were doing the best they could to see that those who turned out regularly and in time got games. It was agreed to forget an incident which had occurred on the previous Sunday.

It seems that all was indeed forgotten shortly afterwards. In mid-December, the Good Counsel game would finally be played, and Lucan would secure a 'magnificent' win that would serve as a massive boost to the whole club. A place in the Corn Céitinn Cup final against Dalgais (also known as Dalcassians and hailing from Balbriggan) now lay in store. The controversy that would follow the final, which was played in the last week of December, would rage on well into 1964. The week before the game had even been played, a committee meeting had decided to 'wait until after Sunday to decide on protesting against Dalgais in the event of an illegal team'.

At the first committee meeting of the New Year then, that decision was made, 'The Junior Hurlers, although beaten, were congratulated on their fine performance in the Corn Céitinn final. It was reported to the meeting that a protest had been lodged against Dalgais on grounds of non registration of players and non registration of club.'

After the initial failure of the appeal, the result went Lucan's way at a meeting of the County Board in early February 1964. The Corn Céitinn, in probably the least desirable way imaginable, would be awarded to Lucan. The news, while welcomed by Lucan, was also well received at Board level, 'The Secretary gave a brief account of the appeal to the County Board which had been successful. It said that the result had been a relatively popular one on at club level. The Corn Céitinn trophy will be passed to Lucan in due course.' That didn't actually happen until late 1964 though, as beaten semi-finalists Crokes had put in an objection of their own.

The team, it appears, had resolved to do their talking on the field in the weeks ahead. After a win in the first round of the Miller Shield, they took on Na Fianna in the semi-final. Old problems would rear their head once again though, the team falling agonisingly short of a much-needed break-through once again. Even in those days, falling just short was acknowledged as being a frustratingly club-wide epidemic:

> The junior hurlers were beaten in a very good game. With a little luck it was a game which could have been won. Tim Delaney proposed a vote of thanks to the players for providing such a sporting game … In examining the game, however, it was felt that if some of the players gave a little extra, especially in the first half of these games, we could win out in many of the ones we're losing … It was agreed to suspend J. Kelly for six months for playing soccer with Celbridge last Sunday instead of turning out for the Miller Shield game.

The footballers had got 1964 off to the ideal start with a solid opening-round Junior Championship win over St Ita's of Portrane over in St Margaret's. In March, they travelled to Mobhi Road to take on Na Fianna and won. Their reward was a clash with neighbours Round Towers in the next round in Ballydowd, and again the result had went the club's way.

Excitement was building in Lucan as the team prepared to take on St

Maur's in Raheny in the last sixteen. A thirty-five-seater bus was arranged to take people to the game. The travelling fans would enjoy the journey home, Lucan emerging with a stunning victory, and for the first time in decades, Lucan Sarsfields found themselves in the quarter-final of the Dublin Junior Football Championship. Naomh Gearoid would provide the opposition, with the game fixed for O'Toole Park in May. There was to be no dream end to the team's run, however, and that would be the end of the footballers' season. It had been a highly encouraging season though, and the breakthrough seemed closer than it ever had been before.

Back in the junior hurling league, Lucan had been making steady prog-ress, and by mid-June they found themselves in a lofty position in the Junior B Hurling League table. Lying in third, they were preparing to take on table toppers Fontenoys. A big crowd showed up and the team delivered a bril-liant win to keep their league hopes alive.

Their fine run would lead to a semi-final date with Ballyfermot in September at Islandbridge. The team posed for a team photo before the game in commemoration of the Corn Céitinn having been awarded their way some months before, but their focus was on the serious business of a place in the league final. Club spirit, it was reported to the committee a week later, had led the team to wonderful victory:

> The Junior hurling team, after a very hard game, had a thrilling one-point win over Ballyfermot and the Chairman congratulated them on their display but stressed that the team required more training. He said he wanted to mention one of the panel, J. Kearns, who after having been stripped and available for selection [but not picked] had instantly handed over his togs so that another player could field. Such club spirit is what's required to make Lucan Sarsfields a top-class club.

Typically, that was far from the end of the Ballyfermot matter. At the fol-lowing week's executive meeting it was revealed that the referee's report had been submitted to the board indicating that Lucan had had sixteen players on the field at two points in the game and had used four subs.

Despite the game having initially been awarded to Lucan and the final fixed for that October, Ballyfermot would have their appeal upheld a few weeks later at a Senior Board meeting, and the game refixed. It mattered little in the end though, Lucan went on to win the replay by eight points and booked a date in the league final against Port and Docks in Croke Park at the end of October.

Heartbreakingly once again, the team would get beaten by a superior side in that final, but that would not be the last the team would see of Port and Docks. They would go on to lose to the same opposition the following season in the semi-final of the Miller Shield, after losing out to Dalkey Mitchells in a championship replay. In 1966, however, a much-needed breakthrough would finally arrive.

An encouraging product of the team's fine run the year before, and the strength coming through at underage level in hurling, resulted in a second junior team being entered in the league for the very first time in 1964. One of the first team's stars, Desie O'Brien, would also make the county junior panel that year, before going on to be selected on the county football panel the following season. Things were beginning to look up all round.

While the minor and under-21 football teams were struggling for numbers (the under-21 team were withdrawn in March), things were really beginning to improve at the younger grades. In March, under-13 and under-15 football and hurling teams were entered in the South Dublin Leagues, and in 1966 success would finally come to the juvenile grades.

A building boom had hit Lucan in the mid-sixties, which culminated in the development of new housing estates such as Hillcrest in the early seventies. By 1966, the club was fielding two camogie teams, one junior hurling team (the second team was not entered in the 1966 competition), two junior football teams, one under-16½ football team, and under-13 and under-15 football and hurling teams. These were indeed boom days for the club.

The club had been reorganised at an AGM in February 1966, at which D. Molloy and T. Speight were handed the reins of the under-13 and under-15 teams. Success was almost immediate, and in late 1966 the under-13 footballers would go on to win the South Dublin League, beating St Martin's in Brittas in the final by 7-16 to no score. The same team would go on to win runners-up medals in the hurling league.

Some of the younger generation were then co-opted onto the club's second team, which was re-entered in the Junior C League ahead of the 1966/67 season. Alan Higgins, an under-16½ star at the time, was one of those drafted onto the adult team. He recalls well his debut for the team in October 1966:

> I was sixteen when our mentors decided to 'blood' a few of the young lads in the junior hurling team, which was a very appropriate term to describe Dublin junior hurling at the time. Because of the small population in the area at the time, we didn't always have enough players to enter the juvenile leagues each year, so my only league experience was at under-16½ level.

The team was made up of footballers who played hurling occasionally, hurlers who were no longer good enough to play with the first team, and, when needed, any spectators who happened to be around at the time of throw-in. Needless to say, we weren't in contention for honours.

The first game I played was against Brothers Pearses in Langan's field, who have long since disappeared. They were in a similar league position to ourselves at the time so there was nothing really at stake apart from pride. That was a great day for me, and it actually marked the first of twenty years of adult hurling for the club.

I had played most of my games at left-half back, but for this game I was thrown in at corner forward, and the full-forward that day was a man named Jack O'Brien. Jack's two sons would have been playing with the first team at the time, and I would actually go on to play with them a few years later. Jack scored four goals that day.

The game that day was a close one, but we lost by a point. I actually remember having a chance to snatch a draw, but I dropped my shot short into the keeper's hands. My main memory of that game came at half time. Both teams and sets of mentors, as well as all the spectators and the referee, marched into Langan's Bar to watch the Prix de l'Arc de Triumph.

There we stood, thirty players in togs with hurlies in hand, alongside regular patrons of the bar, watching the race, while Ma Langan, a small grey-haired woman with a perpetual cough and a woodbine cigarette hanging from her bottom lip, was dishing out the pints. The whole situation just seemed so unreal to me. A horse called Bon Mot won the race anyway, and off we marched back out to finish the game. I played a lot of games for Lucan Sarsfields after that, but none that had a half-time break in the pub.

While the juveniles were beginning to make their mark, the Junior A hurlers were building up a tremendous run in the Junior B League, despite exiting the championship at the hands of Ballyfermot in June. The team had followed that defeat with a solid win over Peadar Moran's in the league and a request to the board that games be fixed for 12p.m. and not 11.30a.m., to facilitate players who attended a later Mass, also went forward. It didn't seem to have much impact straight away, as the team went on to lose their next game to St Columba's, but by the end of the year the team had reached a league final.

A thrilling 3-9 to 2-6 win over St Columba's in the semi-final had seen them reach a decider, where St Colmcille's were to provide the opposition at O'Toole Park. It turned out to barely be a contest, and with their tails well and truly up, Lucan dismantled their opponents by 8-5 to 0-9 in a massive day for Lucan Sarsfields that had been a long time in coming. And rather incredibly, especially considering the scoreline, Lucan had been the underdogs that day.

The club dinner dance took place in December 1966 in the Spa Hotel, where the *Evening Herald*'s Tom Kelly reported on the celebrations of what had been a wonderful year for the club:

> Founded as far back as 1886, Lucan made slow but encouraging progress and after a short break really got down to business in 1953 and have since then gone from strength to strength. They won the league in 1956 and the following year carried off the Special Competition. In 1958 they again took league honours and three years ago made their mark in the Corn Céitinn competition only to narrowly miss the league title again in 1964.
>
> Since then, however, titles have been slow to come their way, but they reaped the rewards for their persistence and great club spirit when this year they took the Junior B League and in so doing put the club right back on the hurling map. The success of their junior hurlers was all the more sweet when it is realised that they were given little chance against champions Colmcille, who in turn had put paid to such an outstanding side as Whitehall Gaels in the championship final. Not only were the Lucan boys good enough to match strokes with the champions, but they proved with the ease of their success that they are good enough to hurl alongside the best that Dublin can produce.
>
> Running down the honours list in an effort to put forward those worthy of special mention, I find it difficult to single out any particular players, as Lucan's recent success has only been brought about through loyalty on the part of all concerned. However, if a special mention is to be made of any particular players I think that Desie O'Brien, who played a real captain's part throughout the year, Eddie Waters, Tommy McCormack and Jimmy Connolly fill the bill.
>
> The club's footballers have also proven their worth in recent years when they narrowly missed getting into the honours list and it seems only a matter of time before they eventually make their mark. The juveniles, thanks to the splendid work of Dinny Malone, have also shown that they are a force to be reckoned with in winning the under-13 football league and occupying the runners-up spot in the South County League.
>
> The club's camogie team repeated their feat of last year when they won the Intermediate B Championship and league, and there was a great round of applause when their captain and star player Ann Foley was presented with the trophies by Fr Herlihy, who despite only coming to Lucan a short time ago, has shown great interest in the affairs of the club.

The only regret at last Friday's function was the absence of 'Mr GAA Lucan' Tom Slattery, who unfortunately is in hospital recovering from a traffic accident. His esteem could be measured by the applause when club chairman Mr Jack O'Brien expressed the hopes of everyone that Tom would make a speedy recovery and be back soon with all his friends in Lucan.

Success on the field continued in 1967 when the under-16½ footballers won their league undefeated, and in their ranks was a young man named Kevin Synnott. In 1970, Kevin would go on to win a Leinster Minor Football Championship medal with the county, and in 1974 he would bring the first ever All-Ireland Senior medal to the club after the Dubs brought Sam Maguire back to the capital.

The sixties petered out with more of a whimper than a bang on the field of play. In 1968, the junior footballers put in a solid performance, in losing out in the Plant Cup final to senior side Cú Chullains and in May of that year the latest edition of the club newsletter recorded the state of affairs in the club:

We are just now fielding under-13 and under-15 teams in the South County Leagues with minor and junior hurling and football teams in the Dublin Junior Leagues and Championships. Both Junior teams are in the A section of the league.

Our minor football side have now completed their league and finished third out of 11 teams to start. Indeed, we were unlucky to lose to eventual competition winners An Caisleán in our only defeat of the year. Many of the players showed good form all through, and in Martin Greene, John Handibode, John Byrne, Alan Higgins and the Doyle brothers among others, the club can look forward with some confidence. Greene, Handibode and Higgins have played in trials for the Dublin minor football and hurling teams.

The junior footballers are having in-and-out form. We have lost one or two games we should have won. Just now the selectors are trying to blend in some of the minors, and it is the intention to use the remainder of the league to sort out the problem areas so that we can go after league and championship honours in the coming year … Now playing some of the best football of his career is Tom Speight and in recent games his high fielding has been a feature. Also playing well are Mick Molloy, Bob Dardis, Bill Kane and Jim O'Brien to name but a few.

The junior hurlers have been in great form for the last few weeks but again have not had the luck to be in front at the end of their games. An example was last Sunday against Moindearg at Ballydowd when, after a disastrous start, we came back into the game, and with a little bit more in our forward line might have won it.

The previous two games against Aer Lingus and Clan na nGael were extremely fine displays of hurling. In fact, some neutral spectators said they were the best games of junior hurling they had seen all year. Some players to catch the eye in these games were Des O'Brien, Pat Delaney, Aidan Dardis, Joe Dooley, Lar Downes, Noel Feeney and Tom McCormack. However, all are playing well, and on Sunday last we were unfortunate to be without our most dangerous forward Eddie Waters. Selectors Mick Dowling, Jack O'Brien and Don Dardis are using the talent available to the best of their ability. We look forward to finishing up in the top half of the league.

In 1969, the junior footballers, captained by Billy Gogarty, would round out the decade with a trophy after winning the Phoenix Cup in Dalkey (they also lost out in the final of the Conlon Cup to St Oliver Plunkett's that same year). The hurlers, meanwhile, lost a top-four final to old enemies New Irelands in 1969 by 6-7 to 4-5, to end the decade on somewhat of a sour note.

It was reported to the committee that the 'Junior Hurling team were beaten in top-four playoff by New Irelands. The chairman congratulated the team for a fine sporting performance, though beaten by a team consisting of senior players and also some illegal ones too. As our own team was also out of order our cause is a lost one.' As a result, no appeal followed.

The decade, which had seemed so promising, had largely disappointed. It was once again a case of so near, yet so far, but a breakthrough was in the offing, with quality youngsters finally beginning to come through the ranks, and the 1970s would finally provide some much-needed on-field success for the long-suffering members of a club that for far too long had promised much but delivered little.

All the while, the playing fields at Ballydowd had been the topic of much discussion. The Junior and Senior Boards had been meeting intermittently with Mrs Langan with the view to securing a long-term lease on the site so that proper facilities could be erected and a more secure future ensured. To that end, it was agreed in January 1969 that a proposal be sent to the board requesting that senior club Seán MacDermott's come on board to divide the cost and that they also be allowed use the venue as their home ground.

The concept of marrying up senior and junior clubs for such purposes was becoming a more common practice at the time, and would eventually lead to the amalgamations of Kilmacud and Crokes, Ballyboden and St Enda's,

Ballymun and Kickhams, to name but a few. A few weeks later, six members of MacDermott's, along with County Board chairman Mr J. Grey, met at the club and agreed that:

> Both clubs would form a joint committee to improve playing facilities at the venue immediately, work as independent units in the Co Board as regards team composition, provide as near as possible equal labour finance and know-how for the proposed improved facilities, and have equal use of the facility for games.

Lucan Sarsfields G.A.A. Club
LIMITED SWEEPSTAKE
Irish Sweeps Derby
TO BE RUN AT CURRAGH ON JUNE 28th, 1969
RESULT SHEET

| 1st HORSE £15 | 2nd HORSE £10 |
| 3rd HORSE £5 | 4th HORSE £3 |

Cards to be returned to;— HON. SEC., before FRIDAY, 27th JUNE, 1969

Draw will take place on FRIDAY, 27th JUNE, at 8 p.m.
IN TOWN HALL
FULL CARD £1.

CARD + LINE Nº	NAME — BLOCK CAPITALS PLEASE —	HORSE	
85-2	Stephen Kenny, No 2 McJoseph	BEAUGENCY	
13-11	Miss Y McCormack, 20 Pearse Lower, Ballymun	AUGUSTUS	
29-19	P. Brady Dodsboro	SANTAMOSS	
7-18	Noel Leeney Eske, Lawns	BLAKENEY	④
76-14	Frank Dunne Elm Hall	VIVADARI	
67-10	Thomas Clarke 20 Dodsboro	MOON MOUNTAIN	
60-22	J Gordon Newcastle	ONANDAGA	
37-1	Julia Connolly Luttrelstown	REINDEER	③
29-11	Thomas McCormack Lucan	RIBOFILIO	②
12-20	Mr Fox, 35 Annamoe Lee Dublin	NORTHERN MIST	
83-7	P. Keenan 70 Ben Bulben Rd. Drimnagh	DEEP RUN	
80-11	B. Keegan C/o C.P.I	TANZARA	
76-18	P. Dunne Elm Hall	BALLANTINE	
83-10	J. McElroy 154 Blackditch Rd B'fermot	BUNKERED	
95-11	Jim Shaw C/o H. Doyle	PRINCE REGENT	①
13-7	John Murray, 77 Dodsboro	SELKO	

Sweep ticket, 1969.

Dinny Malone, Chappy Malone and Eddie
Dunne, left of groom Tommy McCormack
and bride Nancy Clinton, and Peter Doyle,
Peadar Condron and Dinny Malone Snr
to the right. Lucan Sarsfields hurlers give a
guard of honour for the couple's special day
in Lucan on 9 September 1969.

The County Board chairman added that:

> … he would be delighted if both clubs could work together in harmony
> to provide the facilities, and while in no way desiring any amalgamation he
> expressed the hope that in a number of years' time both clubs might provide
> for the area a senior, junior, minor complex which could do much to attract
> the youth to the GAA.

It was agreed that the cost of two years' rent payable to Mrs Langan of
£275 be provided to the clubs by the County Board as a loan, and in
February a galvanised shed was purchased and delivered to Ballydowd.
All of a sudden, the future of Gaelic games in Lucan looked that much
brighter, and over the course of 1969, work on water pipes and installing
new goalposts was undertaken at the site in Ballydowd, and Hermitage
Golf Club were contacted to inquire about the possibility of the provision
of parking nearby.

However, by the end of the year, all was not well with the project. The
promised funds from the board still hadn't arrived, and the relationship
with Seán MacDermott's was beginning to falter. St Patrick's GAA Club
in Palmerstown had made an offer of rent on the juvenile field for the
year ahead, but apart from that development things were beginning to fall
apart. What had initially appeared to be a marriage made in heaven and a
future definitively secured, would in 1970 become an absolute nightmare
for the club.

PLAYERS OF THE ERA

Under-14 football league medal winners, 1952: N. Fallon, R. Murphy, J. Egan, T. Egan, F. Barr, W. Kane, S. Lowe, S. Smith, P. Smith, D. Buggle, E. Kelly, A. Deighnam, D. Malone, C. Kavanagh, D. Galvin, S. Lawlor, A. McLoughlin, D. Malone (S. Walsh withdrew name to allow additional medal for younger boys).

Under-15 football league medal winners, 1952: N. Fallon, R. Murphy, J. Egan, O. Monaghan, E. Burchill, S. Lowe, S. Smith, P. Smith, D. Buggle, W. McLoughlin, W. Hood, S. Walsh, D. Galvin, C. Keogh, N. Buggle, M. Malone, M. Martin, P. Slaughter.

Junior football league medal winners, 1952: W. Malone, P. Condron, M. Merriman, J.J. Condron, P. Slattery, J. Foley, K. Condron, J. Massey, T. Slattery, J. Core, D. O'Reilly, S. Smith, P. Craven, A. O'Toole, P. Foley, D. Hegarty, T. McCormack, L. Earls, T. Malone, P. Doyle, F. Condron, H. Condron, S. Walsh.

Junior hurlers, 1953/54: B. Heffernan, V. Walsh, Peter Byrne, M. Dobbyn, M. Reidy, D. Dardis, P. Slattery, Paddy Byrne, K. Duke, J. Heffernan, J. O'Brien, D. Smith, P. Condron, T. McCormack.

Junior D hurling league finalists v. Portrane, 1954/55 (lost by 6-2 to 2-11): M. Dobbin, P. McCarthy, S. Walsh, K. Duke, P. Craven, P. Byrne, J. Byrne, S. Gorry, F. McNally, P. Slattery, P. Condron, P. Foley, T. Malone, T. McCormack, D. Dardis, M. Reidy.

Veterans' football team, 1955: M. Lacey, P. Slattery, J. Colins, D. Byrne, E. Moffett, M. Mahady, P. Byrne. J. Buggle, N. Clarke, G. Behan, Little Joe Dignam, J.J. Condron, J. O'Brien, D. Malone.

Junior hurling league medal winners, 1956: J. O'Brien, P. Craven, D. Dardis, Pat Byrne, P. Condron, T. McCormack, M. Reidy, J. Malone, K. Duke, M. Dobbyn, D. O'Brien, F. Farrell, J. O'Brien, P. Slattery, P. Murphy, E. Watters, J. Lestrange, J. Doran, J. Connolly, C. Minogue, D. Smith, N. O'Neill, E. Duke.

Junior football league medal winners, 1956: P. Doyle, P. Foley, D. Dardis, C. Walsh, J. Walsh, B. Dardis, P. Condron, J. Collins, D. Malone, M. Gogarty, T. McCormack, T. Malone, C. Kane, P. Fitzgerald, P. Walsh, E. Watters, M. Markey, S. Healy, P. Kavanagh, C. Nolan, J. McCannon, B. Kelly, W. Kane.

St Mary's BNS Miller Shield winners, 1958: Tom Buggle, Larry Downes, T. Speight, Jimmy Dowling, Aiden Buggle, Jimmy Byrne, Tom Harris, Tommy Thompson, Paddy Kelly, Ollie Malone, Richie Croake, S. Mulhall, Jonnie Byrne, Jonnie Shanahan, Thomas Goff.

Junior hurling league winners, 1958/59: D. Malone, J. Connolly, L. Downes, B. Bannon, A. Dardis, P. Delaney, J. Kelly, D. Dardis, E. Moffett, P. Condron, P. Cassells, S. McGilloway, P. McGilloway, E. Watters, M. Reidy, H. O'Neill, D. O'Brien, T. McCormack, John Collins, N. Feeney.

Junior/Inter camogie team, early/mid-1960s: Margaret O'Brien, Róisín Dardis, Patricia O'Brien, Mary Buggle, Nora Gogarty, Mary Feeney, Patricia Kelly, Marcella Muldowney, Lily Condron, Breda Condron, Bernie Dooley, Anne Foley, Nuala Behan, Helen Kiernan, Peggy Kemp, Marie Murphy, Sis Jackman, Sheila Lister, Irene Slattery, Helen Nohilly, Alice Rogers, Rose O'Donovan, Kathleen Shepard, Marie Keatley.

Junior B hurling league winners, 1963/64: C. Fogarty, J. Collins, T. Birmingham, P. Brosnan, T. Crough, A. Dardis, J. Connolly, E. Watters, L. Downes, H. O'Neill, N. Feeney, T. McCormack, D. O'Brien, T. Harris, F. Kiely, P. Condron, E. Dunne, B. Bannon.

Junior hurlers, September 1964: T. Malone, P. Doyle, T. Slattery, C. Fogarty, Joe Collins, B. Grant, T. Bermingham, John Condron, P. Brosnan, T. Crouch, A. Dardis, E. Stafford, J. Connolly, J. Kearns, F. Kelly, L. Condron, D. Dardis, M. Lally, B. Dardis, J. O'Brien, E. Waters, L. Downes, A. O'Neill, N. Feeney, T. McCormack, D. O'Brien, T. Harris, P. Condron, E. Dunne, B. Bannon, D. Byrne.

Junior A camogie league and championship winners, 1964: Mary Feeney, Pat Kelly, Ann Foley, Alice Rodgers, Róisín Dardis, Lily Condron, Bernie Dooley, Ann Leech, Helen Kiernan, Marian Murphy, Marian Langan, Mary O'Brien, Patricia O'Brien, Peggy Kemp, Nuala Behan, Mary Buggle.

Full list of adult members, September, 1965: J. Collins Snr, P. Condron, J. Gaffney, T. Higgins, D. Dardis, D. Malone, J. O'Brien, John Collins, Joe Collins, B. Bannon, C. Molloy Snr, G. Behan, J. Buggle, M. Dowling, J. Handibode, S. Condron, W. Kelly, M. Lacey, T. Slattery, N. Feeney, D. Molloy, M. Molloy, T. McCormack, P. Doyle, D. O'Brien, P. Delaney, H. O'Neill, L. Downes, E. Watters, P. Brosnan, T. Harris.

Junior B footballers, 1965: Billy Malone (manager), Aidan Buggle, Pat Carr, Bob Dardis, John Dobbs, Dennis Byne, Dick Byrne, Barney Bannon, Mongey Behan (trainer), Peadar Condron, Mick Gogarty, Dinny Malone, Larry Downes, Tommy McCormack, Seán Bonas, Dick Fallon, Frank Scarff.

Junior B hurling league winners, 1966: Frank Kiely, Liam Lacey, Tommy McCormack, Aidan Dardis, Barney Bannon, Eddie Dunne, Pat Delaney, Larry Downes, Desie O'Brien, Jimmy Connolly, Jimmy O'Brien, Dick Barron, Noel Feeney, Eddie Watters, Andy Kelly.

Under-16 football league medal winners, 1967: M. Keenan, L. Doyle, John Doyle, Jim Doyle, J. McKeown, J. Handibode, M. Mulhall, J. Byrne, K. Synnott, M. Greene, J. Mahon, T. Egan, T. Slattery, A. Higgins, T. McNeill, E. O'Connor.

'THE SARSFIELDS SONG' BY DON DARDIS

Air: 'By Lough Sheelin Side'

Verse 1

As I sit here in the clubhouse grand,
my friends around and my glass in hand,
My mind goes back down through the years,
of joys and sorrows, thrills and tears,
For 100 years we have kept the flag,
flying high, never let it drag,
With supporters few in some dark days
we battled on, that the spark might blaze.

Chorus

So here's to you my Lucan team, to do or die in your jerseys green,
To rise again when e'er you fall, for the Sarsfields club is the best of all.

Verse 2

How proud I was on that day,
the captain said on the team you play,
To take my place and give my all,
to win the game for our village small,
No tracksuit then, no dressing room,
a friendly hedge half proved a boon,
To own our ground no hope was seen,
a clubhouse then was a far-off dream.

Verse 3

But those days are gone and a good job too,
and the youth today are loyal and true,
They train and play for our growing town,
and soon I know they will win the crown,
And if I'm gone, as it might be,
up to the land of eternity,
I hope the boss with me will bear,
if my loud hooray disturbs all there.

THREE

1970-1979
PAIN AND PROGRESS

The 1970s began with frayed nerves and much frustration in the club. Work on the Ballydowd project was all but at a standstill, and the County Board's failure to pay rent owed to Mrs Langan had by 8 January led to a solicitor's letter being read out at a committee meeting. The situation was growing more and more dire by the day:

> A full report on money owed to Mrs Langan regarding rates and rent was obtained from her solicitor and read, and from the discussion following it was proposed by T. Higgins that an invitation be extended to J. Grey [Senior Board Chairman] and to notify Seán MacDermott's and St Patrick's to have one, or not more than two, representatives present at this meeting when dates had been arranged with J. Grey …

… the committee heard, as they decided what to do.

A date had been arranged for the meeting, but Mr Grey failed to show, and in March, with things beginning to spiral out of control, 'it was proposed that a request for a deputation to the Dublin County Board to put facts before them and to get those matters settled' be organised.

A few weeks later, the relationship with Seán MacDermott's had fully soured as well, 'After a short discussion re Ballydowd affairs it was proposed that the Secretary write to Seán MacDermott's requesting a meeting with the aim of withdrawing our agreement and settling any monies owed or incurred by them on the Ballydowd project.'

Lucan were hanging in the wind, and things finally hit rock bottom in late March, when a trespassing order was posted on the Ballydowd grounds by Mrs Langan, and a series of games fixed for that following Sunday were postponed, 'to avoid adding more fuel to the fire'.

Noel Feeney, Billy Gogarty and K. Callaghan finally got in front of the County Board in early April, at which, 'a complete breakdown of debts owed to Mrs Langan was given to them'. After much discussion, the County Board agreed to contact Mrs Langan's solicitor with a view to paying off the balance owed of £150. And yet, some weeks later, the situation had still not been resolved. A committee meeting on 16 April heard:

> ...that the goalposts in the field had been taken down and that there had been no information from the County Board re payments to Mrs Langan.
>
> During a discussion on the possibility of selling the structure we have in Ballydowd the chairman proposed that we should contact Seán MacDermott's through Mr Kelly with a proposal that both or one of the clubs should try and sell this building so that at least we might get some of the money spent on it back. Because, at the present moment in time, it is slowly deteriorating or diminishing for all we know.

That was that. Ballydowd, having served the club so well and for so many years since 1952, and which only a year previously had been the bright star in the club's long-term future, was gone forever. The relationship with Mrs Langan had been soured beyond the point of recovery, despite the best efforts of the club. All of a sudden, and through no real fault of its own, Lucan Sarsfields GAA Club found itself completely homeless. Just like back in the days before Ballydowd had become available to the club, Lucan would return to playing their home games in the Phoenix Park. Mick Molloy recalls the whole debacle:

> In the '50s and '60s we never thought we would ever leave Ballydowd. Then a new law was proposed where if a ground was used as a sports ground it could not be rezoned for another use. That, and a combination of the Dublin County Board not paying the rent, was why we were locked out really. Having put in the foundations and structures for new dressing rooms and a proposed amalgamation with Seán MacDermott's – a senior football club mainly made up of inter-county mentors and players – all was abandoned and we moved to Dodsboro.

It was a trying time for the club, but matters got worse when Noel Feeney resigned from his role as vice-chairman. His name had appeared in parish notes as a committee member of Lucan Soccer Club, and the club executive had not taken it well. After it was pointed out to Mr Feeney that it was 'not a practical thing to serve both sides', he resigned his position. Things were just going from bad to worse.

Thankfully, back on the playing field, things were slightly better. The footballers had begun the new decade in winning style, opening their campaign with victories over St Enda's, An Caisleán and Foxrock Geraldines in the Conlon Cup, and Ballyboden and St Columba's in the league. However, as the year went on, numbers began to dwindle, and a cracked collar bone to county star Kevin Synnott in a July game against Stars of Erin certainly didn't help matters.

The juvenile section was beginning to creak too. So bad were things, in fact, that a letter was sent to St Patrick's in Palmerstown, 'requesting a meeting of delegates re possible amalgamation of junior teams with no interference to their juvenile teams'.

In late 1970, Lucan then received a letter from St Pat's requesting something similar on the minor front, in which Seamus Murray from the Palmerstown club wrote:

> We understand that your club has no minor team in hurling or football this year. St Patrick's have entered minor football and hurling teams for the coming leagues, but for a number of reasons we are short a few players for these teams.
>
> The club, therefore, are anxious to acquire the services of any of your minor players on the clear understanding that they will revert to membership of your club on completion of the leagues. There is no question of getting them transferred.

It was a far from ideal situation for Lucan, and one that would lead to many of the club's future hurlers, in particular, playing all of their underage games with St Pat's.

Things were going just as badly in relation to numbers on the adult hurling front in 1970. A special meeting had been organised to discuss the team's future, but only ten people showed up. It was a close call in the end, but after much discussion it was decided to make a special effort to continue the hurling team in the club.

All the same, the club as a whole somehow survived the bout of ill-fortune that had seemingly taken hold in the early part of the new decade, and after a period of time in the Phoenix Park, a new field was found in

REDDY, CHARLTON & McKNIGHT,
(INCORPORATING CHARLES J. REDDY & SON)

GERARD CHARLTON, B.A.,
JOHN McKNIGHT, B.A., L.L.B.,
COMMISSIONERS FOR OATHS.

SOLICITORS.

TELEPHONES :
DUBLIN 62706/7/8

12, FITZWILLIAM PLACE
DUBLIN 2,

OUR REF : JMcK/MD
YOUR REF :

6th July, 1970

RE: Gaelic Athletic Association
Lucan Sarsfields and Sean McDermotts

Dear Sir,

With further reference to this matter we have received a
letter from Mrs.Langan's solicitors which is rather disturbing.
The letter states that Mrs.Langan will not agree at this stage to
accept the rent and her instructions are to proceed with the ejectment
proceedings. This is quite serious as no defence can be offered.
Irrespective of anything else, both the old agreement and the existing
agreement were expressly made for the temporary convenience of both
parties but in particular for the temporary convenience of the Landlord.
In the light of this provision the question of whether or not any defence
would succeed does not arise. If Mrs.Langan is determined to get
possession she does not have to rely upon the result of any Court proceedings.
She merely has to serve three months notice. We feel that those who have
been in touch with Mrs.Langan on this matter should go to her again
immediately and try and have this matter resolved once and for all. There
is hardly need for us to emphasise the urgency of this.

Yours faithfully,
REDDY, CHARLTON & McKNIGHT

Solicitor's letter, 1970, concerning the eviction of the club from Ballydowd.

Dodsboro on what is now the site of the Airlie Heights estate.

Things began to settle down a bit after that, but in 1972 the club would be
dealt another blow with the death of hurler Cormac Fogarty, in an accident. He
had been on the 1962 Corn Céitinn winning team and a keen club member. A
year later the club would present the Corn Fogarty to the County Board in his
honour, which was won by Ballyboden in its first year after they beat Lucan in
the semi-finals. The trophy is still played for in junior hurling.

It was indeed a dark time for the club, but one particular highlight helped
lift the gloom. In September 1971, Christine Dignam, one of the stars of the
tremendously successful Lucan camogie revolution, lined out for the Dubs
in the All-Ireland junior final. Two weeks before the final, a note in the
newsletter wished the Dodsboro girl well:

Dublin were surprise winners of the All-Ireland junior camogie semi-final
in Croke Park last Sunday when they beat last year's finalists Armagh by 4-2
to 1-2. As winners of the title last year, Dublin had to field a completely new
side this season. Local girl Christine Dignam, [from] Dodsboro, at midfield

for her county for the first time, played her part in this good victory. We will be keeping our fingers crossed for Christine and Dublin in the final in Croke Park on September 19.

Dublin went on to win that decider after an epic tussle against old rivals Cork, emerging victorious by 2-2 to 1-2, and Christine returned to Lucan with the club's first ever All-Ireland medal at any grade since the introduction of selected county teams.

The renaissance on the football side had been bolstered by the arrival of John Timmons from the recently disbanded Seán McDermott's club. John had been a member of the successful Dublin senior football panel of the 1960s (and 1963 All-Ireland Championship winners), and his arrival to the club was a huge boost. At a much more fundamental level, however, a much-needed juvenile section revolution was also beginning to get into full swing.

In the latter years of the previous decade, the club's underage teams had begun to fall away, but by 1973 the club would once again be able to field football teams at under-14, under-15 and under-16 level, as well as an under-16 hurling side. By 1974, the club had recovered to the point where they were now fielding under-13 and under-15 football teams, under-16 hurling and football teams, a minor football team, and under-14 parish leagues. The 1975 under-13 footballers, who won their league, were described in reports from the time as, 'one of the best teams ever to represent Lucan at juvenile level'.

It had all come about largely due to efforts in the early 1970s to rejuvenate the juvenile section, a development that simply would not have been possible without the contribution of St Mary's Boys' national school, and the efforts of its teachers.

'I was but a short time teaching in Lucan BNS when I was approached by Billy Kelly asking me to get involved with the club,' former St Mary's BNS teacher, Offaly native and club stalwart, Vincent O'Connor, recalls of the time:

Some time later Billy Malone invited me to the club's weekly Thursday night meeting in the Muintir na Tíre Hall. Both he and club secretary Billy Gogarty felt that the establishment of underage football was to be given top priority.

Following discussions with Joe Collins and Aidan Crean we suggested that an under-15 team would be the best option for a number of reasons. Firstly, most people were willing and available to provide transport and support on a Sunday morning.

And secondly, Coláiste Phádraig was newly established and we felt that a strong school-club link was vital for the long-term development of underage football in

Junior football team, 1971: B. Malone, M. Greene, T. Egan, B. Kane, T. Speight, B. Dardis, J. Byrne, J. Walsh, K. Synnott, C. Molloy, G. Behan. Front: C. Fogarty, D. O'Brien, N. Feeney, B. Gogarty, K. Callaghan, D. Malone, P. Delaney.

the area. Thirdly, it ensured that players from a number of successful Lucan BNS teams have the opportunity to continue playing Gaelic football with the club.

I remember the team's opening game was an away fixture against Good Counsel in September 1971. Any doubts or misgivings we had about the team's ability to compete at that level were very quickly dispelled as we ran out facile winners. Working off a small panel, the team had a very successful league campaign and were in contention for honours right to the end of the season.

Players like H. Tully, Seán McCaffrey, Mick Malone, W. Kilduff, C. Hannibal, C. Coyle, D. Tansey, S. Jackson, P. Croke, G. and M. Condron, F. and W. Stapleton, J. Byrne, E. Slattery, J. Mullarkey, J. Irwin and B. Keenan were a match for any opposition really. Lucan BNS captured the under-13 Corn na Laoch that year too, and team captain Richie Crean, along with L. Fleming, K. Graham, B. Hannigan, G. Croke and M. Byrne, very quickly established themselves in that team.

At the start of the season we purchased a set of jerseys in Sarsfields' traditional green and white colours. However, we broke somewhat with tradition in going for a more modern style of jersey with a round neck and all white sleeves. I remember being rebuked by an irate Round Towers mentor one Sunday morning over in Moyle Park.

The team had just scored a narrow win over Towers, and at the end of the game this particular individual loudly declared that our jerseys weren't proper GAA jerseys and that he would be bringing the matter to the attention of the board.

For the 1972/73 season then the club made the decision to enter both under-15 and under-16 teams. Sunday afternoon fixtures were always problematic though, and not just for us but for a number of clubs working off small panels of players. Fortunately we had a group of really dedicated lads and to their credit the under-15 players would always turn up when the under-16s were short.

Both teams did well in their respective leagues, and I always felt that with this particular group of players we would bring a firm foundation for underage success in the club. The committee gave us every support and encouragement with everything and that really helped.

At the same time, Coláiste Phádraig were playing their part in the underage revival just as vividly. A report in the club's first *Irisleabhar* in March 1973 summed up the progress being made in the Christian Brothers' school at the time:

The 1971/72 school year was a very successful one in many ways for Coláiste Phádraig. Starting the present year, the school mantelpiece sported three trophies at under-14C football and under-14C hurling and under-15C hurling. As a result of their success last year, the school competed this year in the under-14B division.

A panel of some twenty-two players took to training and they gave an excellent account of themselves in the league section of the championship, finishing on full points, after beating St Declan's Cabra, Moyle Park, Parnell Road CBS and Coláiste Mhuire. The team faced Árd Scoil Rís in the semi-final at Islandbridge but they proved too strong and recorded a 4-3 to 1-3 victory.

From that team, Kieran Stephenson, Michael O'Brien and Declan Tansey would go on to help Dublin capture their first Leinster under-14 title.

'The under-15 team also finished the league section on full points with wins over Ballyroan CBS, De La Salle Raheny and De La Salle Roebuck, as well as walkovers over James Street and De La Salle Skerries', the report in the *Irisleabhar* continued, 'The team defeated St Laurence's in Loughlinstown by 2-10 to 1-2 in the semi-final but were mastered in the final by De La Salle Raheny by 4-5 to 0-8.'

The vast improvements in the club's fortunes at underage level were summed up in a report in the 18 December 1974 edition of the *Evening*

Herald, under the headline 'Lucan On Way to the Top Four':

> Four years ago, Lucan Sarsfields were unknown in South City juvenile com-
> petition … To rectify this, the club decided in 1971 to reorganise juvenile
> activities and started by entering an under-15 team in the South City League.
> From this small beginning, juvenile football has grown and developed in a
> remarkable way under the guidance of the special juvenile committee.

A report from a Dublin GAA annual, *c.*1972, signalled the improving fortunes of the club even further:

> The future of any club, of course, depends on the schoolboys, the seniors of
> tomorrow. And, in this regard, an important development, and one that augurs
> well for Lucan Sarsfields, is the fact that Mr Vincent O'Connor, National
> School Teacher, has organised a juvenile team within the club.
>
>   This is proving a most successful venture, and one that is certain to reap rich
> dividends in the years ahead. But then, the Lucan club has always been con-
> scious of the need to promote the interests of youth. Among the developments
> in this direction have been Street Leagues to encourage school leavers …
>
>   The juveniles have made their imprint. The team associated with Lucan
> National Schools won such important titles as the Millar Shield, and, in 1970
> and again in 1972, at under-12 football, the coveted Corn na Laoch. Nor does
> the story end there. This is a club that sets a nationwide headline in that it also
> has a camogie section.
>
>   Hardly surprising, of course, for the club has also a long history in the
> national women's game. Way back in 1905, for instance, a club team won
> the Dublin Camogie Championship. This section of the club was revived in
> recent years and took only two seasons in competitive fare to gain intermedi-
> ate status – a splendid achievement by any measurement.

Richie Crean, who would go on to win an All-Ireland with Dublin in 1983,
recalls how his own footballing career began while attending St Mary's
BNS:

> I got involved in Lucan Sarsfields through the school, and through Vincent
> O'Connor and Tom Roche and Noel Noonan, in particular. The school would
> have had no more than 120 pupils at the time so it was a very small school. We
> got to numerous finals in Croke Park so it was a great time for us, we were
> there nearly every year I was there. We must have won three or four trophies.

I think the first underage game I played for the club was up behind Ma Langan's, but that wouldn't have been until we were around under-14, though I would only have been around eleven or so myself, because there wouldn't have been a huge amount of underage at the time. The school would really have been the real breeding ground for the club, and St Mary's was the only school in the village at the time.

I don't remember winning many trophies with the club, but there were other age groups that did. I know the team that had Tommy Carr and Jack Sheedy on it under Martin Lacey would have won all around them. They were a really top-class team.

Tommy Carr, who would go on to win a National League title with Dublin and an All-Star award in 1991, before captaining the Dubs to a second National League in 1993 while playing with Ballymun Kickams, has equally fond memories of the club's first 'nursery' at St Mary's:

I ended up playing hurling with Palmerstown when I was young because my father used to work up in King's Hospital, but I did all my football with Lucan Sarsfields. I went to St Mary's BNS in Lucan so I played football with the school there too. I think there were only five classrooms in the school at the time.

I remember the very first game of Gaelic football I ever played was actually for St Mary's against Bluebell, so my love of football was really born out of Lucan. From there, of course, I ended up playing with Lucan Sarsfields. I would have played an awful lot of football with Jack Sheedy at the time, and myself and Jack would have backboned a lot of underage teams growing up.

Sheedy, who actually went to primary school in Moyle Park in Clondalkin, has fond memories of that particularly strong Lucan underage team, and the uprising of underage talent within the club:

My first memories of the club would be going over to play under-12s in the 1970s. My Dad, Aidan Crean, and Martin Lacey and Paddy Carr would have been involved, and I would have been playing with Tom Carr and Eoin Mullarkey who would have been the same age as me. We would all have been around eleven. I didn't go to school with the lads at the time though, as I went to Moyle Park, which would have been a lot handier to get to from Balgaddy, where we lived.

We had a super team back in those days, I think we went the best part of two years losing maybe two games. We had Martin Murphy from Balgaddy, Barry Dardis, John and Pat Coyle – we all played together. My family involvement would have been scarce enough though, as my father Jack would have been more into the farming and the boxing than the football really.

He started to get involved when I started playing though and it sort of went from there. I remember going to a match in Thomas Davis and we only had two cars and Dad came over and picked some of us up. People just wouldn't have really had cars in those days; you might only have two parents at a game.

Alan Clarke would have been on that team, he was a super footballer. He actually went on to play for Leeds United. He even played in the Bundesliga in Germany. There were a lot of good soccer lads so there were some clashes there. We had some team, but a lot of the lads wouldn't have even played on long enough with the club to play minor.

A lot of the lads would have gone to St Mary's and they had a very strong school team. They played in Croke Park a few times. That developed through under-12, -13, -14, -15, and we won pretty much everything along the way. We didn't train or anything, we just played. There was very little other distraction in those days, no telly or anything. If you weren't playing football you were playing soccer and that's just the way it was.

I remember playing a trial for South Dublin under-14 with Tommy Carr. I forgot my gear that day and when I got down there to Islandbridge I couldn't find it. There were no mobile phones or anything like that, so I had to run around and try to and cobble some gear together.

I ended up only playing the second half of that game, and that really ruined my chances of making the team. Tommy and Martin Murphy would have made that team. Martin would have been corner back and Tommy would have been wing back. I never made it though. I don't know who was thicker over that, me or my Dad.

While the club's future stars were still cutting their teeth, another of the club's brightest prospects, Kevin Synnott, was making a serious name for himself, winning a Leinster Minor Championship with the county in 1970.

'I remember that year well, but not in the best of ways,' Kevin recalls of his first county season. 'I was on the panel alright but I broke my collar bone up in a tournament in Tallaght. We were beaten in the All-Ireland semi-final that year by Galway. That was the only season I played with the minors.'

Synnott, who had played for the club from under-13 level, would go on to make his debut for the county at senior level in May 1974 in a challenge game against Sligo, and after a 1-14 to 1-9 win over Meath in the Leinster final, and a 2-11 to 1-8 win over Cork in the semi-final, the Dubs brought Sam home with a 0-14 to 1-6 victory over Galway.

It was an amazing achievement, and after nearly a century of producing teams and players, Lucan Sarsfields finally had an All-Ireland senior championship medal in the club. And it had come from the ground up. Kevin fondly recalls his journey from tag-along underage footballer to inter-county superstar:

I'd say it was around 1965 or 1966 when I first got involved with the club, and it would have come about through the Bannons who would have lived up in Westmanstown at the time. I would have been around fourteen or so.

I've lived in Clonsilla all my life, and I suppose St Brigid's would have been the local club to me. But I went out to a match one evening with the Bannons and I never left Lucan Sarsfields after that. I enjoyed every minute of my time playing with the club.

We were doing reasonably well with the club at the time [early 1970s] but we weren't winning anything. Somehow I got my chance with the Dublin team in 1974 under Kevin Heffernan, and I think Nudger [Lucan manager John Timmons] would have been instrumental in that. I went out there and it was a total change of scenery for me from what I would have been used to with playing junior football for the club.

Heffernan changed the whole face of the GAA at the time. He was a disciplinarian – you'd nearly be afraid of him like. If he said jump you just jumped. There were times when you just had to sit and lick your wounds, because you weren't really allowed play much club football, which wouldn't have suited me. But if you wanted to stay on the Dublin panel that was what you had to do.

I played once or twice for the club and sure word got back to him. He told me not to even show up to club games in future and I wouldn't have the problem of being asked to play. I wouldn't swap the experience I had with that Dublin team despite it all. Sure even after we'd all finished playing we'd meet up and play challenge games and charity matches just to get to play together again. I don't know if Dublin will ever have a group of lads like that again.

I didn't actually start in the All-Ireland final against Galway in 1974. I started one year in Leinster, but it was harder sometimes to get off that team than it was to get onto it. Most of that team nearly picked itself. I got two All-Irelands out of it all but I never actually played in an All-Ireland. My All-Ireland was really a National League we won in 1976.

My county career came to an end then really in late 1976. I went over to Chicago and busted all the ligaments in my ankle. I arrived there on a Wednesday and I was on crutches by the Friday. Not only was that the first time I'd played on an all-weather pitch, I'd say it was the first time I ever even saw one. I came home early from that trip to get the ankle sorted out, but that was the end for me.

I was told I'd never play football again, but I continued on with the club for another good few years. I should have quit playing with Dublin a year earlier than I did and just gone back to the club. I was getting no enjoyment trekking around the country, but I suppose the lads in the club would have encouraged me to stay on as well. It was one big happy family up there. I might have played with some of the best players ever for Dublin, but I was never happier than when I was back in Lucan.

While Kevin was bringing glory to the club at county senior level, the club's junior football team was finally beginning to replicate their biggest star's success. After forty years of heartbreak, the Junior A Football League title would finally wing its way back to Lucan in 1974. After a painstaking 1-6 to 1-6 draw with O'Toole's in the county final, Lucan came good in the replay to emerge 2-14 to 1-3 winners. It was a day in November that the club would never forget.

The replay was marred by one particularly ugly incident which resulted in the dismissal of an O'Toole's player, but in the end, Lucan came good thanks to fine performances from Martin Greene, F. Brennan and Charlie O'Connor in particular.

'The whole club was nearly carried by the same lads who played football and hurling,' Synnott recalls of the adult section of the club at the time and the 1974 league win:

Some of the lads could be playing hurling matches in the mornings and football matches that afternoon. That was a team that played together for nearly ten years. Desie O'Brien, Mick Molloy, Billy Gogarty, Martin Greene, they were the nucleus of the club for years. So to finally win something was great for those lads in particular.

But while the league win was a tremendous victory for the club, it could have actually been so much better that same year. A run to the championship final, and the manner with which it was achieved, had lifted the entire area. In September, the team had put in a stunning quarter-final display to defeat Clontarf by 2-9 to 1-3, putting Lucan in a Junior Football Championship semi-final for the first time since 1934.

The run didn't end there, and in February 1975 Lucan found themselves in a county final. That was as far as the dream would go, however, and despite a Trojan effort against hugely strong opposition from Beann Eadair, they fell at the final hurdle, 1-7 to 0-6.

A defeat in the Conlon Cup final at the hands of Thomas Davis a few weeks later added insult to injury. All the same, promotion to the intermediate league had finally been secured for the 1975 season, a development that would stand to the club in the historic years to come.

Meanwhile, the issue of playing fields continued. The club had been playing in Dodsboro since the early part of the decade and it was a place of happy memories for many of the juvenile teams in particular. Mick Molloy recalls a humerous incident at an under-14 game there in the mid-'70s:

> We were playing Ballyfermot in an under-14 game in Dodsboro. I was looking after the team, and I remember during the match one of the Ballyfermot lads went over to the ditch to relieve himself and he discovered a bush full of blackberries and before we knew what was happening, the rest of the Ballyfermot team had left the field of play and followed him over to eat the blackberries leaving the referee and the Lucan lads standing in wonder.

Mick recalls another incident from being involved with juvenile teams that portrays the different ethos of the era:

> I remember one day we were were going to a match with a group of young lads, under-13 or -14 I think, and myself and Paul Heneghan packed them all into our two cars down at the national school. I was travelling behind Paul when I noticed a lot of smoke coming from the car and I thought it was on fire. I flagged him to stop to investigate what was wrong. Paul assured me that the car was fine and it was only the young lads smoking in the back! One of the lads was young McMorrow from Sarsfields Park.

Despite the many amusing interludes and enjoyable experiences of the era, the more serious business of securing playing fields and a permanent home was still lurking. By late 1977, however, the club was closer to a satisfactory long-term resolution than ever before, curiously with the help of two Golden Labradors. Mick Molloy takes up the story:

> Having been there [Dodsboro] for a number of years, the council decided that we should move to Arthur Griffith. It was decided that an old ruin there should be refurbished for dressing rooms, which was done voluntarily by all clubs concerned. We put huge work into it and when they were almost

complete we had a meeting with the council where we requested keys for one of the rooms to lock up equipment, but we were refused. This all happened around 1974/75.

I was absolutely furious so I set in motion a committee to look into the possibility of finding a ground of our own, and the committee formed was Billy Gogarty, Bob Dardis, Charlie O'Connor and myself. We looked and enquired about grounds around Lucan, Ballydowd, and the Liffey Mills' ground on the lower road, but without success. Then, by accident, I came across the lands at the 12th Lock. I had a Golden Labrador bitch that had escaped to go 'courting' with a Labrador dog that was owned by the Jameson family (of whiskey fame), and I was out looking for the dogs when I came across the 12th Lock land. It was not in use, a derelict pigsty and cow shed was all that was on the site, and the grounds were overgrown.

I contacted Mick Anderson, a member and player who was working in the adjacent mill, to see if he knew who owned the site. Mick informed me that it was owned by Shackletons, the mill owners, and he told me to talk to Chappy Malone. He in turn told me to talk to Joe Collins, as he knew the Shackletons well, so that I did and Joe and John Collins had a meeting with Shackletons and negotiated a price.

We then had to have an EGM [October, 1977] where we had to convince everybody to back the project. We approached the County Board and the bank we had been dealing with. The County Board wase supportive, but after two or three weeks the bank refused. We got this word on a Thursday and we had to have confirmation if we were going ahead with the project the following Monday.

I had a discussion with Billy Gogarty and we decided to try a different bank and a different approach. We contacted some local business people to see if they would support us at a meeting which we arranged on the following Friday with AIB manager Noel Clarke. Joe Collins, Bill Griffin, Colm Moran, Billy Gogarty and myself met Mr Clarke and explained the situation, but left the bank that evening not knowing how we were fixed.

The bank manager rang me on the Sunday then to give us the go ahead on the basis that a down payment was required, so we set out to raise the money. We decided to ask every member for an interest-free loan. So we collected this and the down payment was paid to the bank. That was the easy part, then the work to get the place into shape to play games and provide dressing rooms, etc., had to begin. The rest is history!

Of course, it would all cost money.

'The population of Lucan was growing at the time, and the membership in the club was steadily expanding,' Padraig McGarrigle, chairman of the club from 1981-1985, recalls:

The possibility of purchasing our own grounds was high on the agenda, but there were a fair few Doubting Thomases around at the time who thought this was just absolutely ridiculous and that we were fine the way we were. The majority ruled and the day finally came when we had a home of our own.

Two other major events happened around that time that in my opinion had a huge impact on the development of the club. First was the foundation, or rejuvenation, of the juvenile section, and the other was the setting up of a finance committee.

The finance committee met for the first time in my house, I remember, and it consisted of Paddy Kelly, Jim McCarthy, Jim O'Brien, Mick Hurley, Tony Strong, Dan McCarthy, Martin Murtagh, Mick Molloy and Joan Fitzharris. We worked our way along pretty quietly, but it was pretty difficult to get funds because there was a fair bit of unemployment around at the time.

The juvenile committee, meanwhile, consisted of a few local teachers like Seán Nolan and Vincent O'Connor, as well Paul Heneghan, Paddy Kelly, Joan Fitzharris, Tony Tobin and the hugely influential John McCaffrey.

We reckoned we needed to have about £2,000 in the bank to be able to secure the purchase of the field. One of the novel schemes the finance committee came up with was to get forty good people to make a contribution of £50 each. It was done in bond form so as anyone could come looking for that money back from us at any time, but suffice to say that nobody ever did. We bought the ground then, and it was really all made possible thanks in no small part to Noel Clarke, who was the manager of the local AIB bank at the time.

He had a great interest in GAA despite the fact that rugby was his own game; he was actually an inter-provincial rugby referee at the time. He was hugely helpful and in a lot of ways it probably couldn't have happened without him, or certainly not as speedily anyway.

Finally, in early 1978, the 12th Lock grounds were purchased from the Shackletons for £51,500. It was quite a moment for the club.

Back on the playing fields, the hurlers had made a Lazarus-like recovery from the lows of the early 1970s, and in 1974 had improved to the point where they reached the Corn Céitinn, Corn Fogarty and Junior League finals. The league title, after so many years of waiting, would finally be winging its way back to the club.

It had been a long time in coming, seventy years in fact, but after almost a century of heartache, in January 1975, Lucan Sarsfields finally won the Junior A Hurling League of 1974/75. A report on the final, published in the *Evening Herald*, described their stunning 4-8 to 3-2 win over Grocers:

Putting on a top-class performance, Lucan Sarsfields won the Junior A League title after a lapse of seventy years when they defeated Grocers in a very sporting game in O'Toole Park on Sunday. The Michael Smith Cup, which was presented to the winners after the game by Junior Hurling Board Chairman Pat McCarthy, was first competed for in the 03/04 competition when it was won by the Céitinn club.

The following season, Lucan Sarsfields took the title and the cup, and one of the stars of that great win was the late Michael Downes who was associated

Lucan's historic win

Lucan Sarsfields, 4-8;
Grocers, 3-2

PUTTING ON a top class performance Lucan Sarsfields won the Junior "A" League title after a lapse of seventy years when they defeated Grocers in a very sporting game in O'Toole Park on Sunday.

The Michael Smith Cup, which was presented to the winners after the game by Junior Hurling Board Chairman Pat McCarthy, was first competed for in the 1903-4 competition when it was won by the Céitinn club.

The following season Lucan Sarsfields took the title and the cup and one of the stars of that great win was the late Michael Downes who was associated with the activities of this great West County club all his life and two of whose grandsons, Larry Downes and Des O'Brien, shone in this latest win.

Another link on Sunday with that 1905 win was eighty-six-year-old (or young!) Club president Tom Slattery who roared and shouted his team on to victory from the sideline like any two-year-old. Tom was a playing member of Sarsfields in 1905 but was too young then for the junior hurling side.

Grocers, with the strong wind to help them in the first half, kept the Lucan defence under constant pressure. Despite great work by Billy Gogarty, Pat Delaney, Charlie Synott and Tom McCarthy kept picking off their scores and were 3-2 to 0-1 in front at the interval.

However, right from the start of the second half Sarsfields set about reducing the arrears. Showing great determination and spirit and producing some top class hurling they soon wore down Grocers' defence.

Inspired by a great goal from Martin Greene the Lucan forwards clicked into top gear and with a point from a free by Des O'Brien followed immediately by another sparkling Greene goal they were on the way to victory.

There was just no holding Lucan and goals from Michael Heffernan and Martin Ryan, along with points from Des O'Brien and Kevin Synott, put the issue beyond doubt entering the last quarter.

Others to shine for Sarsfields were Noel Feeney, Michael Nealon, Barney Bannon and Willie Kennedy. Best for Grocers were J. McDonnell, D. Fitzgerald, B. Dwyer, Sean Carey, Declan Fitzgerald and P. Phelan.

The main attraction of next Sunday's programme will be the replay of the semi-final of the 1974 Corn Céitinn competition in O'Toole Park between Lucan Sarsfields and St. Brigid's.

Last time out Lucan did everything required to win but didn't! This time they should make no mistake.

The 1975 Corn also gets underway with plenty of interesting games down for decision.

All clubs are reminded that as and from next Sunday referees must be paid 75p expenses by each team BEFORE the start of the game.

Defaulting teams will automatically forfeit the game and be also liable to a fine of £5 if the expenses are still unpaid by the following Wednesday. The expenses must also be paid to referees for all challenge and tournament games.

The first full meeting of the Junior Hurling Board of 1975 takes place on Tuesday in 6 North Great George's Street at 8 p.m.

The suggested groupings for the four regional teams for the Senior Hurling Championship are as follows:
Group A—Aer Lingus, Erin's Isle, Trinity College, St. Ita's, Lusk.

Group "B" — St. Brigid's, SS. Michael and James, Lucan Sarsfields, An Caislean, Round Towers.

Group "C" — Cuala Casements, Geraldine Patrick Morans, Father Murphys, Young Irelands, Kevins, Dundrum.

Group "D"—Commercials, Grocers, Raheny, Scoil Ui Chonaill, Parnells.

Evening Herald report on Lucan's Junior A League title win.

St Mary's BNS team, 1974: D. Ryan, N. O'Neill, D. McDonald, J. Crean, P. Thompson, M. Murphy, M. Woods, M. McStay, R. Callen. Front: B. Hassett, A. Crean, A. Clarke, B. Dardis, S. McNamee, P. Keating, D. Brady, T. Carr, T. Newcombe, J. Coyle.

with the activities of this great west county club all his life, and two of his grandsons, Larry Downes and Des O'Brien, shone in this latest win. Another link on Sunday with that 1905 win was eighty-six-year-old (or young!) club president Tom Slattery who roared and shouted his team on to victory from the sideline like any two year old. Tom was a playing member of Sarsfields in 1905 but was too young then for the junior hurling side.

Grocers, with the strong wind to help them in the first half, kept the Lucan defence under pressure. Despite great work by Billy Gogarty, Pat Delaney, Charlie Synnott and Tom McCarthy, Grocers kept picking off their scores and were 3-2 to 0-1 in front at the interval. However, right from the start of the second half, Sarsfields set about reducing the arrears. Showing great determination and spirit and producing some top-class hurling, they soon wore down Grocers' defence.

Inspired by a great goal from Martin Greene, the Lucan forwards clicked into gear, and with a point from a free by Des O'Brien, followed immediately by another sparkling Greene goal, they were on the way to victory. There was just no holding Lucan, and goals from Michael Heffernan and Martin Ryan, along with points from Des O'Brien and Kevin Synnott, put the issue beyond doubt entering the last quarter. Others to shine for Sarsfields were Noel Feeney, Michael Nealon, Barney Bannon and Willie Kennedy.

Slattery's almost childlike and infectious enthusiasm was nothing new to the players. Aidan Dardis remembers him landing on the sideline at a club game in the Phoenix Park around that time and giving his two cents to the goings-on on the field:

> I was playing at corner back one day and I remember I held off the corner forward to allow the ball to go wide. The referee decided I'd fouled him and gave a free in. I looked around anyway and there, standing behind the posts, leaning on his bike, was Tom Slattery, who, in very strong language, expressed his disagreement with the referee.
>
> The ref ordered him away from goals, but Tom refused, saying it was a public park and that the ref had no authority to move him on … So the referee said he was going to get a park ranger to move him, to which Tom replied, 'You can go get a f★★★ing Texas Ranger, I'm not moving anywhere.' And he didn't.

While those young players were being nurtured through the juvenile section, there was always scope for 'outside' recruitment. Even into the 1980s, people like Paul Heneghan would have the jersey on random lads and the ball thrown in before the poor sods even knew what was happening. He recalls of one incident some years later:

> We went over with a Junior B team to Clondalkin, I think it was Deansrath, one day, and we hadn't a full team. Dinny Malone was looking after the team at that stage and we were looking for players. There was a Travellers' site beside the pitches, and I rambled over and asked one of them would they play with Lucan Sarsfields. Jesus, sure they were only too delighted to play!
>
> We ended up getting two of the Travellers over, but we were only short one player, so one of them started for us. It was the biggest crowd we had around a Junior B pitch for years I'd say. He was nearly the best player on the field! We never heard from him again, but we had some audience that day.

On another couple of occasions it was Bob Dardis doing the recruiting. Going out for a walk with the dog in the park could lead to lining out at corner-forward for a team from the other side of the county as he recalls here:

I remember one day we had to play Crumlin in the cup and we went over to play them in Marlay Park. When we got there we only had thirteen people, and that included myself. There were only eleven players really, so I dragged in a few lads we saw kicking a ball around the place. I don't know who they were, but they were two fliers, and I remember the forward line that day … there was Padraig McGarrigle, myself and Dinny Malone. We beat Crumlin by two points.

Another time, out in Glenalbyn, we played Kilmacud Crokes, and some of the lads got lost on the way so we only had thirteen. There were these two lads with boots wandering around ready to play, so I shouted over at them asking if they were ready to play. They were actually on their way to Kilmacud to play against us. They were two very good players, and it was only when the match was over that we discovered who they were or what they were and that they were supposed to be playing for the opposition.

Meanwhile, the hurling progress was continuing and the league success of 1974 was nearly followed with a championship. But despite the remarkable improvements in the side, Erin's Isle would prove too strong in the championship final which was played in March 1975. Lucan had been slow to settle in the early stages, as the nerves of the big occasion ran riot, and Isles had raced into a three-goal lead before Lucan had ever really got their bearings.

Trailing by 4-4 to 1-5 at the break, it was too little too late for the Sarsfields men, and despite a gallant effort, the Finglas outfit emerged with the honours by virtue of a 6-10 to 3-7 win. It was another gutting defeat for Lucan, but it wasn't all grim.

The journey to that point had been most encouraging. A win over St Vincent's in the championship had been a massive fillip. Trailing by 1-8 to 0-3 at half time, Lucan were playing into the wind in the second half, and to add to their plight they conceded an early goal shortly after the restart.

From nowhere, and led by Michael Nealon, Cha O'Connor and Des O'Brien, the team somehow dragged themselves back into the contest thanks to goals from Martin Ryan and P. Feeney, and with five minutes left Sarsfields led by five points.

Vincent's struck a late goal to keep their hopes alive, but Lucan held on to claim a famous victory under selectors Tommy McCormack, Andy Kelly and P.J. Ryan. Tom Slattery famously commented at the time that this was the best Lucan team he'd ever seen.

In September 1975, continuing on from where they'd left off, and after a thrilling final against St Ita's from which they emerged 4-8 to 2-3 winners, Sarsfields brought the Corn Fogarty, a trophy named in honour of one of the club's fallen young hurlers of the 1960s, back to Lucan for the first time.

It had been a special occasion, with Tom Slattery throwing in the ball and the Clondalkin Pipe Band providing the music. That night both teams made their way up to the Spa Hotel, where Cormac Fogarty's father presented the cup to Lucan. It was one of the most emotional victories in the history of the club.

Although bolstered by this tremendous success, the hurlers hadn't got long to settle down before the championship was once again upon them in October. Having lost the previous season's championship final earlier in the same calendar year, it was another heartbreaking day out for the club. This time New Irelands would prove the villains. A valiant effort had seen Lucan come up just short again, losing out this time by 2-14 to 1-12.

While the Junior Championship had once again eluded the hurlers, the team's first season in the intermediate ranks saw them reach a top-four semi-final, losing out to rivals Commercials by 2-9 to 3-5. Another bitter pill to swallow it might well have been, but compared to the state the club had been in just six years earlier, these were heady times for Lucan Sarsfields.

Fr Tommy McCarthy had scored all three of Lucan's goals in that inter semi-final loss, and one of the stars of that team, Barney Bannon, recalls another one of his own favourite characters from the era:

> The man I remember most that I got the most laughs out of was big Andy Kelly. I remember one day Andy happened to be on the sideline and we were getting badly trounced in a hurling game … With about ten minutes to go it was decided to spring Andy from the sideline … The first thing he did when he came on to the pitch was he ran over to the referee and says 'Ref, how much time is left here?' as if he was going to turn the whole game around on his own … As it happened, he didn't manage to do anything for us, but he was a funny guy. He was a comical man to talk to.

Another character, recalls Bob Dardis, was junior football manager John Timmons:

> I remember a match when John was playing with us and he got put off. The referee was a little small fella, and John called him a little Orange b★★tard. Whatever went on, we were over at a board meeting the following Tuesday evening and we were told that a very bad report had come in from the referee and that John would have to come in the following week.
>
> I was saying to myself, 'this is going to be fun alright', so I went in along

with him and I briefed him. I had to go in first and plead his case and all that, but I came out and I said to him that we might get away with it and that he might get a fortnight suspension or whatever.

He was called in to the meeting then in front of the whole board, and there would have been sixty or seventy fellas there. 'John Timmons, we've a report here from a match there recently where the referee says he put you off and you called him a little Orange b★★tard.' 'He *is* a little Orange b★★tard!' says John, and sure the whole place erupted!

The hurlers began their 1976 campaign in ideal fashion, beating a strong St Vincent's side in the opening round of the championship. 'This was an excellent display of hurling by a Lucan team,' the committee heard, 'and if we continue with this form our chances in the championship rate very high.'

A 3-14 to 2-7 quarter-final win over Na Fianna saw them book a place in the last four against Ballyboden, but that was as far as they would get once again. The team fell five points short of an appearance in yet another county final, but things were going well in the league, and playing at a higher level was far from hurting a developing team.

The junior footballers, meanwhile, who were enjoying their first season at intermediate league level, were on yet another championship run. The year had started incredibly brightly with a squad of thirty-two players, the most in many years, turning up for the team's opening round win over St Columba's, after having already secured a Loving Cup win over a strong Thomas Davis side and an Inter League win over Civil Service.

Despite some early season issues with attendances and training, the team really gelled after a Loving Cup clash with neighbours St Finian's. The game had to be abandoned, 'because of a flare up five minutes from the end of the game', but the team's performance had been described as a 'very good display', and despite team coach John Timmons 'apologising for this unsavoury happening', the players had been knit that much closer together.

At a club meeting in March, Timmons expressed succinctly the positivity racing through the veins of the club at the time, saying that, 'he felt the club has gone from strength to strength in the past six months. This club is now one of the strongest in the county and he felt that we have attained a privileged position although contesting three county finals and with nothing to show.'

Timmons, with plenty of experience at the highest level, was bringing a whole new approach to training, 'The new procedure [for training] will be more strict and anyone who feels he is doing enough ... it is up to the trainers to decide that.' Timmons told the committee of his intentions for the year ahead:

Coiste Conndae Ath Cliath

Lucan Sarsfields. 21 1976

CUMANN LUITHCHLEAS GAEDHEAL

Club	Name & Address of Hon. Sec.
Air Corps F.C.	Sergt.K.Browne, Baldonnell Aerodrome,Clondalkin.
Aer-Corp H.C.	Seamus Ua Fheanchaillligh, Baldonnell,Clondalkin.
Army F.C.	Coy.Sgt.Micheal O Caoinlean,McKee Barracks,Dublin
Aer Lingus	Eoin Mac Alinden, Aerphort, Atha Cliath.
Aer Lingus	Padraig O Duibhir, 4 Hampstead Park, Glasnevin.
Banba F.C.	Albert O'Beirne, 46 North Avenue, Mt.Merrion.
Ballyboughal Rangers F.C.	Padraig B. Corra, Ballyboughal, Co. Dublin.
Ben Edair	Daibheid Mac Camhaoil, 1 Hillside Terrace,Howth.
Bros.Pearse	Proinnsias Mac Eochaidh, 15 Elm Park , Terenure.
Benburbs F.C.	M. Pope, 7 Beach Hill, Donnybrook. (ean
Colaiste Albert	Micheal M.Breathnach,Colaiste Albert,Glasnaoidh-
Collins F.C.	S.S. O Raghailligh, Collins Barracks, Dublin.
Clann na nOg	Sean O Cuimin, 331 Clogher Road. Dolphins Barn.
Columcille H.C.	Fintan Donnellan, Palmerstown, Chapelizod,Co.Dub.
Colmcille F.C.	Patrick O'Brien, 19 Crescent Gardens, West Road.
Clanna Gael (Minor)	Diarmuid O Suibhne, 118 Quarry Road.
Clanna Gael	Liam Donovan, 39 Greygates, Mount Merrion.
Crokes	Sean Roche, 235 Upper Rathmines Road.
College of Pharmacy	Liam Bourke, 162 Pearse Street, Dublin.
Civil Service F.C.	Caoimhin Mac Philib, 7 Ontario Tce., Rathmines.
Civil Service H.C. (H.C.	Seamus O hAodain, 160 Crumlin Road.
Dublin Port & Docks Bd.	R.Lawlor, 6 Millmount Place. Drumcondra.
Dal Cais	Diarmuid Mac Raghnaaill, Drogheda At.Drogheda.
Eoghan Ruadh H.C.	B.O'Rourke, Esq., 21 Annamoe Road, Cabra.
Erin's Isle	James Maloney, Dubber, Finglas.
Fingall Rovers	Sean Donnelly, Oldtown, Co. Dublin.
Fr. Murphy H.C.	James Sheehan, 13 Plas Ui Mhanachain, Baile Phib
Fontenoy H.C.	M.Fletcher, 16 Dolphin Road, Dolphins Barn.
Fingallians F.C.	Patrick McKitterick, 4 The Green, Swords.
Faughs H.C.	P. O Fearghail, 37 New Ireland Rd., Dublin.
Geraldines	Sean Byrne, 20 Torlough Gardens, Fairview.
Guinnesses F.C.	Seamus O Liathain, 17 Bothar Doilfin.
Garda F.C.	Bernard Byrne, Sundrive Road,Garda Station.
Garda H.C.	Richard O'Shea, 16 Adrian Avenue, Harolds Cross
Grocers H.C.	John Carey,24 Terenure Rd.,East.
Inrisfail G.F.C.	Seamus Barnes, Balgriffin, Co. Dublin.
Independent H.C.	Peadar O Rinn, 242 Phibsborough Road.
Kickhams H.C. & F.C.	A.Carr, 24 Carlingford Road, Drumcondra.
Kevins H.C.	Padraig McGrath, 25 Leinster Street, Phibsboro
Lucan Sarsfields F.C.& H.C.	H.D.Dardis, 1 Lucan Road, Palmerstown,Co.Dublin.
Maurice O'Neills H.C.& F.C.	Sean O Cadhain, 49 Derrynane Gardens,Sandymount.
Man o' War F.C.	John Jones, Man o' War, Skerries. (Croimlinn
Moindearg	M.P.de Hindeberg,Sliabh Ruadh,Pairc San Mora,
Naomh Fionnbarr H.C.& F.C.	Seamus O Nuallain, 38 Bothar an Bhainbh,Cabrach.
Naomh Eanna F.C.	Sean O Broin, Teach Franshaw, Crumlin Rd.
New Ireland Ass.Co. H.C.	Michael F.Brennan,16 Lr.Brigid's Rd.,Drumcondra.
O'Donovan Rossa H.C.	Austin Harrington, 67 Jamestown Rd., Inchicore.
O'Moores H.C. & F.C.	Padraig O Meachair, 10 Connolly Gardens, do.
O'Dwyers F.C.	Traolach O Coinlean, 30 Craoibhin Park,Baile Brign
O'Connell's Boys H.& F.C.	G. McGurk, 9 Seville Place.
Palmerstown Gaels	Thomas Dardis, 1 Lucan Rd., Palmerstown,Co.Dublin

Full list of Dublin contacts, 1976.

Under-11A football team of 1976, before a league clash with Thomas Davis.

Players not turning up in time for training have an adverse effect on their own team. Allowances will have to be made so that everyone comes in time. It is basically [about] the mental approach to the club and to the game.

Each and everyone should have his own gear prepared in time and not be searching on the day of a game for a loan of gear. Players spending two nights training must appreciate that the pub is not the place to spend the rest of the time.

Well, some things never change, it seems. It was all about the attitude for John though. All about a winning mentality that had thus far eluded a storied club with very few happy stories to tell:

Our ambition should be to attain senior status and be prepared to get this into our minds that winning should be our prime aim. If players meet outside of games they should chat among themselves in a way of encouragement and advice. The rest is all important … fitness, both mentally and physically. Smoking should be reduced if one smokes. Now that the evenings are getting longer everyone should look forward to training, even if you are not feeling well, come up to the ground only to show his face to his other club members and create a proper atmosphere among one another.

Seán Nolan remembers Timmons' impact on the team:

John was a great character. His move to the club was huge for us. I suppose it was just a pity that he was towards the end of his own playing career. He had a great input as coach though. We'd be looking forward to the training sessions. We really prospered under John. He was a big man, sometimes it took two of us to put the jersey on him, but he was a great man and he really contributed a huge amount to the club.

This new attitude seemed to be making inroads. Having beaten O'Connell Boys in the quarter-final of the championship, the team soon found themselves in the county decider thanks to a 0-12 to 1-7 semi-final win over Man-O-War. St Vincent's would provide the opposition in the final, this time in Parnell Park, but once again that final breakthrough win eluded the club. Vinny's would emerge 2-9 to 2-4 winners, amazingly the Marino giants' first ever Junior Football Championship title. A whopping seventy-four teams had taken part in that competition.

It was yet another blow to a club on the up and up. 'This was a case of beating ourselves, yet it was a great achievement in getting to the final,' the committee were told. 'A very bad start to the game and the many missed chances added to our downfall.'

'That was a serious let down for us,' Kevin Synnott recalls. 'It was a bad day at the office. Vincent's were probably a better team on the day, but a lack of experience in finals really got to a lot of lads that day I think.'

Despite the disappointment of having fallen short once again, the seeds had been sewn in this group of players. Finally, after so many years of almost getting there, 1977 would prove the year that it would all come good at long last. It would be a year to seriously savour for the long-suffering supporters of Lucan Sarsfields.

A quality crop of youngsters were coming through the ranks, with the under-21 footballers getting their season off to a winning start in November, beating St Fergal's in the first round of the championship. They would lose in the following round to a very strong Erin's Isle side, but the stage was set for an extraordinarily successful 1977 for everyone in the footballing fraternity in the club.

It began in December 1976 with an opening-round tie against Erin's Isle in the Junior Championship in Ashtown. The team emerged impressive victors with a performance that was described as 'a welcome return to our best form', and everyone went into the Christmas break in high spirits. By February, the club's youngsters were beginning to break through at county level, with S. Downes, K. Coyle, B. Hannigan and Richie Crean all put forward for trials, and Hannigan and Crean both making the 1977 Dublin minor football team.

St Mary's BNS Cumann na nGael winners, 1977. Includes: Larry O'Toole, ___, Aaron Callaghan, David O'Toole, Gilmore, ___, Ronan Duke, ___, Stuart Clarke. Front row: Ronan O'Flynn, Brian Malone, James Clifford, Donal Griffin, Niall Doyle, Mark Dardis, Declan Kane, ___, Coyle.

The second round of the Junior Championship arrived in March, and a full turnout led to a hard-earned win over Casement Gaels. Lucan were really taking this charge seriously, and at a meeting in late March it was decided that they would protect their only senior inter-county star when, 'it was agreed that where championship fixtures are involved, we will not play unless Kevin Synnott is available and free from county duty'.

It did the trick. An epic one-point semi-final win over championship favourites and bitter rivals St Vincent's saw Lucan through to a Junior Championship Final with the club's best chance of winning the competition within the team's reach. The entire area was buzzing with anticipation.

At the same time, the under-21 footballers, starring M. Dwyer, G. Canavan, Liam Fleming, N. Rankin and Richie Crean in particular, had progressed to the final of the South City Division 2 league, and on another massive day for the club they beat Good Counsel by 2-7 to 3-3 at O'Toole Park. With John McCaffrey and Jim Quinn at the reins, the team had gone one better than the year before, and it was a special moment for the club, mostly because the team had been together as a unit since under-15. It was a development vital to the prospects of the future. The stage was set for that much-awaited breakthrough at adult level.

It had felt like a lifetime in coming, but finally, in October 1977, Lucan Sarsfields, 'at long last won the much-coveted Dublin Junior Championship' by virtue of a 1-18 to 0-6 hammering of Park Rangers in the county final (seventy-seven teams had started out in the competition). It was the club's first ever Junior Football Championship, and with it came the even bigger prize of a place in the intermediate ranks. A report in the *Evening Herald* on 9 October, under the headline 'Lucan trounce Park Rangers', told the story of what had been a completely one-sided final and a hugely historic day for Lucan Sarsfields:

> The fans at Parnell Park on Sunday were sorely disappointed as the game, apart from the fine football by the Lucan side, was a complete flop, as at no time were Rangers ever in the hunt. Rangers started with a flourish and took the lead with a point but when Lucan settled in they played superb football and they had the game double wrapped up by half time when they led by 1-10 to 0-2.
>
> The second-half was just a practice run for Lucan, who gave a perfect performance. Their scorers were B. Lennon (1-1), J. Lydon (0-6), M. Greene (0-4), D. O'Brien (0-2), Stephenson (0-2), A. Coyle (0-1), K. Synnott (0-1) and D. Tracey (0-1).

After years of being robbed and denied by teams full of illegal players and mercenary outsiders, it seemed only fitting that Lucan had beaten a team made up almost entirely of players from the country. Bob Dardis recalls going into that decider knowing full well what the opposition were planning:

> We used to go to watch Park Rangers matches quite a fair bit when our matches would be finished. We'd start off early in the morning with our own match and then we'd have a few pints and then head across to watch them play. I'll always remember on the eve of the junior championship final when I decided to go into Weir's, and John [Timmons] said he was coming in later with somebody else.
>
> I was in there and Paddy Hartnett, who used to run Park Rangers at the time, walked in, and I says 'Paddy, you know I'll know every player you put out, and I don't mind you putting out fellas that I know are on, but if you bring up any strangers and you beat us out of sight I'll bloody protest!' He turns to me and he says, 'Bobby, if any team comes up I'll put the bloody jerseys on them!' He did bring on a few bangers that day; I remember they had a fella from Westmeath who played in the centre of the field who was brilliant. But we beat them anyway.

Kevin Synnott lists that day in Parnell Park as his finest in a long and storied career with the club:

The day we won the junior championship is definitely my happiest memory with the club. I had won medals along the way playing with Dublin in National Leagues and Leinster championships and All-Irelands, but to see the likes of Desie O'Brien, Mick Molloy, Mick Anderson, Charlie Molloy and those lads, lads who had put their hearts and souls into the club and who were involved in every aspect of it from running it to playing for it, to see those lads finally get something out of it was very special.

We got to something like five finals one year, and the only two we won were two of the lesser ones. The year we won that championship was just so special because I think the Dublin Junior Championship is probably the hardest one to win in the whole of Ireland. That was the sweetest one, from my point of view anyway.

Lucan captain that day, Seán Nolan, also points to that famous victory as a massive career highlight:

The Junior Championship was just so hard to win. There would have been around 100 teams competing in the junior championship at any time. We'd often reach the advanced stages, but it wasn't until 1977 that we finally won it. I was captain that day, and although I know I certainly didn't play all that well, it was a huge honour for me.

There were great characters on that team. The likes of the Molloys, Kevin Synnott, Billy Gogarty, Mick Casey, Martin Greene (a great Clare man) and Padraig McGarrigle was there too. We beat Park Rangers in that final, but I think our great achievement that year was actually beating St Vincent's in a low-scoring semi-final. I think it was 0-6 to 0-5 it finished, but we knew once we'd beaten them that we'd go on to win the whole thing.

After so many years of trying, Lucan had finally made the breakthrough. And with it, in 1978, the club would be playing in the Intermediate Football Championship. The debut that followed was nothing short of sensational.

A brilliant run led them to a semi-final date with Blanchardstown rivals St Brigid's. Lucan ran the northsiders off their feet in the opening minutes, racing into a 1-2 to no score lead after five minutes, inspired by the half-back line of Cha O'Connor, Mick Casey and Joe Murray. From there the team drove on, and scores from Seán Nolan, Liam Fleming and Eddie Mescall led them to an impressive, and very convincing, 3-10 to 1-4 win.

The town was buzzing, and Lucan, after years of aspiring to their ultimate goal, now found themselves just sixty minutes away from the senior ranks in just their first attempt at the Intermediate Championship. Alas, the gap would prove just too big to breach. Despite a gutsy effort, the class of opponents Kilmacud shone through in the 16 July decider, as the southsiders, who were unbeaten in the senior ranks of the league, emerged 3-10 to 0-11 winners.

'We lost that final more than they won it. Nerves got to us again that day. Lads that we needed to play well just didn't play well,' Synnott recalls. 'We still had a very strong team, and we were very unfortunate to lose that match by just a couple of points to a very strong Kilmacud team,' Seán Nolan agrees. 'We stayed inter for a good few years, but it was very difficult to get up senior.'

It wasn't all bad news though. Lucan was blooding yet another star of the future. Richie Crean had made his adult debut with the club in that 1977 final, and was building a wealth of invaluable experience representing the county:

> I got on the Dublin minor panel in 1976, and then on the team proper in 1977, the same year we won the Junior Championship with the club. The only game I played that year was the final, and that was a fantastic day. Some of the fellas I was playing with on that team … well suffice it to say that I was happier playing with them than against them!

Despite the disappointment, progress was most certainly being made. Another breakthrough, though still a few years away, would follow early in the following decade. The club's hurlers, meanwhile, were doing more than just surviving in the Intermediate league in the late seventies.

In March 1977, they reached the top-four semi-final, only to lose out at the hands of Kevin's by just two points, while the under-21s had also enjoyed a solid championship run before losing out to SS Michael and James in the latter stages of the competition.

The decade wound down in disappointment for the small ball game in the club. After reaching the quarter-final of the 1978 Junior Championship, they threw away a golden opportunity to beat one of the competition's favourites, Kevin's, drawing on a scoreline of 3-8 to 1-14. They were hammered by twelve points in the replay, and the wait for success with the small ball would continue into the 1980s.

The club's hurling section was in serious trouble by that stage in the late seventies. Jim Quinn, a native of Castlecomer in County Kilkenny, had come to Lucan in 1970 and it was his intervention that had stopped the rot just in time. He had played with the club all through the seventies, and when the club's hour of need came to rescue the national game in the parish, he stepped up to the plate:

I was thirty-six when I came to Lucan, but I carried on playing for a few years anyway. I played hurling until I was fifty-eight. I think I'm probably the oldest to have played for Lucan.

I would have played with the likes of Desie O'Brien, who played until he was forty-six or so himself, Martin Greene, Larry Downes, Noel Feeney, Paddy and Kevin Mulkerrins, and Billy Gogarty who would have been the goalkeeper. I didn't play much football, but there would have been a few lads playing dual and playing football under John Timmons, like Desie O'Brien and Cha O'Connor.

Jack O'Brien, Desie's father, would have been looking after the hurling team at the time. He was there for a number of years, but the likes of Tommy McCormack and Eddie Waters would have been retired by that stage, they didn't play after 1970. The team went bad around 1977; we fell apart all together and didn't have a team at all that year. I went to Arthur Griffith one day to play, but nobody showed up only myself and Jack so that was the end of that.

Mick Molloy was chairman at the time, and he asked me to go in and try to sort out the hurling team. I sort of didn't want to, I wanted to continue playing a bit myself, but I took it on in the end anyway. We started a seven-a-side competition down in Arthur Griffith and got a load of lads up in the field after a few months' work, a mixture of lads that would have been over the hill or that maybe wouldn't have played with us.

We got about fifty-five or fifty-six players together in the end. We had seven teams and there were medals and all. Galway hurler Sylvie Linnane was on the winning team that year. He was living up in Lucan at the time, but he wouldn't hurl with the club. He was still playing down in Galway, but he played in that alright.

We got things going again after that. We never failed to get a team together again, and a few years later we had enough to get a second team going. There were no mentors around at the time at all though. There was no one else around to do a line or an umpire or anything like that at all at the time. Somehow we kept everything going though.

Around that time the club also tried to establish an under-21 hurling team, soliciting the help of the club's neighbours in Palmerstown:

We tried to get an under-21 hurling team going in 1978. We would have had a very weak team though, so myself and Billy Gogarty and Desie O'Brien went up to Palmerstown to see if they would amalgamate with us. They would have had a very weak team too.

We spoke for two hours with a Mr Daly in Palmerstown, and we'd even reached the point where we'd agreed to call the team Patrick Sarsfields. It was only for under-21 hurling and just for the year, but in the end we couldn't agree on anything else so we just went home.

We got a team going in the end, and of course the first team we were drawn to play against was Palmerstown up in Arthur Griffith. They only had fourteen, and we had about twenty with footballers and everything. One of our lads, who would have been a footballer, came up to play. He was still drunk from the night before though so I wouldn't let him play.

He would have gone to Coláiste Phádraig so he knew all the Palmerstown lads, so he went over to play with them instead because they were one short. He had a point to prove that day and he was throwing himself in front of everything. Of course, he ended up getting an awful wallop on the head and ended up getting sixty-seven stitches. I had to bring him to the hospital.

Despite the hard slog that became the final few years of the decade for Jim and the hurling fraternity, the Kilkenny man has some very fond memories of that era in the club, when it came to the small ball game:

It was a great club all the same, and I played with some brilliant hurlers. I suppose the player with the biggest name that I would have hurled with was Joe Dooley who played for Offaly. He was a great player. Mícheál Moylan was a fantastic player too. He got a few runs for Offaly, but he was living up here and he didn't want to go down the country all the time to do the training and that. He was a lovely hurler though.

Cha O'Connor was a very good player too; he would have been centre back in the old days. We had a goalie from Galway called Jarlath Burke, he was inter-county standard. Jerry Fahy would have been very good too, but he had a bad groin injury that he carried for about five years and he just couldn't get it right.

Despite all that we just couldn't win a thing. The way hurling was done in Dublin at the time you hadn't a hope, it was full of bangers. We had a lot of country lads, but they were all transferred up and everything was done right. Lucan played in a final in Croke Park a few years before I got there in 1970 against New Irelands, and sure they had half of Tipperary playing against them. Those lads wouldn't have been hurling with them normally, they were just brought up for the day. They beat Lucan of course.

Overall, it had been a good ten years for the club, with promotion to the intermediate football ranks, huge progress on the juvenile front and a rescue from the point of oblivion for the club's adult hurling team.

In 1979, meanwhile, another major milestone was reached when one of the club's brightest underage talents secured the club's first, and to this day only, All-Ireland Minor Football Championship medal. Paddy McCabe, a product of Coláiste Phádraig, featured as part of the Dublin minor team that defeated Kerry by 0-10 to 1-6 in a thrilling All-Ireland final. It was a fitting end to a decade that had seen so much progress on and off the field, but particularly at juvenile level. The stage was now set for the club to make that giant leap forward.

A report from the *Lucan Newsletter* in late 1979 summed up the progress that had been made in the decade gone:

Objectively reviewing the Lucan Sarsfields Club over the past decade is a near impossible task if one has been involved in the week-to-week running of affairs. The obvious and pertinent questions would be: what progress has been made? Has the club adapted to changing times? How have we catered to the youth? Success on the playing fields? Every individual will have their own yardstick in assessing the club's progress.

For many, achievements on the field tell the story. Yes, it has been a good ten years – the winning of the elusive Junior Football Championship, promotion to the Intermediate grade in both hurling and football, and the capture of the under-21 football league title were certainly the high points. However, a club's success should not be measured solely on the prizes won. In fact, the most significant changes have taken place away from the playing fields. Ten years ago, Lucan Sarsfields were very much a small rural-type club, similar to many others in County Dublin. The club was built around the team, or teams, as the case may be.

The reforming of the juvenile section within the club in the early seventies changed the whole structure, organisation and aim of Lucan Sarsfields. The challenge of catering for the increasing population in the area was certainly a formidable one – a challenge Sarsfields met in a most satisfactory manner. Today, any young player interested in Gaelic games is assured of regular competition with the club's numerous teams. The influx of young players into the club means we can now realistically set our sights on becoming a senior club. The glamour and glory of senior status is everyone's ultimate ambition.

Facilities befitting a senior club are now a must. Here, again, the acquisition of our own playing fields at the 12th Lock will prove to be the most significant milestone in the club's progress in the '70s. We can look forward to the coming years, confident in the knowledge that the foundations for the development of Lucan Sarsfields, catering for members of the community of all ages, have been laid.

The future, and the onrushing 1980s, looked bright for Lucan Sarsfields.

PLAYERS OF THE ERA

Junior football team, 1971: M. Greene, T. Egan, B. Kane, T. Speight, B. Dardis, J. Byrne, J. Walsh, K. Synnott, C. Molloy, G. Behan, C. Fogarty, D. O'Brien, N. Feeney, B. Gogarty, K. Callaghan, D. Malone.

Coláiste Phádraig under-14 football panel, 1972: C. Ó Muirí, J. Beggan, F. Behan, G. Brady, M. Byrne, P. Coffey, E. Coyle, R. Crean, D. Cully, T. Curran, J. Dowling, J. Doyle, K. Graham, M. Kelly, K. McAllister, P. McCabe, P. Mullarkey, T. O'Brien, F. Reidy, J. Ronan, J. Temple, R. Verner.

Coláiste Phádraig under-15 hurling panel, 1972: K. Stephenson, M. Carney, E. Condell, P. Coffey, K. Coyle, J. Doyle, L. Fleming, M. Garvey, J. Hegarty, J. Kelly, J. Mullarkey, M. O'Brien, C. Ó Muirí, B. O'Shea, F. Reidy, M. Reidy, J. Ronan, D. Ruane, F. Russell, E. Slattery, D. Tansey.

Coláiste Phádraig under-17 football panel (13-a-side), 1972: S. Brady, M. Beatty, J. Connolly, M. Doherty, M. Duncan, C. Durham, V. Keating, S. McCaffrey, T. McGiff, V. Mahon, M. Malone, C. Ó Muirí, E. Rogers, W. Stanley, K. Stephenson, H. Tully, G. Watkins, F. Stapleton.

Junior A football league winners and Conlon Cup and junior championship runners-up, 1974: B. Murphy, S. McCaffrey, A. Collins, J. Leydon, O. Davitt, T. Speight, M. Anderson, M. Molloy, C. O'Connor, C. Synnott, P. Delaney, K. Synnott, W. Gogarty, S. Nolan, N. Feeney, M. Ruane, F. Brennan, J. Murray, D. O'Brien.

St Mary's BNS team, 1974: D. Ryan, N. O'Neill, D. McDonald, J. Crean, P. Thompson, M. Murphy, M. Woods, M. McStay, R. Callen, B. Hassett, A. Crean, A. Clarke, B. Dardis, S. McNamee, P. Keating, D. Brady, T. Carr, T. Newcombe, J. Coyle.

Full list of adult members, January 1978: Jim McCarthy, J. Gaffney, J. O'Brien, Mr Coyle, A. Coyle, K. Coyle, V. O'Connor, T. Higgins, M. Molloy, John McCaffrey, N. Feeney, J. Sheedy, B. Dardis, J. Connolly, A. Dignam, S. Walsh, C. Leahy, Tom Malone, Joe Byrne, P. Heneghan, Joe Dunne, Jim Brady, C. Savage, F. Farrell, G. Condron, C. O'Connor, Joe Murray, J. Tansey, E. Ó Mathúna, P. O'Connell, W. Griffin, P. Kavanagh, J. Moran, Seán McCaffrey, L. Cullen, T. Malone, M. Corway, Joe Collins, John Collins,

S. Nolan, D. Enright, B. McGowan, C. McCormack, Fr McCarthy, D. Hughes, M. Hever, F. Slaughter, T. Speight, P. McGarrigle, John Ryan, Tony Sourke, M. Farrell, M. Greene, D. Farrelly, J. Quinn, C. Molloy, B. Gannon, E. Mescall, W. Gogarty, D. O'Brien, B. Fassnidge, E. Gilmartin, T. Carey, P. Hallisey, D. Gilligan, G. O'Neill, P. Martin, B. Mohan, C. O'Keeffe, P. Brady, T. McCarthy, Pat Finnerty, J. Burke, T. Tobin, C. Moran, Joe Lennane, N. Clarke.

Intermediate football league v. Clontarf, June 1979: N. Cullen, M. Anderson, B. Murphy, K. Synnott, M. Casey, C. O'Connor, D. Tansey, R. Crean, J. Connolly, S. Nolan, T. Dennehy, P. Mulhern, P. Carney, A. Coyle, M. O'Sullivan, L. Fleming, L. Coyle, J. Brennan, G. Butler, J. Murray, B. Hannigan, E. Mescall.

Junior 3B football squad, 1978/79: A. Sourke, P. McGarrigle, D. Enright, M. Molloy, J. Brady, G. Coakley, G. Canavan, T. Speight, D. Malone, J. O'Toole, E. Coleman, N. McKelvey, C. Gannon, F. Farrell, M. Farrell, B. Gannon, J. Ryan, J. Byrne, G. Condron, J. Burke, P. Mulkerrins, C. Savage, M. Kearns, K. Mulkerrins, J. Callaghan, S. McCaffrey, H. O'Neill, C. Molloy, J. Quinn, B. Clarke, J. O'Reilly, B. Haragan, J. Timmons.

Intermediate football squad, 1978/79: B. Hannigan, N. Cullen, B. Murphy, M. Anderson, K. Synnott, G. Butler, M. Casey, C. O'Connor, J. Brennan, P. Carney, A. Coyle, M. Greene, D. Tansey, P. Mulhern, K. Coyle, D. O'Brien, R. Crean, L. Fleming, G. Watchorn, J. Connolly, S. Nolan, E. Mescall, T. Dennehy, J. Murray.

FOUR

1980-1989
A FIELD OF OUR OWN

The dream has come true. Lucan Sarsfields now have a clubhouse – a centre they can call their GAA home. Starting from modest beginnings, due to the weekly work and contributions of some members and thanks to the Trojan efforts of Eddie Mescall and his merry men in the last few months, Lucan Sarsfields, for the first time ever, now have a centre they can really be proud of.

In the next few weeks, dressing rooms, complete with showers, will be finished, and from then on we only await the grass to grow on three superbly laid out pitches, to have the nucleus of a vibrant GAA centre, which will be an enormous help in promoting the basic aims of the GAA, i.e. our national games, our national language, our national culture, our community environment, our national industry. Make no mistake about it; the GAA in Lucan is on the move.

Lucan Newsletter, January 1983.

The ownership of the 12th Lock officially passed into the hands of the club, namely to the trustees Mick Molloy, Billy Gogarty, Joseph Gaffney and Seamus McConraoi (of the County Board), on 5 December 1979. The certificate itself arrived in March 1980, and from there it was all about making the most of what the club now had. That, of course, required money.

'The people of Lucan, and especially local businesses, have always been incredibly supportive of the club, whether it was for purchasing jerseys, sponsoring cups or contributing towards annual dinner dances, even prior to the purchase of the 12th Lock', says Seamus Clandillon:

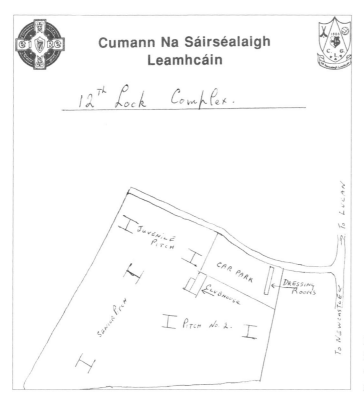

Cumann Na Sáirséalaigh Leamhcáin

12ᵀʰ Lock Complex.

Early imaginings of 12ᵗʰ Lock grounds, 1978.

But after the club had secured the grounds there was a serious push on to raise some funds. The club had to come up with more varied forms of fundraising, and that was done through once-off draws, monthly draws, annual dinner dances, race nights, American tea parties, poker classics, céilís, ballad groups, dramatic events, fashion shows, table quizzes and many more such activities.

The monthly 500 draw was set up in 1981 and ran until 1986. The tickets were £5 per month and there was a great range of cash prizes. In October, 1986 the first £100 ticket draw was launched. A total of 2,000 tickets were sold for twelve monthly draws, beginning in January, 1987. Four locally supplied new cars and six exotic holidays were up for grabs and there were a host of other cash and value prizes too.

They were tricky times financially for the club, with a series of race nights, cabarets and poker classics held all throughout 1980 and 1981 in a bid to raise much-needed funds to meet the bank repayments. Added to the mix in 1981 was a proposed levy on all Dublin clubs to help with the development of the County Board's headquarters at Parnell Park.

95

Above: Lucan juvenile camogie team, early 1980s.

Left: Car draw, 1987.

It was estimated that Lucan would, all things told, have to fork out somewhere in the region of £1,500. The timing was less than ideal, but despite the added burden, the club continued to support other ventures in the community, with donations and raffles held for the support of everything from the local church-building fund to the Stardust Disaster Fund.

By May, however, the club had raised just £6,199 and had paid out £11,144 on everything from materials for the new clubhouse to loan repayments and support for Ciste Gael, the profits from which went to the County Board. This was a common theme, with the club donating monies to many local organisations at regular intervals, including Peamount, Stewarts and St Loman's Hospitals.

With the bank chasing hard, the committee put their heads down and drove on with a series of further fundraising projects. The 500 Club Draw was officially launched in the Spa Hotel in February 1982 by former

Jay Maher, Babs Keating and Chappie Malone at a visit of the Tipperary Senior hurling team to the 12th Lock in the late 1980s.

Dublin goalkeeper Paddy Cullen, alongside club secretary Billy Gogarty, Seán McCaffrey of the club's finance committee and club chairman Padraig McGarrigle. It proved to be a massive success. As always within the GAA, volunteerism was vital to its success.

The ladies of the club were doing their share also. After the 12th Lock was acquired, chairman Mick Molloy had initiated the formation of a Ladies Committee, which was the first social committee in the club. It was chaired by Una McCaffrey and included Joan Molloy, Een O'Connell, Bríd Greene, Joan Fitzharris, Breda Malone, Millie Travers, Marie Murtagh, Agnes Dignam, Breda Kelly and many others. They ran dances and other social events in the new club. The first barn dance they ran made a profit of £400, which was a tidy sum at that time.

Eddie Mescall, in a club newsletter of April 1981, was named club person of the month for his efforts. The glowing report read that:

> Eddie took on the task of grounds man this year and has proved more than able for the job which involves the large building programme which Lucan Sarsfields are undertaking. A carpenter by trade, Eddie has put in countless hours working on the dressing rooms and the hall.
>
> Eddie also organises the buying of the building materials and also plays intermediate football for the club, operating as target man at full-forward. For his all-round enthusiasm and application to the building programme, for his dedication to training and turnout at matches, and for his no-nonsense lead-by-example approach, Eddie is a deserved club person of the month.

Every little helped, and Lucan was on a sound footing as the 1980s got into full swing. Pat Mulhern, who had recently moved to the area from Leitrim to take up a post in Lucan Garda station, recalls 'supervising' a part of the project around the time in the new grounds:

> When I arrived in Lucan the work was well underway. Paddy Kelly's input was savage. You couldn't say no to him when he asked you to do something. He deserves great credit. His life was Lucan Sarsfields. But I remember putting in the first set of lights ever in the club, myself, Jack Sheedy Snr, and Aiden Crean dug out the holes. Joe Dooley did the electrical work, and Paddy McCormack from Saggart, whose son played with the club at the time, provided the poles. They were only training lights but they were the first ever.

The AGM of 26 September 1982 reported how:

> ... over the year we relied on the 500 Club Draw for our bulk of finance, our commitments to AIB and Croke Park have been met to date, and in relation to the bank we are still paying off interest. Our new pitches will be second to none, but unless we have the support we need nothing will be achieved. Together we must do this; no other way can we survive.

A report in late 1983, after the hall had finally been opened, thanked all those involved:

> We would like to thank Eddie Mescall, Martin Greene, and Michael Molloy and all others involved in getting the hall opened. Also we would like to thank the following for their help and hard work during the year; Christy Leahy, Seán McCaffrey, Billy Gogarty, Paul Heneghan, Paddy Kelly, Mick Molloy and a special word of thanks to our chairman Padraig McGarrigle.

The club hall was, by now, proving a real asset to the community too. As an executive meeting in March 1983, heard, 'The club hall is in use two evenings per week by a rock band for rehearsals. A number of youths have been co-opted onto the social committee and they intend to organise games and discos in the hall at regular intervals.' The centre of the community was fast becoming a community centre.

With the finishing touches to Phase One of the 12th Lock project now completed, it was time to move on to Phase Two. A special booklet on the plans for the second stage of development was published in July 1985, laying out exactly what lay in store in the coming years:

> The club is presently catering for approximately 450 juvenile players, both boys and girls from the ages of nine upwards. The adult membership is 180 and on the increase each year. In 1979 we purchased our own grounds in the 12th Lock and set about implementing our development programme.
>
> Phase One: the provision of a senior playing pitch up to county standards, dressing rooms with toilets, washing facilities (showers) and the construction of a compact clubhouse so that our members could have a meeting place of their own. All of these items were completed by May, 1984.

Phase Two, the booklet went on to explain, was to, 'provide an extension to the existing clubhouse so as to have a lounge/bar and catering facilities and a social centre where our members can meet and enjoy themselves'. Phase Three, meanwhile, would aim to, 'provide handball, tennis, squash and basketball courts' and also, 'to provide a green area suitable for croquet and bowls. As soon as Phase Two has been completed, no amount of effort will be spared in order to implement Phase Three immediately.'

To finance Phase Two, the club introduced life memberships for the first time. 'This is a unique opportunity for you to become a life patron of Lucan Sarsfields,' the brochure explained:

> Your subscription at this important stage of our development is the most direct way you can secure our future. A once-only subscription of £250 entitled you to a Life Membership Card and allows your family full use of our club's facilities.
>
> As a life patron your name will be inscribed on the Patrons Roll of Honour to be installed in the club, thus ensuring you will be associated with our club in a very special and permanent way … All members who donate £250 will become life members of Lucan Sarsfields. This will be a family membership to include children up to the age of 21 years.

The club also appealed to the local business community:

> Lucan Sarsfields is providing a basic amenity for the Lucan area and therefore recreation facilities for many of your staff. At this crucial fund-raising stage your firm has a unique opportunity to enhance company prestige locally. A business subscription of £500 will clearly establish your firm as one of those giving us support with this worthwhile development.

Your firm's name will be entered permanently on the Patrons Roll of Honour, entitling you to the full use of the club's facilities. A framed certificate of Patronage will be issued for display on your company's premises.

Phase Three would never really come to fruition as it had been originally envisaged, but the clubhouse extension would follow and a bar licence would arrive in 1988, with Christy Leahy taking the lead on legal affairs from the club side and former Junior hurling team captain Victor Blake acting as club solicitor.

Since the hall had been finished it hosted many social functions and club occasions, but the majority of the club's major social events and fundraisers had taken place in surrounding hotels such as the Spa and the Springfield. Now, however, and in conjunction with Lucan Pitch and Putt Club across the road in the 12th Lock, a licence was granted for the sale of alcohol. It was a big leap forward, especially as a new source of revenue for the club.

Back on the field, Lucan's first foray into the Intermediate Football Championship in the new decade ended in July after a 3-5 to 3-4 defeat to St Brendan's in a quarter-final replay. The *Evening Herald* featured that game the following week:

St Brendan's had to pull out all the stops to overcome a Lucan Sarsfields side by a single point in their Intermediate Football Championship quarter-final replay at Parnell Park on Sunday. In contrast to their first encounter, this match was most enjoyable to watch. St Brendan's, strengthened by the return of Willie Shanley and John Hughes, were expected to record a comfortable victory, and for much of the game this prediction seemed likely to be proved correct.

Surprisingly it was Lucan who scored first. From a Seán McCaffrey cross, Seamus Mulhern fisted the ball into the net to put his side a goal ahead. St Brendan's struck back. Grant Spellman burst through a static defence to score an excellent goal and thus level the scores. Points from Ray Kelly, Georgie Hayes and Willie Walsh extended St Brendan's lead to three points before a Richie Crean '50' and a Seán Nolan point reduced the deficit to a single point at the interval.

At the start of the second half, Richie Crean equalised with a point from 35 yards and at this stage an upset seemed possible. But St Brendan's quickly found their rhythm again and Eugene Griffin rocketed a shot into the net to put them a goal ahead and the same player extended the lead with a further point. Shortly after, substitute Mick O'Donnell was put through by Peter Storey and he scored a lovely goal to put the Grangegorman side seven points clear.

Five minutes from the end Richie Crean converted a penalty to leave just four points in it and then, with just seconds remaining, it was Crean again who latched on to a loose clearance in the St Brendan's defence to slide the ball into the net. But it was just too late to save Sarsfields.

All the same, Lucan were holding their own in the intermediate ranks, with most of the same group of players that had seen them win the Junior Championship in 1977, and in 1980/81 they came close to going senior when beaten in the top-four Intermediate Football League playoffs, 1–10 to 1–7, by Naomh Barróg. The following season though, the club's biggest breakthrough to date would finally arrive.

After an epic 1981/82 season, in which the intermediate league had run into March 1982, Lucan would finally find themselves promoted to the ranks of senior thanks to an epic inter final replay win over St Anne's.

'We had a very good team at that time, a team that really could have competed at any level of football,' recalls Pat Mulhern, who would have been one of the stars of the team:

Jack O'Shea was training the team, he was brought in late in the season, and the selectors would have been Mick Molloy, Billy Gogarty and Bob Dardis.

There was great unity and friendship in the team; my brother Seamus played midfield with John Connolly but we had fine footballers all over the field. We had seven hard games against northside clubs like Garristown and Man-O-War on the way to that final. We eventually got there though and won it in extra time.

I remember there was a bust up in extra time that day. Joe McNally's father came on to the field and it all sort of kicked off from there. We actually had two great lads from Palmerstown on that team too – Noel Lally and Fergal Christie – and they were big additions to the team. Jack Sheedy and all those lads had come through by that stage too, so it really was a serious team.

A note in the Palmerstown newsletter from Joe Buggy of St Patrick's extended the warmest of congratulations to their friends down the road on their momentous achievement. Having shared so much at underage level all through the 1970s, and with many of the driving forces behind Lucan Sarsfields – the Dardises as well as Billy Gogarty and Desie O'Brien – all originally hailing from the area, it was a time of celebration for the whole of the west of the county:

On behalf of all the old and young Gaels in Palmerstown and Chapelizod

I would like to congratulate Lucan Sarsfields on gaining promotion to senior football when they beat their old south county rivals St Anne's of Bohernabreena (after a replay) to win the inter league.

We cannot but admire Sarsfields who kept going through thick and thin and the men who put so much time and effort into building up the club. Particularly, I remember the Condron family and Billy and Tommy Malone, of course from Palmerstown they have Don and Bob Dardis, sons of Louis from the Main Road who were also prominent in GAA activities in Palmerstown before moving to Lucan. (Who remembers Green Flags of Chapelizod and Clann Tighe Guaire of Palmerstown before St Pat's were formed?)

Sarsfields have acquired their own grounds at the 12th Lock and in a few years' time will be celebrating their centenary. We wish them lots of success both in developing their new ground and in their newfound senior status.

Unfortunately, that new-found senior status wouldn't last long, as after just one season in the senior league, and before even the end of the 1982 calendar year, Lucan would be relegated once more back down to intermediate.

Seán Nolan, one of the team's senior players, believes the quick relegation came about because of the lack of depth in a club which was still relying heavily on the same core of players:

> Our main problem at the time would have been that our panel was quite small and there had been a big delay in running that league final. Because of that we had to play a series of six or seven senior league games in a very short space of time. Because of injuries and everything else that came with that we were unable to stay up and we went back down very quickly. You couldn't question the quality of the team; it really just came down to numbers.
>
> We were an aging team too, that was essentially the same team that had been trying to win the junior championship for years, but I think it definitely came down to numbers.

Richie Crean agrees with the reasons for the club's all-too-speedy relegation, but the achievement of reaching the senior ranks had been momentous all the same. The club, at least, now knew it was possible. The mental block was gone, though the scars of immediate relegation took a long time to fully heal.

'I went off with a hamstring injury that day, but I came on again then in extra time and thankfully kicked a couple of points. That was a fantastic team,' Richie recalls the Inter League final and the senior campaign that followed:

> That final was played so late in the year. I think it would have been only about two weeks later that we played our first senior game. We drew with Vincent's that day I remember, but the matches just came too thick and fast after that.
>
> From 1977 on we were on an upward turn, but I think what really knocked us back was that senior league campaign. People would have different opinions on it, but I think that the season became so condensed that we never really got a chance to draw breath. We really needed to recharge our batteries, but we never got that chance. The season was over before we realised what had happened, and the few years after that were very difficult.
>
> We needed a break. As a club, we never got to settle down and say, 'Right, we're senior now, everything we do has to be of a higher standard.' We were thrown in at the deep end. We never had a chance to get ourselves ready and that had a big impact on us.
>
> In terms of an atmosphere around Lucan, I think that time we went senior was the best. I remember being around the village and everybody was just so delighted. Then, just four or five months later, we were down to intermediate again. Sometimes things like that just conspired against the club.

Padraig McGarrigle, chairman of the club at the time, summed up the sense of achievement within the team in reaching the senior ranks for the first time in the twentieth century and also the lack of energy that remained for the battle to stay in the top flight:

> I was chairman at the time and I remember a few of the lads coming to me in the days after we won that intermediate league. A couple of them said they were going back down the country to play for their clubs at home, and another few of them felt they were getting a bit too old and they'd achieved what they'd wanted to achieve.
>
> In terms of Lucan, the league final win in 1982 was huge.

Kevin Synnott hadn't been a part of the team that year, but he remembers the campaign well, a campaign that ultimately had shaken the club's footballing fraternity to its foundations, despite the massively successful nature of the whole enterprise overall:

I missed that league campaign that brought us up senior. I didn't play, but we came straight back down again which was a killer blow. I think one of our first games was against one of the Vincent's teams, they would have had two teams senior at the time I think, and we drew with them in our first game. After that it just didn't happen for us. We were lacking a bit in player power again I think.

We had the makings of a good team, but for some unknown reason we just couldn't get through the door. We could get to the door, but not through the door. If you look at the facilities the club has now, sure we were like cowboys going around in those days.

Lucan certainly had the players. Crean had been the team's leading light, and in 1983, after a few years on and off the Dublin senior and junior panels, he would bring the club's second All-Ireland medal back to Lucan Sarsfields after being part of the Dubs' All-Ireland winning campaign:

I was on the Dublin junior team in 1978, and I was on the under-21 team in 1979 and 1980. We actually won Leinster in 1980 but we were beaten in the All-Ireland final by Cork.

In 1981 then, when I was in college in Maynooth, I managed to get on to the combined universities team and that was a huge honour for me because that was a particularly difficult team to get on to. And then later that year I finally broke through on to the Dublin senior team properly.

My time with the Dublin seniors was great, though I would have liked to have played more matches. Any time I got a run of games in league matches I seemed to be interrupted with injuries. I loved every bit of it. We had our twenty-fifth reunion there a few years ago, and it was like we'd never been apart from one another.

Kevin Heffernan would have been in charge the whole time I was involved with Dublin. He was fantastic. I was coming from a junior club, and you'd have doubts about yourself, but he would always be telling you that you were good enough. It was a great time to be coming on to a Dublin team; the guts of that great team from the '70s would still have been there.

My first senior game for Dublin was in 1979 at the opening of a pitch in Swinford in Mayo. That was some day for me. I was playing corner forward, John McCarthy was in the other corner, and Jimmy Keaveney was full forward. David Hickey, Tony Hanahoe and Anton O'Toole made up the rest of the forward line. You were in awe of these fellas, so in a way it was a bit difficult.

I remember 1983 was a crazy year. We played Kerry in an All-Ireland junior final that year in Nenagh. That was played the week before the senior final and we drew with them. The senior final was the following week, when we beat Galway, and then the week after that we played the junior final replay in Ennis and they beat us. Three All-Ireland finals in three weeks was fairly manic alright. I think I was the only junior player on the senior panel at the time, so it was a busy few weeks for me.

The early eighties were golden years for Lucan Sarsfields' footballers, with another crop of top-quality players coming through. And with the adult team doing the business, it was the ideal environment for a young footballer to be making that transition. Jack Sheedy remembers his first few years making the breakthrough with the club, and shortly afterwards embarking on his own inter-county career:

Some of the older lads would have had a huge influence on us young fellas coming through. The likes of Seán Connolly, Mick Anderson, Pat Mulhern, they all had a huge impact on us. And lads like Charlie O'Connor, Kevin Synnott and Mick Casey, we would have looked up to these guys and they would have taught us an awful lot.

There were so many people that were just vital to the club at the time and in driving it forward and putting in structures. People like Frankie Farrell, Padraig McGarrigle, Eddie Mescall, they all would have made huge contributions.

Indeed, Jack's own minor football team were making strides in the 1981 season, with team captain Eoin Mullarkey, who actually had played much of his underage hurling with St Pat's, having been selected at full back on the Dublin minor team. Eoin would also go on to follow in the tradition of Lucan referees John Brennan and Frank Brophy in the 2000s when taking charge of the county hurling final.

The April 1981 newssheet takes up the story of that year's minors:

Having suffered some initial teething problems in so far as mentors were difficult to find, John McCaffrey stepped into the breach and the [minor football] team has settled well. They have played nine league matches, losing only to league leaders Round Towers, while in the championship they beat Fingallians in the first round only to bow out to Division 1 side Ballyboden St Enda's, but only after a strong struggle.

The panel has a good blend of young and old players with seven members having played under-21 football and five players still in the under-16 ranks, and they have the necessary backbone to qualify for the playoff stages of the league.

Elsewhere at underage level, the early eighties had been incredibly successful for the club. One of Lucan's and Coláiste Phádraig's brightest stars, Rory Leahy, whose father Christy would be heavily involved in acquiring the club's first bar licence some years later, was chosen to travel to Australia as part of the Dublin Colleges team in 1983 (alongside former Republic of Ireland soccer star Niall Quinn). A report on the juvenile section of the club in the April 1981 newsletter gave a glowing synopsis of the state of play in the club in that era:

> Congratulations to Alan O'Brien and Michael Travers on their selection on the Dublin South City under-14 team. The current under-15 side have had an outstanding season with players like Ronan Duke, Ronan O'Flynn, Aidan Mahady, Donal Walsh and David Dowling really coming into their own. The future at under-16 and minor level looks secure. Seven of the present panel are eligible for under-15 again next season.
>
> Our under-16 team were unlucky in defeat to An Caisleán in the championship, but even in defeat this team has proved a great success this season. Many of the panel have already played minor and under-21, while most are still under-15. Our under-21 team has shown great promise of late, and with youth very much on their side the future looks bright for next season.

At lower underage level, though, came the most success, when the club enjoyed a clean sweep of the West Regional Board, as a report from the board in 1983 stated, 'It was a great year for Lucan Sarsfields, winning all league competitions at under-10, under-11 and under-12 levels. The under-10 league turned out to be a tremendous competition. In a great final played in Lucan, the home side were very thankful to hear the full-time whistle which halted a great comeback from St Patrick's of Palmerstown.' The team had been managed by Jim O'Brien and his huge core of assistants, John Curley, Fachtna Murphy, Pat Crummy, Charlie McGuire, Mrs O'Donovan, John Bresnan, Mr Norris, Mr Scully, Mr O'Riordan, Mick Griffin, Mr Morley, P. Kelly and Mrs Farrelly.

At under-11 level, Seamus Farrelly had been in charge, but although not quite as extensive as the under-10s', his assistants, C. O'Brien, J. Ryan, Phil Kehoe, J. O'Connell and Mick Griffin, were still numerous. Not only were more players coming along to the club, the mentors that had for so long been lacking were now beginning to appear in spades.

'While 10 teams competed in the under-11 competition, the standard was quite low with Lucan head and shoulders above the opposition,' the report continued:

> The final turned out to be the finest match of the competition with gallant Inchicore side St Michael and James fighting for every ball until the final whistle. The victorious Lucan side can look to their greater strength and overall experience for their success. The same team had won both the league and the Corrigan Cup twelve months earlier. In the under-12 competition, Lucan came back from a half-time deficit to turn the tide in the second half and defeat An Caisleán.

Sadly, in late 1982, one of the club's most dynamic supporters of the juvenile section passed away. John McCaffrey, who had been involved in countless underage teams throughout the years, died in November, and was fittingly remembered in a note in the newsletter the following week:

> Lucan Sarsfields wish to extend to Mrs McCaffrey, family and relations, their deepest sympathy on the recent death of their and our beloved John. Every single member man and boy had the greatest respect for the amiable John McCaffrey. After many years of unselfish and untiring support in all sections of the GAA in Lucan and about the community, he will be sadly missed by us all.

In April 1983, John's son Seán presented the John McCaffrey Cup to the Minor Board to be competed for at under-21 football. The newsletter reported that John's family, 'have presented the Minor Board with the trophy which ensures John – the heart and soul of the GAA in Lucan – is remembered in Dublin's GAA world'.

The first year in which the new trophy was to be competed for, Lucan nearly did the unthinkable under the management of Pat Mulhern in almost winning it. After winning out the Division 2 South section of the competition, northside group winners Kilmore ruined the fairytale by defeating a gallant Lucan side. It had still been a sterling season for the young team though, and medals would wing their way to the club in April 1984, presented to the players by Dublin legend Paddy Cullen.

'I was involved with the under-21 team when we won the Division 2 league,' Pat Mulhern recalls:

> The selectors would have been Jack Sheedy Snr and Aiden Crean who were

just fantastic clubmen. Jack Sheedy Jnr was on the team, Pascal Jackman, Tommy Carr, Barry Dardis, Mark Dardis, so it was a very strong team.

Pat O'Toole from Dodsboro was a great part of the team too; David Lynch, the Gannons, and Paddy McCabe, of course, who had won an All-Ireland minor medal with Dublin a few years earlier.

We had a function in the clubhouse after we won it and I remember there had been an event on the night before up there. There was beer left over from that do, so rather than spend the night down in the village we decided to come up to the club instead and we were pretty much the first ones to celebrate a win actually in the clubhouse. In think Bob Carroll's supplied a few beers for us that night too.

Things were developing at an amazing pace on the field of play, but Lucan Sarsfields were extending their gaze far beyond even that at this point. One of those new outlets was the setting up of a golf society in mid-1981. The newsletter reported:

Yes you have read correctly, Sarsfields are branching into the golf scene. This idea has been around for quite a while and the main driving forces behind the society are men like Bob Dardis, Dinny Malone and Mick Molloy. Their first official outing is on Munster Final weekend, 17-19 July, in Killarney.

The society came in and out of focus in the intervening years, but in 1987 it really began to take shape when Bob Dardis became the first captain. While it proved a tremendous social aspect to the club, it also served as a wonderful way to keep retired players involved with Lucan Sarsfields. Some years later, in the early part of the next century, it would go on to become a massive source of fundraising for the club's next big leap into the future.

Mick Roche and Seán Walsh take up the story of the Lucan Sarsfields' Golf Society from its early beginnings right up to the 2010 successful club classic:

Some people may find it hard to understand how the game of golf finds a place in the history of a GAA club. Perhaps the answer may be found in a rewriting of the old adage – old GAA players never die, they just turn to playing golf. Or maybe even, when there's funding that can be raised from anything even peripherally associated with Gaelic games, GAA people will find a way to deliver these funds back into their club to help run its core games.

Leaving financial aspects aside for the moment, the genesis of Lucan Sarsfields Golf Society is to be found in a touring party to a Munster football

Lucan CBS colleges reps
to Australia, Tom Donovan
and Rory Leahy, 1983.

final back in the last century. This subsequently became an annual pilgrimage by such noteworthy golfers as Denis Malone, Bob Dardis, the Molloy
brothers (Michael and Charles) and Joe Murray, and grew into what is now a
thriving unit in the activities of the club.

The initial outing was organised for Bandon Golf Club. We can state that
the society embraced formality in 1987, with the election of its first Captain,
the well-known and effervescent Bob Dardis. Since then, the society has
gone from strength to strength, with its own well-attended AGM, and with
many established figures within the club taking on the mantle of captain over
the last twenty-four years.

Stories abound of the adventures of the early golfing pioneers as they travelled around the golfing paradise of Ireland, often in luxury coaches. One
such example is the society's visit to Arklow Golf Club when the transport
featured no windscreen wipers and also boasted a leaking roof – a situation
not helped by a downpour on the homeward journey.

Another tale from the society also features transport, though this time
during the round of golf itself, rather than on the way home. This concerns a
former club chairman who regularly encountered difficulty at the par-3 sev-
enth hole at Lucan Golf Club. Tubber Lane crosses the fairway and inevitably
this misfortunate man would do something daft here – such as hitting his
ball into the drain a few feet from the tee-box, or over-hitting the ball in the
direction of the first tee-box, or destroying the branches of the very fine tree
just to the right of the tee-box.

On this occasion, the club's annual Golf Classic, he failed to notice that a
car was approaching slowly, carefully and indeed quietly, on Tubber Lane. In his
defence, it should be noted that his playing partners also failed to see the car. The

The 1983 Under-10B footballers with team mentor Tony Strong.

golf ball struck and cracked the car window and bounced off. After humble pie had been eaten (and thankfully, nobody was injured), the three-ball made its way across the public road to the hole, with the errant golfer hardly in an enthusiastic mood. However, to his joy, he discovered his ball at the edge of a very tricky green, and proceeded to make what was a rare par on that hole.

Excellent camaraderie has long been a feature of the golf society, and the banter and wisecracks are a constant and most enjoyable feature. There is also tremendous loyalty among this sporting group who look out for each other on the away trips almost like a platoon of soldiers on a battlefield mission.

On an outing to Dunmurray Springs in relatively recent years, when weather conditions made playing on impossible, the organising committee (who hadn't yet started their round) drove the length and breadth of the course to bring all our golfers home. However, on this occasion, one member of the (usually effective) committee was most surprised, and indeed disappointed, a couple of hours later, to get an angry phone call from a member of one four-ball who claimed that his group had been 'left behind in the field' by the completely irresponsible organising committee.

The society, which is open to gents and ladies, hosts a number of outings each year and, notwithstanding the occasional omission that can be represented as bordering on treachery, is almost completely devoted to increasing the pleasure and enjoyment of its members. It is fully self-financing and, in fact, has established a fine tradition of giving a financial donation (currently €500) to the club each year.

This is awarded on the strict proviso that the money is used to purchase sliotars for the juvenile hurling and camogie section; this is possible because those far-seeing early golf promoters believed that improving skills within the club with the small ball would also help the growth and standards of the smaller ball game!

The society takes great pride in visiting a broad range of golf clubs, and even greater pride in going where there's value for money to be had. Notwithstanding this, great relationships have been established with many golf clubs over the years. It is appropriate to mention Lucan Golf Club in particular, where, despite the occasional damage to vehicles on adjoining roads, proximity and common membership have led to a very warm and mutually beneficial relationship that continues to endure, despite the many and on-going changes of officials on both sides.

The annual Golf Classic is the major event and has been going now since the early 1990s. This is an excellent fundraiser for the club; over the period from 1996 to 2010, Golf Classics have raised over €150,000 in funds for the club. The years 2000 and 2001 are especially notable – these coincided with the major new club-house development at the 12th Lock – and clearly the Golf Classic Committee cranked up its efforts to deliver very substantial funds in these years.

The Golf Classic has enjoyed tremendous support over the years, with up to forty teams playing, at rates of up to €825 per team in some of those years. Again, the personnel has changed quite a bit through the years, with John Mills Snr in particular providing many teams through his numerous business contacts in the early years, and then Colm Moran using his vast network of family and business leads to generate many teams and much sponsorship.

In more recent years, with the deterioration of the economy, corporate support has dropped off significantly, but the Classic has responded by reducing the rate per team to as little as €200; this saw thirty-nine teams take part in the 2010 Classic, with many coming from among the Club's members.

While financial returns in the past two years are down, the loyalty and goodwill shown by supporters of the Classic is such that it is fully expected that the vast majority of these teams will return year after year. As such, the future of the Golf Classic should be assured.

Another off-field development that would prove massively successful took place in early 1981, when Lucan Sarsfields held their first Scór competition in the Spa Hotel on March 21. A whopping thirty-seven entries from céilí dancing to recitation, ballad group singing and set dancing all took to the stage in what would prove an incredibly successful first foray into the area for the club.

So successful, in fact, that even before the first Scór Sinsear had been held an underage equivalent had already been planned. A message from the Scór Committee on the back of the Spa Hotel programme for the senior event explained how the committee had been so 'overwhelmed by the enthusiasm of the young people of Lucan, in all aspects of Irish culture' that 'they are holding a Scór-structured competition in all eight sections for young boys and girls of Lucan in May of this year'.

The driving force behind the Scór na nÓg was Paddy Kelly, and he arranged the event which would eventually take place in St Joseph's College in June. According to the newsletter, 'the event is really geared towards our younger members who may not have had a chance in the last [Scór Sinsear] event. A big effort is being made to try and encourage as many boys as well as girls to take part.' Needless to say, it would prove another big success for the club.

The biggest victory on the Scór front came in 1983, when the club took home an incredible two All-Ireland Scór titles from the national finals at the National Stadium in Dublin on 30 April. Having already secured the Dublin and Leinster crowns in instrumental music and in the novelty act, the club's two teams secured Lucan Sarsfields' first ever national titles in a hugely memorable evening for everyone in the club. Seamus Clandillon recalls:

> The club has a great record of taking part in the Scór since our first foray into the competition in 1983 with the nua cleas team of Pearse O'Connell, Ewan O'Flynn, Dinny Malone, Donal Healy, Pete Brady, Jane Doran. The late Joan O'Flynn was the genius behind the hilarious act that year that saw the team win the All-Ireland title. That group brought the house down.
>
> It didn't end there though. In the traditional instrumental section the group of Patsy Toland, Brendan Begley and Larry Kinsella took out the All-Ireland that same night, so the celebrations went on late into the night.
>
> In those days the late Paddy Kelly, past chairman of the club, was to the fore in promoting not only the senior Scór but also the juvenile Scór. He would leave no stone unturned when it came to that. His bus, which became known as the Sarsfields Express, would be used to bring people here and there.

A report on the front page of the *Lucan Newsletter* on 8 May 1983, recorded the moment forever in time:

The National Stadium was the scene on Saturday of a quite unique double for Lucan Sarsfields GAA Club. The club's entries for two out of seven events in the All-Ireland finals of Scór won out. The club took Craobh na hÉireann twice.

Three Comhaltas [Ceoltóirí] members wove magic in instrumental traditional music. The experience of Lucan Dramatic Society members and make-up expertise helped win the novelty act with a clever musical production of *Sive*. It was a rewarding night for Padraig Kelly. His belief in Lucan talent and enthusiasm for junior and senior Scór over recent years has been dramatically vindicated. The club entries enjoyed great support from the strong Lucan contingent in the huge attendance. The 12th Lock was running red with the Dark Rosaleen later in the night.

In 1985, Lucan was once again to the fore in the Scór, with Marie Corway winning the Dublin Senior Championship for solo singers. That same year Ruairí Mullarkey and Kevin Farrell won the county crown for music, while the quiz team of John Egan, Michael Corry and Senan Kelly won the quiz title at the Scór na nÓg. In this year also the Lucan Sarsfields Youth Band struck up for the first time, visiting Irish centres in Boston, New York, Philadelphia and Washington as part of a trip to the States.

The club had an interest in Scór again in 1986, with the ballad group of Mary and Fidelma Kelly, Margaret Collins, Barry Kavanagh and Terry O'Brien winning Dublin and Leinster titles. In 2008, the team of Donal Downes, Joe Whyte, Donal Healy, Seaghan Ó Lanagáin, Seán Ó Conghaile, Seamus Clandillon, Brian Flynn and Gerry McGarry would once again win the nua cleas Leinster title, while in 2010 the club's most recent All-Ireland crown arrived in Tráth na gCeist thanks to the team of Declan O'Neill, Seán Ó Ceallaigh, Ollie Mann and Annette Healy.

'In 2007 it was decided to really give it a go. We entered all categories in Scór Sinsear and did reasonably well in all,' Seaghan Ó Lanagáin recalls:

The nua chleas team won the first of four successive county titles, and having won the Leinster title in 2008, narrowly missed out in the All-Ireland final to an impressive cast from Tyrone.

The themes depicted in comedy over this period were 'Improving your Hurling through Céilí', 'A Match for Anyone', 'Rumble in the Jungle' and 'Junket to Lima'. The artistes to represent the club included Greg O'Neill, Seamus Clandillon, Tom Flannery, Gillian Flannery, Joe Whyte, Jerome Twomey, Brian Flynn, Seaghan Ó Lanagáin, Dónal Healy, Seán Ó Conghaile, Dónal Downes, Gerard McGarry, Helen Ryan, Michael O'Grady, Seán Flynn,

Above: The 1983 All-Ireland Scór Sinsear winning team: Jane Doran, Dinny Malone, Donal Healy, Ewan O'Flynn, Pearse O'Connell, Agnes McMahon.

Below: The newsletter reports on Scór success, 1983.

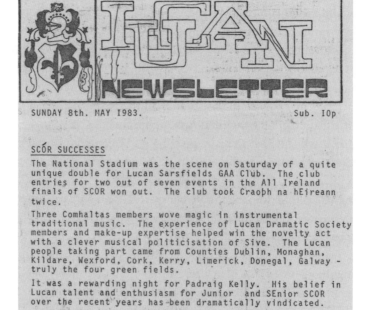

NEWSLETTER

SUNDAY 8th. MAY 1983.   Sub. 10p

SCÓR SUCCESSES

The National Stadium was the scene on Saturday of a quite unique double for Lucan Sarsfields GAA Club. The club entries for two out of seven events in the All Ireland finals of SCOR won out. The club took Craoþh na hEireann twice.

Three Comhaltas members wove magic in instrumental traditional music. The experience of Lucan Dramatic Society members and make-up expertise helped win the novelty act with a clever musical politicisation of Sive. The Lucan people taking part came from Counties Dublin, Monaghan, Kildare, Wexford, Cork, Kerry, Limerick, Donegal, Galway - truly the four green fields.

It was a rewarding night for Padraig Kelly. His belief in Lucan talent and enthusiasm for Junior and SEnior SCOR over the recent years has been dramatically vindicated.

The Club entries enjoyed great gallery from the strong Lucan contingent in the huge attendance. The 12th. Lock was running red with the Dark Rosaleen later in the night.

Eoin Mullarkey and Stíofán Ó Conghaile.

These thespians strutted their stuff on the boards to the enjoyment of many, but, in truth, they thoroughly enjoyed great craic themselves on their comical theatrical odyssey.

The early eighties were great times for the club on the social side, but things weren't going badly on the field of play either. Camogie was finally beginning to win its place back at the forefront of the hearts and minds of Lucan's youths, thanks largely to the efforts of Patricia Dowling, Joan Fitzharris and Laurie French. And in 1983, an almost immediate breakthrough followed the game's latest resurgence.

The club's Junior C team won the league after a run of eight victories on the trot and a 3-0 to 1-0 win over Kilmore in the final, and they almost made it an historic double when just missing out in the championship final, losing by a point to Thomas Davis. The signs were good that the small ball ladies' game was on its way back to the top in the club. Again, in 1984, the team would win their section of the league.

Of course, that rejuvenation hadn't happened overnight, with the foundations having been laid in the early eighties, and the future now also looking bright with the growth of underage camogie in the club. Joan Fitzharris, secretary of the club's juvenile section, revealed the state of affairs in in her report of 1982/83:

> Camogie seems to be gaining interest as we had three teams entered in the league this year. Even though none of the teams were successful, they all accounted for themselves very well, in particular the under-12s. We have a few promising players at this level. Thanks to Laurie French, Patricia Dowling, team managers, and Ursula Billings. Much interest has been shown by a big number of girls and we hope to see better things in the future.

By 1988, the club had an under-12 and under-14 team, with the junior team being run by Padraig McGarrigle along with Kathleen McGarrigle and John Ryan. And a visit from his home club in Ballyshannon, County Donegal, offered a welcome change of pace. These were the building blocks for what would go on to become the club's most successful ever underage section.

All the while, hurling was on its way back from the lows of the late 1970s and strides were being made at underage level. A juvenile committee report to the executive in 1983 summed up the progress that had been made in the early part of the 1980s:

Two years ago hurling was almost non-existent at this level. Now, for the second year in succession, we had good results in hurling. The under-12s had a very good league run, only losing one match; they finished runners-up. The under-13s have yet to finish their league, but hopes are high for Lucan to do well as they have won all their matches. We look forward eagerly to the remaining matches. Both of these teams are under the management of Dan McCarthy, Eoin Mullarkey, Tony Byrne and Mrs Donohue.

The under-15s did very well in winning a number of matches. This was a great achievement for manager Paul Heneghan and assistant Paddy McCormack as they had a very small panel of players to pick from.

The real strides were coming at the most fundamental level though, as the report went on to show:

Brother Kinsella organised a very successful hurling street league, at the beginning and end of the season. With about 80 boys in the under-10 and under-11 age group involved things look good for the future of hurling in Lucan. Our thanks to Brother Kinsella, Vincent O'Connor, Jim McCarthy, Michael Griffin, Jim O'Brien, Seamus Farrelly and all those who helped in any other way. We extend our special thanks to Michael O'Sullivan for all his help and getting the pupils of Esker involved.

At adult level, things were beginning to take shape too. In 1980/81 the junior hurlers lost out to Crumlin in the semi-final of the Corn Fogarty by 3-11 to 1-10. It was the first of a series of heartbreaking defeats for the team that had come so far and probably deserved better.

The first major disappointment came in 1982 when the team won their section of the intermediate hurling league only to lose to Kilmacud Crokes in a play-off to go senior, and another gutting defeat followed shortly after in 1984, when the side lost by two points to Faughs in the Junior Hurling Championship final after a run that had seen them defeat Whitehall Colmcilles, Ballyfermot and New Irelands.

These were testing times, but compared to the state of affairs in the small ball game in the late 1970s, things were at least moving in the right direction. Jim Quinn recalls those painful years when a breakthrough seemed so near and yet so far, especially that Faughs defeat:

We were red-hot favourites to beat them, we had a great team at the time. Faughs would have been a good club though, they would have had country lads but it would all have been done legally. We were beaten by two points that day. They had a couple of senior lads on the day though, so we objected to that. Every objection lodged to the County Board at that time would have been ruled out of order though so we hadn't a hope with it.

That was some team we had. Jarlath Burke was in goals, Joe Dooley was full-back, Tom Stewart was corner back, and Alan Higgins was in the other corner. He was a great Lucan man, and a great hurler. He wouldn't give you an inch.

Eoin Mullarkey would have been wing back, and Mícheál Moylan was centre back. Desie O'Brien Jnr would have played in the middle of the field, and Desie Snr was in the corner. Noel Flynn would have been on that team too, and a Limerick man called Noel O'Dwyer. Jim Walsh was wing-forward, and John O'Toole from Wexford and Gerry Fahy made up the rest of the team.

There were some really good Dublin teams at the time too. Finbarr's in Cabra had a great team and Erin's Isle had a great team, without any foreigners on it. There were teams like us and Ballyfermot and An Caisleán that just couldn't win anything. Anytime you even got to a final the odds would be loaded against you.

One of Lucan's stars from that time, Mícheál Moylan, was enjoying his first season with the club in 1984. It was a disappointing start to a long career with the club that would sadly prove fruitless for the Offaly man, on the playing field at least:

I was coming from St Rynagh's and we were going for three senior champi-onships in a row but we were beaten in a semi-final in 1984. I couldn't keep travelling up and down so I decided to join Lucan. At that time Jim Quinn was involved and Pat Delaney was the manager, but it was Jim that got me involved with the club.

I'd say there are an awful lot of hurling people in the club that are com-mitted members of the club now because of Jim. Brother Kinsella came in as manager after that for a while, and Mick Ryan from Waterford was involved for a while too, he was a great organiser.

They were playing intermediate league and junior championship when I arrived and that year we got to the junior final where we were beaten by Faughs. They were an exceptionally good team, and in my opinion the stand-ard of hurling in Dublin at the time would have been very, very high.

That Faughs game was a very tight game, but it was a game we should have won, and deserved to win. It was a very good game, and their goalie that year was Liam O'Mahony and he had one of those days goalies pray to have. He saved everything. I remember Gerry Fahy blazed a shot at him and it hit O'Mahony

Junior Hurling Championship Final 1984

Back Row (L-R): *J. Burke, M. Mockler, J. Dunne, G. Fahy, N. Flynn, J. O'Toole, T. Jones, J. Linnane, R. Duke, P. Delaney.*

Middle Row (L-R): *D. O'Brien (Jun), M. Moylan, E. Mullarkey, V. Blake, D. O'Brien, J. Dooley, N. O'Dwyer, A. Higgins, J. Quinn, D. Fitzgerald.*

Front (L-R): *T. Stewart, P. Mulkerrins, M. Maher, B. Gannon, J. Walsh, S. O'Brien.*

Sairséalaigh Leamhcáin

(1) Iarlaith De Búrca Jarlath Burke

(2) Tomás Stiobhard   (3) Seosamh Dúblaoich   (4) Ailéin Ó hUiginn
   Tom Stewart   Joe Dooley   Alan Higgins

(5) Eoin Ó Maoilearca   (6) Micheál Ó Maoiléan (7) Buach de Bláca (Capt)
   Eoin Mullarkey   MI. Moylan   Victor Blake

(8) Deasún Ó Briain   (9) Nollaig Ó Floinn
   Des O'Brien (Jun)   Noel Flynn

(10) P. Ó Maoilchairáin (11) Nollaig Ó Duibhuir   (12) S. Breathnach
   Paddy Mulkerrins   Noel O'Dwyer   Jim Walsh

(13) Seán Ó Tuathail   (14) Gearóid Ó Fathaigh (15) Deasún Ó Briain
   John O'Toole   Gerry Fahy   Dessie O'Brien

Fir Ionad:
(16) Seán Ó Briain (John O'Brien) (17) Mairtín Ó Meachair (Martin Maher) (18) Finnéin Mac Críosta (Finian Christie) (19) Seán C Doinn (John Dunne) (20) Séamus Ó Coinne (John Quinn) (21) Tomás Mac Seoin (Tom Jones) (22) Barra Fhionnáin (Barry Glennon) (23) Dioraí Mac Gearailt (Derry Fitzgerald) (24) Mairtín Moicléir (Martin Mockler) (25) Seosamh Ó Linneáin (Joe Linnane) (26) Rónán Duke (Ronan Duke) (27) Eoin Breathnach (Eoin Walsh).

Junior Hurling Championship final team, 1984.

in the chest and rebounded wide. He was a fine keeper, but it was just one of those days.

Lucan had a great team then. Joe Dooley was there, Gerry Fahy, Tom Stewart and these lads. Desie O'Brien Jnr and Snr would have been there, and Desie Jnr really would have been a marvellous hurler even though he was very young at the time. He was a tremendous athlete and he had great heart and great skill; he was one of those lads you would have wanted to have in the trenches with you.

I stayed hurling with Lucan then up until about 1995/96, but we won nothing other than in 1993 when Liam Carton, Eddie Bolger and myself won the over-40s Masters with Dublin in the year of that competition's inception.

The breakthrough was still almost fifteen years away for the club's hurlers. The footballers had already enjoyed their day in the sun and were back in the shade once again by the time Lá na gClub came around in 1984 to mark the centenary of the association. An underage blitz competition was organised to mark the occasion on the weekend of 28/29 July, as well as an intermediate hurling nine-a-side competition and a seven-a-side football event.

The timing of the club's respective successes at Scór, inter football, juvenile progress and the opening of the 12th Lock had been perfect, as later that same month (July 1984) a letter reached the club revealing the news that

Lucan Sarsfields had been named as one of the finalists in the AIB GAA Club of the Year Awards. A team of assessors then came out to the club, and later that year Lucan Sarsfields were named as the Division B Dublin Club of the Year for 1982/83.

'I remember we were presented with the award down in Kilkenny,' Padraig McGarrigle recalls. 'I think that was really the start of the good times for the club.'

It was due reward for a club that had come so far in a relatively short space of time, and the first major event to grace the new fields in the 12th Lock provided another red-letter day when, in July 1984, the Jimmy Magee All-Stars came to town. Part fundraiser for the club and part for the Esker Parish Building Fund, it was also the perfect opportunity to show off the club's new facilities.

The All-Star team, which included radio personality Ronan Collins, Eurovision winner Johnny Logan, rugby legend Tony Ward, Kerry star Jack O'Shea and Offaly goal-scoring hero from 1982 Seamus Darby, took on a Dublin selection featuring Lucan quartet Richie Crean, Jack Sheedy, Paddy McCabe and Kevin Synnott.

The game was followed by a cabaret spectacular in the Spa Hotel which featured Johnny Logan and another of the All-Star selection that day, T.R. Dallas. It was a resounding success for the club, leading to a massive profit of £1,331 (£665.50 of which went to the Esker Parish Church Building Fund). All in all, as a committee meeting heard some weeks later when the financial windfall had been finalised, it had been the, 'most enjoyable night ever in Lucan'.

Enjoyable as it might have been, it also marked one of the last occasions on which many of Lucan's star players would be on the field together. The club had won the Maynooth tournament that year, and while the minors had also won their own league undefeated, the future did not look as bright as it once had. Disharmony within the club meant the team that had secured senior status, although briefly, just three years earlier, was about to take a giant leap backwards.

That Maynooth tournament win would provide one of the final highlights in the 1980s, and for Jack Sheedy it had been a day that had almost jeopardised his entire Dublin inter-county senior career. Although his own career with the Dubs would blossom from there, Jack recalls the happenings of the mid-1980s, from his own breakthrough at county junior and senior level to the gradual falling away of the club's footballers:

LUCAN SARSFIELDS GAA CLUB
Present
Grand Charity Football Match
(in aid of)

Esker Church & Club Building Fund

Jimmy Magee ALL STARS
vs.
DUBLIN SELECTION
(PAST & PRESENT)

MONDAY 9th July at 7.30 p.m.
GAA GROUNDS — 12th LOCK
Newcastle Road, Lucan

Left and below: Programme from the visit of Jimmy Magee All-Stars to Lucan in 1983.

JIMMY MAGEE ALL-STARS

Jimmy Magee
Larry Cunningham
Paddy McCormack (Ironman)
Ronan Collins
Greg Hughes
Johnny Logan
Tony Ward
Mick Leech
Jack O'Shea
Fr. Michael Cleary
T. R. Dallas
Gene Stuart
Fr. Brian Darcy
Frankie Byrne
Jody Gunning
Seamus Darby
PLUS Many More Personalities

DUBLIN SELECTION

John O'Leary
Gerry Hargan
Sean Doherty
Jimmy Keaveney
Paddy Cullen
Ciaran Duff
John Caffrey
Joe McNally
Gay O'Driscoll
Richie Crean
Jack Sheedy
Paddy McCabe
Kevin Synott
Pa Connolly
Arthur French
Larry McCormack
Pascall Flynn
Paddy Delaney

Cabaret Spectacular to follow in Spa Hotel from 10.00 p.m. to 2.00 a.m.
Dancing etc.   Adm. £5.00

ARTISTS APPEARING
- Johnny Logan
- Fr. Clery
- Gene Stuart
- T.R. Dallas
- Ronan Collins
- The Memories
- Larry Cunningham
- The Indians
- Johnny Peters
- Fr. Brian Darcy
- Joe Doherty

THE JIMMY MAGEE ALL-STARS

June 6th 1966 was a day just like any other day, or so it seemed to the residents of Ballyjamesduff, Co. Cavan.

But little did they know that all would be changed in a short few hours — for on that night the Jimmy Magee All-Stars descended on the town to play their first-ever game. The cynics said the idea wouldn't last a week, and they were right — it has lasted nineteen seasons and 240 games so far, with the All-Stars having played in all 32 counties, in Britain, and in the United States.

Now in their 241st game, their first visit to Lucan, the All-Stars can look back on a vast amount of money collected for charity — an index-linked half-a-million pounds. For charity, of course. They say it covers a multitude of sins; if it doesn't we're all in trouble!

Liam Campbell, (Hon. Sec. of All-Stars)

When I started playing at adult level the club was intermediate. Richie Crean was on the Dublin senior team in 1983, and because we were only intermediate he could play for the Dublin juniors. He was ineligible to play the following year because they'd made it past the Leinster final in '83, and in 1984 then I made the Dublin junior team, and I actually made the Dublin senior panel that year.

We were beaten in the All-Ireland final. It was unbelievable to make that panel and just to be around the place after they'd won the All-Ireland the year before. Especially as a Lucan man. The only other Lucan Sarsfields men to get near a Dublin senior panel before that were Kevin Synnott and Richie.

To be around guys like Brian Mullins, Anton O'Toole and Tommy Drumm was just surreal. I'd just go into the dressing room, head for the corner, and keep the head down and the mouth shut and say nothing. It was scary being managed by Kevin Heffernan.

The first day I played for Dublin was against Wicklow in Bray. I came on and scored a goal that day so I was asked to come back. I was so green though. There wasn't a huge amount of coaching, you were just expected to be of county standard going in there. I wouldn't have been all that streetwise in a football sense, but it was a good year.

I scored two points off Páidí Ó Sé in a challenge game that year too, so that was a highlight. I didn't really expect to get into the team though, it was just great to be there. I was just so fiercely loyal to the club at the time.

I remember one day we played a league game against St Pat's in Palmerstown, and the same afternoon we were playing a tournament final in Maynooth. Dublin were playing Meath in a challenge game at the same time for the opening of Naomh Barróg's new ground, but I chose to go and play for the club in Maynooth, so that was pretty much the end of me playing for the county under Kevin Heffernan. That was probably a bad call on my behalf.

I got called back for a game in 1985 – there was a challenge match in Longford. There had been a terrible storm in Lucan and all the electricity and the phones were out so I was never contacted, but there was an article on the back of the old *Evening Press* about it. A friend of Dad's, Charlie Byrne, saw the article though, and let me know I was supposed to be playing the next day. I couldn't get in contact with anyone though, so myself and the brother just headed down to Longford on the Sunday morning.

I explained the situation to Tony Hanahoe and to Heffernan, but he didn't really want to know. I was a sub that day but I didn't get a run and that was the end of that really. In hindsight I probably should have gone to Barróg that day and played with Dublin, but I was captain of the club at the time and that tournament had particular significance to us so I felt obliged to do that. If I

had it all to do again I don't honestly know what I'd do. It was all about playing for Lucan for me at the time.

That same year Richie Crean was eligible to play for Dublin juniors again.
He captained the team that year and I was on it too. We won Leinster that
year, but we were beaten in the All-Ireland semi-final by Galway.

Then it all began to fall apart at club level. A gradual disintegration that
would lead to many of the club's leading lights leaving the team:

We were beaten by the Garda in the quarter-final of the intermediate cham-
pionship in 1985 over in O'Toole Park, and that year I went to Templemore.
We had a great team on paper, with Pascal Jackman, Eoin Mullarkey, Mick
Kilduff coming through and with Martin Heneghan, Terry Duignan, and
Martin Woods. Of course Richie Crean, Pat Mulhern, Alan Coyle, Seán
Nolan and Christy Corrigan would have been there still, and Paddy McCabe
too, though he finished when he was about twenty-three.

John McGearailt would have been a central figure on that team too, and
Eddie Mescall, Rory Mulhern and Ollie Murphy, who would have played a
bit with Sligo. Tommy Carr would have been gone by that stage, and there
would have been a lot of country lads around at the time. We really should
have been an awful lot better than we were, looking back!

There just wasn't enough commitment in the club at the time. There was too
much messing going on and a lot of the better lads just got fed up with it and
just left. I was under pressure then to play with the Garda, because they went on
to win that championship and went senior. Richie was living and teaching in
Navan at the time too, and he joined Navan O'Mahony's.

There were lads coming in from all over the place just to play football.
They weren't living in the area or anything and there was no camaraderie
there. These lads had no grá for the whole thing. There were only about five
or six of that great underage team we had that actually went on to play senior
for the club, which was an absolute disgrace.

So I joined the Garda then and we had a couple of great years. It was a bit
difficult because my Dad was a selector with the Lucan inters at the time.
When you're born and raised in a place people expect you to play for the
club, but sometimes circumstances dictate otherwise.

I suppose having been on the Dublin team in 1984 I had seen the other
side of things being done right, and none of my pals in Lucan ever really had
any real problem with me. I was always a Lucan man, I still always went to
their matches.

I played with the Dublin juniors in 1987 when we were beaten in an All-Ireland final. I was actually captain that year. A big crowd from Lucan came down to it, there was a bus organised, so there were no real difficulties there. I played with the Garda then until 1994 when I came back to Lucan.

Richie Crean also remembers that game:

Jack had come onto the Dublin junior team in 1985, and we won the Leinster Junior Championship again when I was captain. Unfortunately Galway beat us in the All-Ireland semi-final. I think Jack captained that team then in 1987 and I think Billy Gogarty was actually involved with running that team as well.

I know Paddy McCabe was on an All-Ireland minor winning team in 1979, they beat Kerry in the final. He came on that day as I recall. We lost Paddy to Leixlip around 1985, and that was another big loss for the club.

The by now somewhat depleted Lucan side battled on, much to their credit, but by the end of the 1980s all they would have to show for their efforts were defeats in consecutive Intermediate Football Championship semi-finals – the second of which was a particularly painful 1-10 to 2-6 defeat at the hands of Kilmore. A league semi-final loss to the same opposition at the end of 1989 put paid to another quality run that had seen the team beat Churchtown, Ballymun (replay) and St Maur's.

Luckily though, better times were just around the corner. It may have felt like a long way back to the lofty heights of early 1982, but the right approach was now being taken. The future of the club would come from within. In 1985, the club made a major decision not to enter the under-10 football leagues and instead to begin an underage coaching scheme. The footballers of that age group would instead be brought up to the 12th Lock every Saturday morning where they would be coached in small groups and street leagues would be run off.

'At the juvenile AGM in June 1985, a motion was passed to withdraw Lucan Sarsfields' two under-10 football teams from weekly league competition in the South-East Board and engage them in a weekly coaching scheme,' recalls Seamus Clandillon:

The motion was proposed by a subcommittee who met over the winter of 1984/85. Their role was to determine how best to improve the football ability of all under-10 footballers. They suggested that a coaching course combined with street leagues be held at the 12th Lock each Saturday morning for approximately

25-30 weeks. Such an experiment/scheme was to be closely monitored and reviewed after one year. It was emphasised that it was only an experiment.

Great thanks must be extended to those committee members and mentors who, over the years since 1976, gave Lucan a firm base for expansion and development by training and managing such great under-10 football teams in the different board competitions. They put Trojan work into these teams, the fruits of which are evident even today.

The coaching scheme came into operation on 7 September 1985. There were 132 boys under the age of 10 years old on 1 September 1985, taking part, half of them attending Our Lady's NS in Esker and the other half attending St Mary's BNS in Lucan village. There were 12 teams each with 11 players under the guide of their own individual coach.

Each Saturday morning, the emphasis was on the development of the players' skill by drill on the various facets of the game. The coaching lasted forty minutes approximately and was followed by a street league in which two teams of eleven combined to play another two elevens. Thus there were three street league games played each week in which the boys could apply what they had learned in the coaching session.

The weaker individuals got a good chance to develop while the better players could improve their basic skills. The players' commitment and dedication was remarkable and their attendance was amazing. For the thirteen weeks in the Christmas phase, an average of 100 boys attended weekly; in the cold Easter six-week phase, the attendance was a steady seventy-five weekly; and in the Summer phase of twenty weeks, the fine weather encouraged almost a full house.

Throughout the coaching, there was a great comradeship between all the boys and mentors alike. We had been thoroughly well served by a dedicated band of mentors who, week after week, took their young charges in hand and saw them improve in football ability and companionship accordingly.

A series of challenge matches took place on three periodic Saturdays. These were a great novelty because of the trip element against outside opposition. The teams showed themselves to be skilful and sporting in these encounters, even in the face of older, fitter and more experienced teams.

Of the 132 players in the first year of the experiment, sixty-nine graduated into a possible three under-11 teams in September 1986 which were involved in league competitions in the South-East Board. The remaining fifty-five boys were still eligible for under-10 coaching in 1986/87. These boys were to be augmented by a new batch of players who were eligible to take part, i.e. be in third class.

The boys were involved in written quizzes and a trip to Croke Park and their parents were more than helpful with transport to matches. The scheme was under constant revision so that improvements could be effected. It ran smoothly due to the fact that the 12th Lock was an ideal and safe venue where the boys could easily identify with Lucan Sarsfields.

The scheme was a good experiment and all agreed it should be on-going. We realised that if continued, success would not be evident for a number of years. Whatever the outcome, it gave pleasure, was a pleasure and mixed all the boys in sporting companionship. The mentors involved were satisfied with its progress and strongly recommended its continuation.

In the last year of its seven-year trial, 1991/2, two under-10 teams were entered in official County Board leagues while the rest of the lads were coached in the 12th Lock on Saturday mornings.

It would prove to be one of the most important decisions in the club's recent history, and in an ever-growing area it served just as successful in getting new mentors and parents involved as it did young players.

Seaghan Ó Lanagáin, a native of Dickboro in Kilkenny, remembers how he first came to be involved with the club and the success of the early coaching programmes:

In the late '80s we had the under-10s coaching up in the club and that's how I got involved. I suppose by 1989/90 we would have had 120 kids up here playing football. There were a lot of people involved – Eoin Walsh, Dermot Russell, Albert Curran, Hugh McGonnigle – and we ran a series of leagues. Remarkably we had three football teams that ran up to minor level.

Out of that initial involvement, Seaghan went on to become involved with many other teams:

I got involved with a team with my own lad Eoin when he was under-12 with John Egan in 1992, so they would have been a product of that. I got involved with a younger hurling team in 1993 with Joe Byrne and Kevin Brennan, and I think that was the last Lucan team to win that under-11 league.

Our first game was against Crumlin and I remember I had to ref it. There was torrential rain that day, people were burying themselves under their umbrellas. Lucan were winning well at that stage and the Crumlin mentors asked me to blow it up early, so I did. Of course it went to the board after that and we ended up having to replay the game. We annihilated them in the final game of the season.

The club's older generation of underage footballers were continuing to make great progress too. In 1984, the minor footballers won out their section of the league undefeated, in 1985 the under-15 and under-16 teams both won their leagues, the under-16s defeating Erin's Isle in the North v. South playoff along the way. The 1986 under-12s, as highlighted in a newsletter report, summed up the strides being made on the field:

> Lucan won the under-12 hurling league last Sunday when they defeated a gallant Trinity Gaels to become the Division 3 league champions. In ideal conditions before a very large crowd in Ringsend Park, Lucan showed plenty of skill and a great eye for scores when they ran out comfortable winners in a very hard fought but sporting match against the North County league winners.
>
> All on the team were stars, including the many subs, and high praise was bestowed on team mentors Paddy Kelly and the solid 'cat' himself Martin Lanigan. Having won Division 3 this term the team have showed that they will be more than a match for any opponent in the higher division in the season ahead. Well done to all concerned.

A year later, in 1987, a very special day came to the club thanks to the efforts of the under-21 footballers. After winning the south section of the competition, they went on to defeat Inisfails in the North v. South playoff and to finally bring the McCaffrey Cup back to Lucan for the first time. A 4-4 to 2-5 win brought great joy to the club, but also an optimism for the more immediate future ahead.

In 1988, the club received a boost when Colm Kelly was selected on the Dublin minor football team, but the real satisfaction that year came from the almost immediate success of the club's pioneering underage coaching structures. That same year, the under-11A footballers won their league undefeated, the under-11Bs finished runners-up, the under-12As, under-14s and under-15s all won their leagues, and the under-13Bs and under-16s finished as runners-up.

Towards the end of 1988, the under-12B team created their own little bit of history when they received both winners and runners-up medals for the same competition. Beaten in the final of the Millennium Shield by a single point, they were presented with the runners-up medals after the game. After an appeal against the opposition's illegal players, the board carried out an investigation and eventually presented the winners' shield and a set of medals to the team.

The future was looking brighter by the minute, with Coláiste Phádraig's

Liffey Valley News 1986

Jim - The Hurley Surgeon

While the clash of the ash may elicit strong emotions from many folk in the country, it regularly prompts an expression of anxiety from Lucan man Jim Quinn.

The reason is simple. Everytime hurleys clash the chances are that repair man Jim will be called upon. Jim operates a hurley hospital from a shed at the rear of his home in Esker Lawns and it is from there that the local club, Sarsfields, and its hurlers are assured of quality implements when they set about their hurling campaigns.

Jim is one of the club's hurling mentors. Originally from Kilkenny, he is well versed in the game but his initiation as a hurley repair man only began with his association with Sarsfields. He moved to Lucan in 1972 and joined the Sarsfields club two years later.

EXPENSIVE

Being involved with the game he saw the need to repair hurleys but his need has grown in recent years to a very large extent because of one obvious reason. "Hurleys are £8 each and they may last maybe two minutes on the field. If

you didn't fix hurleys it would cost a club a fortune," Jim explains.

Some of the larger clubs could field a dozen teams and the hurley bill could amount to a very large figure. Recently, a Kilkenny clubman told Jim they spent over £3,000 a year on hurleys while large clubs could spend in excess of £6,000.

One other reason, of course, for repairing hurleys stems from the fact that most players become attached to a certain stick. If you break your hurley during a match it can put you off your game and Jim feels it is important for players to be able to continue to use old sticks.

UNPAID

Jim, of course, is an unpaid repairman. The tape and other items used to repair broken sticks is paid for out of the kitty contributed by players. He admits he often spending over 20 hours a week repairing hurleys in the garden shed but in the last few years he has cut down on that activity. "I could spend seven days a week repairing hurleys. People came from Celbridge and everywhere and eventually I had to say to them that I could not keep it up," he reveals. But as a hurling mentor

he admits to finding it difficult to turn someone with a broken hurley away from his door.

Nowadays, he concentrates on repairing hurleys for his own clubmen and students from Coláiste Phádraig, a local secondary school. "I might repair maybe 15 or 20 in a week," he confides.

LIFESPAN

And a hurley's lifespan, according to Jim, depends on who is using it. "Some players would get 12 months out of a hurley and another player would go through eight or nine hurleys during the

same time. The more skilful a player is, the less likely he is to need a new stick.

Jim is pleased with the growing popularity of the game, particularly in Lucan. He pays tribute to Paddy Kelly and a local teacher Owen Walsh for nurturing the game among youngsters.

The Sarsfields intermediate team has been close to glory on a number of occasions in recent years. In the last year the side has played 32 games and won 27. No doubt Jim's skill as a repairman has had quite a lot to do with that success.

Jim Quinn.

A *Liffey Valley News* report on club hurling stalwart Jim Quinn and his skill with the repair of hurleys (1986).

Under-11A footballers, 1988/89: T. Clarke, J. O'Sullivan, D. Foley, C. Kealy, S. Hurson, M. Crystal, F. Colgan, C. Hickey, K. Foley, G. Maher, C. Canavan, B. Whelan, C. Corcoran, R. O'Sullivan, G. Doocey, C. Fahy. Front: B. Kealy, S. Kelly, B. Murphy, B. Clarke, D. Hurson, D. Kealy, B. Geraghty, W. Nolan, K. Wade, K. Wright.

footballers winning the under-14B county colleges championship that same year. And with the formation of Lucan Community College in 1987, the club had yet another breeding ground for young players. A set of jerseys was presented to the school from the club before the start of the 1988/89 school year, and with Neil McKelvey, a teacher at the college, informing the club that there were a number of students willing to play for Lucan, things were really looking up.

The club's hurlers, meanwhile, were trucking along quite nicely, but without the major breakthrough they so badly needed. In 1986, the team reached the final of the Doyle Cup and the top-four competition, but once again they were beaten in both.

More misery followed the following year in the exact same circumstances. Trips to the Doyle Cup final and top-four playoff again led to defeats, this time to Na Fianna and Faughs respectively. In October 1988, then, the team was beaten in the Corn Céitinn Cup final by Ballyboden after a fine semi-final win over Crumlin. They just could not catch a break.

After years of service to the club's hurling section, Jim Quinn handed the reins of the inter hurlers over to Seán McCaffrey and Peter Flannery. With Mícheál Moylan appointed captain and Eddie Bolger as vice-captain the future looked a lot rosier, but the decade ended in disappointment once again as the team lost out to St Vincent's in the quarter-final of the Junior Championship.

Success on the underage front of the small ball game was keeping spirits high though, after the club's under-12 team won both the 1985 and 1987

Above: The 1971 Lucan Sarsfields Junior football team.

Below: The 1972 Corn na Laoch winning St Mary's BNS footballers with teacher Vincent O'Connor.

Above: The 1984 Junior hurling championship team that were defeated by Faughs in the county decider.

Below: St Patrick's Esker Under-12 school football team that took part in the club's street leagues in the mid-1980s: Stephen Carroll, Brendan Byrne, Michael Kinsella, Eugene Murtagh, David Cullen, Seán Scully, Daryl McGrath, Noel Murphy, David Rankin, Colm McDermott, Joseph Ward, Larry Kelly, Ian Cunningham, Thomas Dolan, Keith Rothery, Jason Redmond.

Under-10 Coaching, 1985/86. Back row: Jim O'Brien (Coach), Darren Gilbert, Ian Rothery, Keith Battersby, David Herlihy, Justin Colleary, Kevin Lacey. Front row: Richard Dolan, Conor Hughes, Eoin O'Connor, Gregory Hickey, Declan Mulhern, Liam Mulhall, John Corkery.

Under-11 footballers, 1986/87: Pat Glover, Paul Horgan, Lorcan Heneghan, Eugene Nolan, Christopher O'Sullivan, Kevin Walsh, Paul O'Connor, Eoin O'Heir, Conor McGee. Front row: Declan Crummy, Brennie Collis, Michael McGillacuddy, Derek Taylor, Brendan Nestor, Diarmuid Roche, Brendan Glover, Seamus Clandillon.

Under-10 football coaching, 1987/88. Left to right: Peter Faulkner (Coach), Eamon Murphy, Paul Leonard, John Doyle, John Paul Linnane, David O'Brien, Jonathon Rodgers, Liam Morris, Gavin Lennon, Terence Walsh, David Kennedy, Eoin Walsh (Coach), Jarlath McKeever, Gerrard Kelly, Kenneth Wright, Stephen Power, James Morris, Ronan Philips, Colm Comerford, Jesse Brennan, Seamus Tackaberry, Seán Slaughter, Philip Keane, John Mahon, Evan Keane, Ciaran Fahy, Gillian Colgan, Richard Archibold, Neil Walsh, David Faulkner, Niall McKiernan.

The Coláiste Phádraig Under-14B Dublin league winners 1988.

The 1988 Under-15 footballers. Back row: Colin Maguire, Ciaran McGrath, Ronan Hallessey, Noel O'Grady, Conor Bresnan, Derek Maher, Lar Norris, Mel Kelly, Murchada Vaughan. Middle row: Brian Flavin, Kevin O'Brien, Vincent Hargaden, Niall Carroll, Ciaran Colgan. Front row: Emmet Brady, Mark Kelly, Leigh Moore, Shane Brennan.

St Mary's BNS Johnston Mooney & O'Brien Cup Winners, 1989. Back row: Martin O'Halloran, Ian Fitzgerald, Vinny Shanagher, Michael Norris, Niall McGonnigle, Paul Foley, Stephen Corrigan, Keith Brophy, David Herlihey, Terence McMorrow. Front row: Barry O'Neill, Aidan O'Brien, Robert McQuaid, Stephen O'Neill, Patrick Philips, Ciaran Fahy, Simon Doran, Tadhg Clandillon.

The Under-16 footballers of 1990.

The 1991 Minor football team. Back: Martin Lanigan (Mentor), Niall McNulty, Paul Noonan, Donal Lanigan, Paul Horgan, Mark O'Riordan, Paddy Rooney, Ollie O'Brien, Alan Casey, Paddy Mooney, Jonathan Kelly, Pat Keane, Jim Brady (Mentor). Front: Liam Strong, Keith Coughlan, Senan Clandillon, Colin Rigney, Colm Muldoon, Philip Lanigan, Eoghan McGrath, Mick Casey, Darren Gilbert.

Above: The 1991 Under-14 hurling team.

Below: Intermediate Hurling Championship Team v. Faughs, 1992. Back row: Derek Maher, John Grimes, Eoin Mullarkey, Niall Gaffney, Lar Norris, Hugh McNally (RIP), John Mills, Liam Carton, Brendan Healy, Paschal Jackman, Eoin Healy, Paddy Mulkerrins. Front row: M. Hogan, John Hayes, James Coughlan, Declan Kelly, Brendan White, Lochlan McEvoy, Liam Strong, Michael Killeen, Martin Heneghan, Des Hennessey, Christy Tucker.

Early 1990s Intermediate Hurling Team. Back row: Michael Griffin, Liam Carton, Peter Flannery, John Egan, Niall Gaffney, Joe McDonnagh, Eoin Mullarkey, Stephen Farrell, John Hayes, John Clancy, Ultan Tuite, Vinny Shanaghar, P.J. Curtin (Trainer). Front row: Fergal Scully, Gerome O'Connor, Colm Muldoon, Jimmy Walsh, Mick Norris, Brendan White, Michéal Moylan, Phil Cunningham, Kevin Brennan, Declan Kelly.

Under-10 footballers, 1992: Tommy Clyne, Ronan McCarthy, Graham Fitzgerald, Ross Aylward, James Mulhern, Colm Russell, Seán Delaney, Brian Larkin, Ger Gleeson, Ciaran O'Neill, Aiden McKelvey, Brian Quinn. Front row: Ciaran Phillips, Aaron Dunne, Anthony Clarke, Kevin Roche, Aidan Glover, Conor Healy, Terence Smith, Richie Butler, Eoghan McGearailt, Cormac McCarthy.

Above: The ladies senior football team of 1993. Back row: Liz Balfe, Caitriona Heneghan, Bridgie Hurson, Gorana Leahy, Nora Keane, Ann Bresnan, Jackie Buggle, Mary Bresnan, Donal Griffin (Manager). Front row: Gillian Mulqueen, Mags Scully, Maria McGrath, Suzanne Place, Antonette Buggle, Jackie Quinn, Karen O'Toole, Phil Mescall.

Below: St Mary's Cuman na mBunscol senior hurling team, 1994: Vincent O'Connor, Peter Bielenberg, Brian Quinn, Leonard Skelly, Martin Murphy, Seán Quinn, Graham Fitzgerald, Ronan McCarthy, Rowan Kelly, Aiden McKelvey, John Galligan, Shane Donoghue, Ciaran Curley, John Kelly. Front row: Kevin Greene, Daragh Brennan, Joey Byrne, Shane Casey, Aaron Dunne, Andrew Duff, Conor McKeon, Padraig Ward, Philip Linton, Kevin Bielenberg.

Intermediate Football League and Championship double winners that secured senior status for the club for the first time in both league and championship, 1995. Back row: Colm Kelly, Tommy Carr, Conor Bresnan, Fergus McNulty, Damien O'Brien, Damien McGowan, Niall Collins, Jack Sheedy. Front row: David Ryan, John Mills, Donal Lanigan, Ronan O'Flynn, Alan O'Brien, T.J. Briody, Eugene Gorry.

Under-15 camogie team, 1995. Back row: Gillian Flannery, Imelda Smith, Joy Coyle, Elaine Cooney, Patricia McGarrigle, Sarah Bradley, Aideen Casey, Catriona McGarrel, Kathy Wright. Front row: Róisín Hayden, Aoife Sheils, Deirdre King, Gráinne Ní Lanigáin, Elaine Galvin, Caroline Flynn.

St Mary's National School, Cumann na mBunscol Hurling Final, 1995.

Under-14 Division 2 Dublin Féile na nGael hurling title winners, 1996: Mick Power, Brian Quinn, Jerome Twomey, Ger Power, Seán Quinn, James Mulhern, Leonard Skelly, Richie Butler, Aiden McKelvey, Stephen Murphy, Cian Fleming, Terence Smith, Peter Bielenberg, Pat Glover, Joe Byrne. Front row: Joe Healy, Seán McCaffrey, Daragh Brennan, Aidan Glover, Joey Byrne, Kevin Roche, Aaron Dunne, Conor Healy, Ger Gleeson, Daire Reidy, Philip Linton, Andrew Duff, Jim Quinn. Front mascots: Johnny McCaffrey, Matthew McCaffrey, Niall Healy.

The Under-21 hurling team that claimed the 1996 C Hurling Championship crown with a win in the final at Parnell Park. Back row: Dermot Foley, Cathal Corcoran, Declan Mulhern, Conor Griffin, Ian Fitzgerald, Vincent Shanagher, Stephen Kelly, Paul Foley, Alan Mockler, Dan Hickey, Tadhg Clandillon. Front row: Mark Cristal, Aidan O'Brien, Senan Clandillon, Paul Kelly, David Herlihy, Fran Kearns, John Doyle, Martin O'Halloran.

The 1996 Under-13 hurlers with team mentor Tom Duff.

Above: The 1997 Minor hurling team that defeated Ballyboden St Enda's in the quarter-final of the A championship in Pairc Uí Mhurchú: G. McGarry, M. Moore, B. Corcoran, B. Percy, T. Moulton, A. O'Neill, E. Farrelly, B. Byrne, S. Russell, P. Casey, F. Gordon. Front row: P. O'Leary, E. Ó Lanagáin, F. Clandillon, D. Hickey, C. Dooley, A. Barnes, T. Cummins, B. McGarry.

Below: The 1997 Under-10 footballers with mentors Seán McCaffrey and Mick McGrath.

The 1998 Intermediate hurlers, winners of the Corn Fogarty, Corn Céitinn and Keogh Cup. Back row: Liam Carton (Mentor), Hugh McNally, Tadhg Clandillon, Declan Carr, Derek Maher, Vinny Shanagher, Lar Norris, No Pain Kelly, Colm Sunderland, Alan O'Neill, Cro Dooley, Seaghan Ó Lanagáin (Mentor). Front row: Michéal Moylan (Mentor), Seán Quinn, Eoin Ó Lanagáin, Liam Bergin, John Mills, Stevie Farrell, Neville Kelly, Senan Clandillon, Pat Doyle, Phil Lanigan, Colm Mockler, Peter Flannery (Mentor).

Above: The 1998 Under-16 football league winners with captain Richie Butler holding the trophy.

The historic 1999 Intermediate hurling team that secured senior status for the club for the first time, winning the League and Championship double along the way. Back row: Derek Maher, Hugh McNally, Alan O'Neill, Joe McDonnagh, Declan Kelly, Colm Sunderland, Tadhg Clandillon, Vinny Shanagher, John Mills, Declan Carr, Eoin Ó Lanagáin, Cro Dooley. Front row: Seán Quinn, Neville Kelly, Lar Norris, Stevie Farrell, Phil Lanagan, Fintan Clandillon, Alan Mockler, Pat Doyle, Liam Bergin, Ryan Doyle (sitting at front).

The 1999 Under-12 hurlers. Back row: Peter Callaghan, Eoin McCarthy, Kev Reilly, Shane O'Niell, Lorcan O'Connor, Stephen Reilly, Seán Keane, Garry Manning. Front row: Aaron Doonan, Andrew Mockler, Aidan Roche, Garry Coleman, David Byrne, Niall Guy, Darren Anderson.

The historic Under-14 Féile Peil na nÓg Division 1 winning team celebrate their victory in St Vincent's after becoming the first underage team to secure a Division 1 Féile title in 2000.

The 2001 Dublin Minor B Hurling Championship winners. Back row: John Hayes, Kevin Brennan, Joseph McCarthy, Patrick Mulhern, Thomas Hayes, Niall Long, David Coyle, Philip Corcoran, David Corrigan, Kevin O'Reilly, Colm Barrett, Alan Butler, Keith Brennan, Brian Bergin, Joe Byrne, Dave Corrigan, Liam Bergin. Front row: Mark Twomey, Declan O'Shaughnessy, Damien Mitchell, Enda Tucker, Johnny McCaffery, Jerome Twomey, Darragh Brennan, David Mescall, Diarmuid O'Connor, Gerard Twohig, David Scully.

Under-11B Football Division 3 SE Board winners, 1988/89: Tommy Wynne, David
Hurson, Eoin Comerford, Colm Comerford, Cronan Finnegan, Shane Dalton, Alan
Kellegher, David Gannon, Damien O'Halloran, Ronan Phillips. Front row: Sean Slaughter,
Brian Geraghty, Greg Byrne, Fachtna 'Doc' Clandillon, Niall O'Leary, Kenneth Wright,
Brian Murphy, Garret Doocey, Peter Clayton, David Walsh.

leagues undefeated. The minors, in 1987, won their league, and in 1988
the under-12s once again won the league while the under-16s won the B
Championship. The biggest highlight for the underage section of the small
ball game in the club came in 1989, when, under Paddy Kelly, the under-16s
secured an historic league and championship double.

A first-round championship win over Kevin's and a semi-final win over
Thomas Davis in O'Toole Park had secured them a date in the final in
Swords to face Naomh Barróg. After a tense, tight battle, Lucan came out
on top by 1-6 to 0-5. A few weeks later they would go on to complete the
double by beating the same opposition by a single point.

To round things off, the hurlers of St Mary's BNS went on to win the
Johnson, Mooney & O'Brien Cup at Croke Park. The stage was set for the
biggest decade in the history of Lucan Sarsfields.

Off the field, things were beginning to develop on the social side. Don
Dardis recalls one of the early initiatives to bring people from the surrounding areas up to the 12th Lock:

We got the set-dancing up and running in 1989. Classes were held once
a week and a céilí was held each month from September to June which
were really enjoyable occasions. Neil McKelvey, who was teaching in the
Community College, called the sets, while I looked after the publicity and
organised the bands and admission and that side of things. There was really
a great surge in the popularity of set-dancing after that in the early '90s, so

Lucan BNS, Johnston Mooney & O'Brien Cup winners, 1989: M. O'Halloran, I. Fitzgerald, M. Norris, V. Shanagher, N. McGonnigle, P. Foley, K. Brophy, D. Herlihy, T. McMorrow. Front: A. O'Brien, S. Corrigan, R. McCabe, S. O'Neill, T. Clandillon, P. Philips, S. Doran, B. O'Neill, C. Fahy.

much so that people had to be turned away from classes and ceilis. It would slowly lose its appeal though, and it ceased by the end of the 1990s when it was no longer paying its way.

Either way, the club had successfully brought people in through the doors while the good times lasted.

PLAYERS OF THE ERA

Intermediate footballers, v. St Brendan's, championship quarter-final replay, 1980: Noel Cullen, Mick Anderson, Kevin Synnott, Joe Murray, Mick Casey, Charlie O'Connor, Tim O'Donoghue, Seamus Mulhern, Paddy McCabe, Seán Nolan, Richie Crean, Pat Mulhern, Maurice O'Sullivan, Alan Coyle, Seán McCaffrey.

Minor football panel, 1981: Eoin Walsh, Joe Kavanagh, Eoin Mullarkey, Paul Norris, Michael Crean, Jack Sheedy, Mick Murphy, David Lynch, Seán Murray, Brendan Gannon, Mick Kilduff, Vincent Byrne, Niall McCabe, John Murphy, Gerard Curran, Brian Harte, Gerard Dermody.

Junior A hurling championship final team, v. Faughs, 1984: J. Burke, M. Mockler, J. Dunne, G. Fahy, N. Flynn, J. O'Toole, T. Jones, J. Linnane, R. Duke, P. Delaney (manager), D. O'Brien Snr, M. Moylan, E. Mullarkey, V. Blake, D. O'Brien Jnr, J. Dooley, N. Dwyer, A. Higgins, J. Quinn, D. Fitzgerald, T. Stewart, P. Mulkearns, M. Maher, B. Gannon, J. Walsh, S. O'Brien.

Junior hurling championship finalists, 1984, from match programme: (Name, age, occupation, hobbies.) Jarlath Burke, 39, carpenter, squash and golf; Alan Higgins, radio technician, squash and photography; Seán O'Brien, 20, trainee accountant, golf, music, cars and snooker; Noel O'Dwyer, 25, quality engineer, ballads and reading; John O'Toole, 31, civil servant, gardening and decorating; Tom Jones, 28, nurse, television and music; Martin Maher, 23, ESB linesman, discos and boxing; Joe Dooley, 39, company director, squash and jogging; Gerry Fahy, 32, clerical officer, bridge, reading and TV; Tom Stewart, 31, builder, jogging and pony trekking; Joe Linnane, 37, plasterer, whist, dancing and music; Eoin Mullarkey, 21, technician, swimming and music; Mícheál Moylan, 30, clerical officer, gardening and music; Martin Mockler, 36, carpenter, swimming and music; Paddy Mulkerrins, 36, sales rep, golf, jogging and music; Barry Gannon, 30, company director, golf and dogs; Victor Blake, 32, solicitor, gardening and woodcraft; Jim Walsh, 32, nurse tutor, cycling and squash; Noel Flynn, 30, councillor, football, music and TV; Ronan Duke, 18, student, music, cycling and swimming; John Dunne, 27, civil servant, fishing, squash and TV; Eoin Walsh, 19, student, golf and basketball; Des O'Brien Jnr, 19, student, discos, rock music and snooker; Derry Fitzgerald, 30, army officer, jogging and music; Desie O'Brien, 45, engineering planner, golf and squash; Finian Christie, 20, blacksmith, farming and antiques; Pat Delaney, team manager, 31, company director, cooking, golf and cards; Jim Quinn, selector, 51, sales rep, making and repairing hurleys and whist.

Clubhouse development committee, 1985: P. McGarrigle, V. Blake, G. Butler, A. Coyle, R. Crean, D. Dardis, J. Fitzharris, B. Gannon, W. Gogarty, P. Kelly, C. Leahy, J. Sheedy, D. Malone, E. Mescall, M. Molloy, E. Mullarkey, P. Mulhern, S. McCaffrey, P. O'Connell, J. Quinn, J. Smith, T. Tobin, E. Walsh.

Under-10 B footballers, 1984/85: Trevor McHugh, Alan Hughes, Terence Kelly, Paul O'Connor, Oliver O'Brien, Eugene Nolan, Christopher O'Sullivan, Conor McGee, Niall McNulty, Eoin Kenny, Brennie Collis, Mark Creevey, Desmond O'Connor, Darren Burbridge, Pascal Joyce, Diarmuid Roche, Mark Nolan, Liam Smyth, Justin Collery, Stephen Kiernan, Christopher Price, Brendan Nestor, Evin O'Connor, Senan Clandillon, Brendan Glover, Daragh Doohan, Tadhg Clandillon, Connel Duffin, Colm Colclough, James O'Brien, Darren Glover.

Under-10 coaching participants, 1985/86: Liam Smyth, Thomas Germaine, Paul Hogan, Christopher Sullivan, Mark Corkery, David Malone, Daragh Doohan, Colman McGrath, Eoghan McGrath, Paul Kelly, Colm Pattison, Adrian Reidy, David Brennan, Robert McQuaid, Jim O'Brien, Joe Aherne, Darren Gilbert, Ian Rothery, Keith Battersby, David Herlihy, Justin Collery, Kevin Lacey, Richard Dolan, Conor Hughes, Evin O'Connor, Greg Hickey, Declan Mulhern, Liam Mulhall, John Corkery, Robert Heffernan, Ronan McHugh, Ian Fitzgerald, Gaven Eogan, Niall McGonigle, Stephen Geraghty, Peter Geraghty, John Gleeson, James Nealon, David O'Sullivan, Francis

Dillon, Colm Colclough, Edwin O'Byrne, Patrick Campbell, Peter Nealon, Thomas Nolan, Liam Lynch, Mark Creevey, Ian Gordon, Brendan Carthy, David Hartnett, Mark Walsh, Thomas Cummins, Vincent Shanagher, Christopher Price, Martin O'Reilly, James McCormack, Stephen Carolan, Cyril Murtagh, James O'Brien, Darren Glover, Barry Harte, Anthony King, Aidan O'Brien, Eoin Dunne, Seamus Miller, Ronan Kavanagh, John Barrett, Michael O'Sullivan, Jeff Aherne, Mark Slaughter, Gavin O'Neill, Fergal Kelly, Brian Sourke, Senan Clandillon, Eamon Cunningham, Alan Buggle, Niall Eogan, Eoin Kenny, Patrick Kelly, Keith Murphy, Simon Doran, Damien Doolan.

Under-13 B footballers, 1985/86: Ronan Hallissey, Vincent Hargaden, Colin Kelleher, Gareth Burbridge, Ciarán McGrath, Mark Kelly, Murchada Vaughan, Ronan Gavin, Cearbhall O Siochain, Michael Colclough, David Fagan, Ciarán Colgan, Robert Tierney, Emmet Brady, Shane Brennan, Stephen Corrigan, Declan Monaghan, Brian Fagan, Tadhg Clandillon, Edward O'Brien, David Dillon.

Under-11 A footballers, 1985/86: Paul Horgan, Eoin O'Hehir, Lorcan Heneghan, Jim Dowling, Donal Lanigan, Conor Griffin, Donnachadh Vaughan, Conor McGee, John O'Shea, Declan Crummy, Darren O'Reilly, Philip Lanigan, Ciarán Cassidy, Kevin McManus, Brendan Glover, Derek Taylor.

Under-11 A football, 1988: Vincent Shanagher, Aidan O'Brien, Ronan Doolan, Seán Nolan, Niall McGonigle, Barry Prenderville, Desmond Goldrick, Stephen Corrigan, Darren Glover, John Corkery, Martin Butler, Simon Doran, Robert McQuaid, Alan O'Shea, Paul Kelly, Michael Norris, Niall Tully, Tadhg Clandillon.

Under-11 B football Division 3, South-East, 1988/1989: Thomas Wynne, David Hurson, Eoin Comerford, Colm Comerford, Cronan Finnegan, Shane Dalton, Alan Kellegher, David Gannon, Damien O'Halloran, Ronan Phillips, Seán Slaughter, Brian Geraghty, Greg Byrne, Fachtna Clandillon, Niall O'Leary, Kenneth Wright, Brian Murphy, Garret Doocey, Peter Clayton, David Walsh.

Under-11 A footballers, 1988/89: Mark Crystal, Frank Colgan, Colm Hickey, Karl Foley, Gary Maher, Cillian Canavan, Barry Whelan, Cathal Corcoran, Robert O'Sullivan, Garret Doocey, Ciarán Fahy, Brian Kealy (mascot), Stephen Kelly, Brian Murphy, Brian Clarke, David Hurson, David Kealy, Brian Geraghty, Wesley Nolan, Kenneth Wade, Kenneth Wright.

Coaches involved with inaugural under-10 coaching scheme, 1985/86: Richie Crean, Jim O'Brien, Jerry Kenny, Tony Price, Joe Dunne, Joe Ahearne, Kevin O'Reilly, Oliver Meyler, George Butler, Brian Carolan, Eoin Walsh, Séamus Clandillon, Padraic Colleary.

Coaches involved with under-10 coaching scheme, 1986/87: John Carabini, Tom Drohan, Greg Flynn, Mick Mulhall, Joe Dunne, Dermot Flynn, George Butler, Matthew Burke, Barry O'Leary, Brendan Maher, Séamus Clandillon, Eoin Walsh, Jim O'Brien, Tom Kelleher, John O'Shea, Brian Carolan, Frank Chubb, Tony Clarke, Tony Price.

Coaches involved with under-10 coaching scheme 1987/88: Tony Clarke, Shay Hurson, David Flavin, Pat Corbett, Conor Kealy, Joe Fox, Tom Drohan, Eoin Walsh, Peter Faulkner, Séamus Clandillon, Frank Chubb, Brian Gaffney, Philip Coffey, Damien Foley.

Coaches involved with under-10 coaching scheme, 1988/89: Steve Byrne, Dermot Russell, Pat McGrath, Mattie McCabe, Michael Malone, Jim Galvin, John Brien, Seaghan Ó Lanagáin, Denis Clifford, Brian Gaffney, Kevin Whirdy, Albert Curran, Noel Buggie, Joe Fox, Pat Mooney, Eoin Walsh.

Coaches involved with under-10 coaching scheme, 1989/90: Seaghan Ó Lanagáin, Pat Mooney, Jim Galvin, Michael Malone, John Brien, Pat McGrath, Denis Clifford, Albert Curran, Hugh McGonnigle, Joe Fox, Noel Hickey, Pat Carr, Tom Drohan, Mattie McCabe, Kevin Whirdy.

Under-15 footballers, 1988: Colin Maguire, Ciarán McGrath, Ronan Hallessey, Noel O'Grady, Conor Bresnan, Derek Maher, Lar Norris, Mel Kelly, Murchada Vaughan, Brian Flavin, Kevin O'Brien, Vincent Hargaden, Niall Carroll, Ciarán Colgan, Emmet Brady, Mark Kelly, Leigh Moore, Shane Brennan.

Under-16 hurling league and championship double winning team, 1989: Liam Strong, Cathal O'Connor, Fergal Scully, Paul Higgins, Declan Donohue, Lar Norris, Patrick Rooney, Derek Maher, Alan Horgan, Ciarán Nolan, Ciarán McGrath, Conor Bresnan, Mel Kelly, Noel O'Grady, Brian Flavin.

St Mary's BNS, Johnston, Mooney & O'Brien Cup winners, 1989: M. O'Halloran, I. Fitzgerald, M. Norris, V. Shanagher, N. McGonnigle, P. Foley, K. Brophy, D. Herlihy, T. McMorrow, A. O'Brien, S. Corrigan, R. McCabe, S. O'Neill, T. Clandillon, P. Philips, S. Doran, B. O'Neill, C. Fahy.

Lucan Sarsfields golf society captains:

1987: Bob Dardis	1988: Billy Gogarty	1989: Seán McCaffrey
1990: Eoin Mullarkey	1991: Christy Leahy	1992: Donal Walsh
1993: Noel Lally	1994: Denis Malone	1995: Fergal Walsh
1996: John Mills Snr	1997: Colm Moran	1998: Pearse O'Connell
1999: Kevin Duke	2000: Seán Walsh	2001: Dave Murray
2002: Michael Molloy	2003: Christy O'Toole	2004: Pio O'Leary Snr
2005: Ciarán Keogh	2006: Michael Roche	2007: Michael Malone
2008: Pat Keane	2009: Damian O'Brien	2010: Michael O'Grady
2011: Dave Whittle		

FIVE

1990-1999
THE INTER MISSION

The end of the 1980s had been tinged with sadness after the deaths of two of the club's stalwarts. Joe Gaffney, who had been club treasurer in the 1960s and 1970s, and who had played a crucial role in the purchase of the 12th Lock grounds, passed away in 1988. Later that same year, Jack O'Brien, whose tenure as chairman had been highlighted by his passion for the development of underage games, also died. They were sad times for the club, but with the legacies of these great men in mind the club drove on ever forward.

The underage football coaching developments of the late eighties had ensured a steady flow of players coming through the club, and in 1990 a proposal to do the same in hurling had been introduced by Seán McCaffrey. Dave Foley was to come on board as a coach, and by the end of the year he would also be working with under-13s, -14s, -15s, and the minor and under-21 teams. A club newsletter published in May 1990, revealed the progress being made, 'This month will see the launch of the first phase of a three-year coaching scheme for young hurlers. Co-ordinator Seán McCaffrey and the coaching committee have now finalised plans for what will undoubtedly be of tremendous benefit to the game of hurling in the years ahead.'

The same newsletter also summed up where the club stood as it looked ahead to the decade in store:

During the 1989/90 season the club fielded a total of 27 teams, comprising of 14 football, 9 hurling and 4 camogie teams. The development of a strong camogie section has been one of the most heartening features of the past year – our thanks and appreciation to all concerned.

Major refurbishing of the clubhouse and dressing rooms is now nearing completion. We are confident that the alterations will provide a greater degree of comfort and thus ensure larger attendances at social events. With regards to the pitches, the landscaping of the ground's perimeter and the building of a boundary wall has greatly enhanced the general appearance of the area.

The car park has been lined for two tennis courts and we would welcome the assistance of anybody who may be interested in forming a tennis club. The dramatic increase in club membership is indeed most welcome, 215 adults and 515 juvenile members speaks for itself.

The underage football coaching programme, meanwhile, was continuing where it had left off, involving upwards of 110 young players in the club under the guidance of Seaghan Ó Lanagáin and his team of mentors, coaches and parents, while former Dublin star Kevin Synnott was working with the under-14, -15 and -16 teams.

ACC tournament team, 1990: C. McGrath, A. O'Brien, T. Clandillon, M. Norris, A. O'Shea, N. Mulhern, E. Linnane, S. Kelly, M. Butler, E. Dunne, N. Tully. Front: B. Carthy, D. McCabe, P. Nealon, D. Herlihy, M. McHugh, P. Kelly, B. Clarke, F. Kearns, J. Doyle.

The Clubhouse in the 1990s.

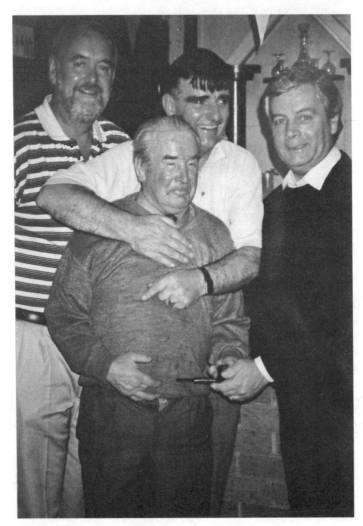

Club stalwarts John Mills Snr (back left) and Mick Molloy (centre) with now departed club legends Tommy Malone (front) and Billy Gogarty.

Cumann Na Sáirséalaigh
Leamhcáin

1991 / 1992 REVIEW   17 June 1992

Lucan Sarsfields fielded thirty four teams in football, hurling and camogie this season. The following is a list of teams, mentors and league placings up to and including Minors. The more senior teams and juvenile hurling teams are still involved in the final games of the different leagues.

	Team	Mentors	League Placings
Football:	U.10A	Tony Clarke, Seán McCaffrey	Won
	U.10B	Michael Malone, Gerome Twomey	
	U.11A	Shay Hurson, Martin Kelly	R/u. R/u.Special
	U.11B	John Flynn, John Carabini, Walter Rice	R/u.
	U.12A	Albert Curran, Hugh McGonigle	R/u.
	U.12B	Ray Barnes, Eamon Cullen	Won
	U.12C	Alan O'Brien, Philip Dowling	
	U.13A	Dermot Russell, Noel Buggie	
	U.13B	Steve Byrne, Gerry Gleeson	
	U.14A	Tony Clarke, Shay Hurson	Won
	U.14B	Martin Walsh, Séamus Clandillon	
	U.15	George Butler, Jim Nealon	R/u.
	U.16	Seán Nolan, Joe Murray	
	U.18	Jim Brady, Pat Keane Mick Casey	
	U.21	Jim McCarthy, John Mills	
	Junior	Tom Brennan, Pat Mescall	
	Intermediate	Paul Kelly, Mick Molloy	
Hurling:	U.10	Seán McCaffrey, Mick Power	In contention for honours.
	U.11	Niall Gaffney, Ciarán McGrath	"
	U.12A	John Egan, Séamus Clandillon	"
	U.12B	Kevin O'Connell	
	U.13	Willie Bray, Michael Murphy	
	U.14	Gerry Fahy, Eamon Corcoran	R/u. Feile "
	U.15	Pat Colgan, Paddy Kearns	"
	U.16	Mick Ryan, Peter Flannery	"
	U.18	Tom Jones, Martin Lanigan	
	U.21	Eddie Waters, John Mills	
	Junior	Mick Ryan, Jim Quinn	
	Intermediate	Christy Tucker, Paddy Mulkerrins, John Mills	
Camogie:	U.13	Séamus Kelly	
	U.14	Cormac O'Brien	
	U.15	Noel Flynn	
	Junior B	Padraig McGarrigle, John Ryan	
Ladies Football:		Donal Griffin	

In addition, a very successful U.8/9/10 Football Coaching Scheme was held on Saturday mornings at the 12th Lock organised by Seaghán O Lanagáin, Mick Casey and co-mentors. Also, the annual Junior and Senior Hurling Street Leagues are reaching their climax, organised by Vincent O'Connor.

We thank all those who have kept this huge games organisation going; including mentors, trainers, drivers, linespeople, umpires, flaggers and netters, jersey washers, grass cutters, referees, board delegates, committee and executive members, social committee, bar committee, and above all, the players, who make it all worth while. We thank you one and all for your time, effort and support throughout the year.

Mentors, 1991/92.

The club bar was operating at full capacity, with volunteerism to the fore once more. 'The bar opened in 1990, and at that stage it was just open on weekends,' recalls Seamus Clandillon:

> The club wasn't in a position to pay a bar manager at the time so it came down to volunteers. Liam Carton, an experienced barman, came in and acted as volunteer manager for years after that, and he was helped out by Frank Chubb, Tommy Clyne and Gerry McNamara, who did some really great work up in the club.

There was hunger for expansion, however, and the wheels were soon set in motion once again to refurbish the clubhouse. 'About two years after the bar got up and running the executive decided to give the place a makeover. Padraig McGarrigle and Jim Quinn were allotted the responsibility of deliveries and the likes so it was all down to volunteerism,' Seamus recalls:

> In 1991 a club development draw limited to 1,500 members at £50 per ticket was held as a once-off draw in June. This was to pay for modernising the dressing rooms and the development of a clubhouse extension. There were three star prizes of £15,000, £7,500 and £5,000, as well as a number of other small prizes. That went really well.
>
> After all these draws the club's major debts were finally cleared, the clubhouse was re-roofed, the entrance was tarmacadamed, the grounds were fenced and work initiated on the juvenile pitches. With all the necessary facilities in place it was now time to make as broad a statement as possible on the field of play.

The club opened its new Members' Bar in 1992.

Back on the field, and ahead of the 1988/89 season, the structures of the Dublin adult club football competitions had been changed. Lucan were now playing in Intermediate section C of the league, and the rejuvenated second team in Junior Division 2 under Alan Coyle. Success, thankfully, was now just around the corner.

The minor footballers, meanwhile, who had lost out narrowly to Erin's Isle in the championship in December 1989, had one of their stars Fergus McNulty called onto the county panel, and John Mills Jnr was called onto the county hurling panel. The underage county structures were changing too, with the county entering under-21 football and hurling teams into inter-county competitions for the first time.

At club level, the inter footballers got the decade off to a bright start with a league win over Robert Emmets in the 12th Lock in January, with some fresh blood coming into the squad from Casement Gaels. By February the junior team had exited the championship at the hands of Wild Geese, but the inters would not taste championship action until late March. Despite the promising start to the decade, however, the team fell short against old rivals St Vincent's in the first round the championship. The signs were promising though, and the team was still very much in league contention.

The Jimmy Magee All-Stars returned to the club on the May Bank Holiday Monday, 1990, when they took on a Dáil Selection in the club, but the first silverware to come the club's way in the nineties came through the inter footballers' win in the Quinlan Cup tournament in September, beating St Mark's in the final.

As they prepared for a run in the league playoffs, and heading into their last-four clash with Raheny, team trainer Gay McCabe stepped down. Mick Casey stepped into the breach at the crucial time and when the game finally came around in O'Toole Park on 11 November, Lucan were ready to perform. The cobwebs got the better of the team the first day out, and after an epic battle the teams finished level. But in the replay in December the team came good to see them book a final date with St Maur's of Rush.

Junior camogie team, 1991.

Left: *Evening Herald* club feature clipping, 1992.

Below: Minor footballers, 1992: Pat Keane, Niall McNulty, Paul Noonan, Donal Lanigan, Paul Horgan, Mark O'Riordan, Patrick Rooney, Oliver O'Brien, Alan Casey, Patrick Rooney, Jonathan Kelly, Pat Keane Jnr, Jim Brady. Front: Liam Strong, Keith Coughlan, Senan Clandillon, Colin Rigney, Colin Muldoon, Philip Lanigan, Eoghan McGrath, Alan Casey, Darren Gilbert.

Cumann Na Sáirséalaigh
Leamhcáin

TEAMS FOR SEASON 1992/93

FOOTBALL

BOARD	TEAM	MENTORS	PITCH	DAY	TIME
South East	IOA	Seán Flynn, Dermot Russell	AGP	Sat.	II.30
" "	IIA	Tony Clarke, Seán McCaffrey	"	"	"
" "	IIB	Michael Malone, Gerome Twomey	"	"	"
" "	I2A	Martin Kelly, Shay Hurson	12th Lock	"	"
" "	I2B	John Flynn, Walter Rice, John Carabini	" "	"	"
South City	I3A	Albert Curran, Hugh McGonigle, Fergus McNulty	" * "	"	3.00
" "	I3B	Ray Barnes, Eamon Cullen	" "	"	"
Coisde na nOg	I4A	Dermot RUssell, Noel Buggie	AGP	"	"
South City	I4B	Steve Byrne, Gerry Gleeson	"	"	"
Coisde na nOg	I5A	Tony Clarke, Shay Hurson	"	"	"
South City	I5B	Martin Walsh, Séamus Clandillon	"	Sun.	II.30
Minor	I6	George Butler, Jim Nealon	"	Sat.	3.00
"	I8	Jim Brady, Mick Casey, Pat Keane	"	Sun.	II.30
"	2I	Tony Tobin, John Mills	12th Lock	Sat.	3.00
Junior Football	Jun.I	Tom Brennan, Pat Mescall	" "	Sun.	am/pm
" "	Jun.2	Jim McCarthy, Jim O'Neill, Frankie Farrell	" "	"	"
" "	Inter.	Paul Kelly, Mick Molloy	" "	"	II.00

Co-ordinators: U.I5 downwards - Shay Hurson. U.I6 upwards - Mick Molloy

HURLING

Juvenile	IOA	To be arranged by March	AGP	Sat.	II.30
Hurling Board	IOB	" " " " "	"	"	"
IO-12	IIA	Seán McCaffrey, Mick Power	"	"	"
	I2A	Niall Gaffney	12th Lock	"	"
Juvenile	I3A	John Egan, Séamus Clandillon, Eamon Cullen	"	"	3.00
Hurling Board	I3B	Roger Nolan, Ciarán Nolan	" "	"	3.00
I3-15	I4	Willie Bray, Michael Murphy	AGP	"	3.00
	I5	Gerry Fahy, Eamon Corcoran, Martin Mockler	"	Sun.	II.30
Minor Board	I6	Pat Colgan, Paddy Kearns	"	Sat.	3.00
" "	I8	Loughlin McEvoy, Liam Strong, Hugh McNally	"	Sun.	II.30
" "	2I	Peter Flannery, Martin Lanigan	12th Lock	Sat.	3.00
Junior Hurling	Jun.	Jerome O'Connor	" "	Sun.	am/pm
Board	Inter.	Peter Flannery, Brendan White, Billy Gogarty Willie O'Neill	12th Lock	"	am/pm

Co-ordinators: U.I5 downwards - Pat Colgan. U.I6 upwards - John Hayes.

CAMOGIE

Minor	I3	Séamus Kelly, Peter Flannery	AGP	Sat.	II.00
"	I5	Cormac O'Brien, Séamus Kelly	. "	"	"
"	I6	Noel Flynn	"	"	"
Senior Camogie	Jun.B.	Pádraig McGarrigle, John Ryan	Phoenix Pk. / AGP	Sun.	I.30
Board					

Co-ordinator: Pádraig McGarrigle

LADIES FOOTBALL

Ladies Football Board		Dónal Griffin	12th Lock	Sun.	p.m.

* Underlined names: Board Delegates.   Paddy Kelly: Treasurer Minor Board
                                       Pat Colgan: Chairman Juvenile Hurling Board I3-15
                                       Tony Clarke: Chairman South East Board.

Mentors, 1992/93.

Lucan CBS Leinster SFC team, 1993: Back row: Peter Duff, Derek Fleming, Robert Brannigan, Colin Rigney, Martin O'Reilly, Liam Smith, Barry Prenderville, Eoin Dunne. Front row: Derek Taylor, Paul Garvey, Michael O'Byrne, Alan Curtis, Michael Norris, Sean Herlihy, Derek Downes.

Under-21 football championship team, 1993.

1994 — BAR ROTA

PHONE	NAME	DAY	JAN	FEB	MAR	APR	MAY	JUNE	JULY	AUG	SEPT	OCT	NOV	DEC	Jan	Feb
6241376	M. MULHALL P. BEHAN M. KELLY	FRI	28	25	25	22	20	17	15	12	9	7	4	2+30		27
6282493 6282849	P. MULKERRINS R. MURPHY P. CUNNINGHAM	SAT	1+29	26	26	23	21	18	16	13	10	8	5	3+31		28
6282084	M. MALONE J. BUGGLE	SUN	2+30	27	27	24	22	19	17	14	11	9	6	4		29
6241328 6241977	S. CLANDILLON P. MESCALL	FRI	7	4	4	1+29	27	24	22	19	16	14	11	9	6	3
6241875 6281072 6241977	G. Mc NAMARA J. RYAN P. MESCALL	SAT	8	5	5	2+30	28	25	23	20	17	15	12	10	7	4
6282020	S. HURSON B. HURSON	SUN	9	6	6	3	1+29	26	24	21	18	16	13	11	8	5
6241324 6241324	W. O' NEILL C. O' NEILL	FRI	14	11	11	8	6	3	1+29	26	23	21	18	16	13	10
6282145 6240456	L. CARTON A. CHUBB M. BARR G. O'SULLIVAN	SAT	15	12	12	9	7	4	2+30	27	24	22	19	17	14	11
6282849	M. CUNNINGHAM M. WALSH	SUN	16	13	13	10	8	5	3+31	28	25	23	20	18	15	12
6260992 6282622	J. O' CONNOR N. REIDY	FRI	21	18	18	15	13	10	8	5	2+30	28	25	23	20	17
6281354	J. MILLS (SEN) P. GLOVER T. McGRATH	SAT	22	19	19	16	14	11	9	6	3	1+29	26	25	21	18
6282622 6280472	L. REIDY S. ROSS	SUN	23	20	20	17	15	12	10	7	4	2+30	27	25	22	19

6281686 L Mc Evoy
6280443 C Bresnan
6281673 R O 'Flynn
6280065 P. Hogan

OPEN 8.30 EVERY NIGHT
PHONE: CLUB HOUSE - 6240744
PLEASE COLLECT AND LEAVE BACK KEYS EVERY NIGHT FOR ALARM.
IF YOU CANT WORK YOUR NIGHT, PLEASE GET REPLACEMENT.
"REMEMBER" IF YOU DONT WORK, SOMEONE ELSE HAS TO.

NE 1463

Bar rota, 1994.

A large crowd flocked to Swords in late March 1991 (Easter Sunday that year) to watch the club's attempt to return to the senior ranks for the first time since 1982. Sadly, once again things conspired against the team and the northsiders ran out victors by 1-7 to 0-7. The *Evening Herald* of 3 April takes up the story:

It was an Easter Sunday to remember for the Saints from Rush. They received the golden ticket to re-enter senior football with a cherished victory in the Intermediate Football League Final at Swords. This time they'll hope their stay in the top grade will last longer than their last visit two years ago. But one thing is for sure – they'll search long and hard to find more sporting opponents than Lucan Sarsfields.

Lucan, who had a short journey in senior ranks themselves over 10 years

ago, lined the exit from the pitch at the end of the match to salute their opponents' triumph. That's the kind of spirit that prevailed all afternoon in a duel
that saw the refereeing of Joe Woods at his most efficient. About 300 spectators didn't see much pretty football, but plenty of heart and courage.

St Maur's were a worried crew at the interval. They led by a mere point, 1-2
to 0-4, after having the stiff breeze at their backs. They had recorded 10 wides
and had wasted abundant good possession that their more direct style created.
Any elegant craft came from Lucan, who moved the ball neatly in attack.

They had every right to feel optimistic at the break, but then they saw
Maur's produce a blistering start to the second period that laid the foundation for their success. Still, Lucan had some very fine chances of taking
the prize in that second half. Excellent free-taker Donal Walsh brought
a marvellous save from Alan Devine, and then was unfortunate to shoot
wide from very close in. And Rory Leahy drove wide a minute from the
close with a shot that many of the Lucan supporters thought was heading
for the net.

They were rare opportunities gained against a very secure Maur's defence
who refused to panic under severe pressure as Lucan tried to force equality.
The game's only goal came after 19 minutes when Ian Mullett, like a fish in
Lucan's hands, turned crisply from eight yards to fire in a wonderful effort
off the post. And two Gary Murphy frees in the first seven minutes of the
resumption helped to confirm Maur's new-found conviction.

It was yet another bitter pill to swallow, but in February 1991 they finally
had some silverware to show for their efforts after they defeated Parnells in
a replay of the Stacey Cup final. The biggest prize in club history now lay
just four years down the road.

The stars of that famous senior team to come, meanwhile, were cutting their teeth with the best in the county. The minor footballers took
care of Naomh Fionnbarra in the first round of the championship in early
November 1990 in a game that bizarrely had to be ended five minutes early
due to a soccer match that was due to take place straight afterwards. All the
same, they got the job done and their reward was a trip to Mobhi Road to
face Na Fianna in the next round. Unfortunately the team fell just short,
but once again there was hope for the future.

A report in the *Lucan Newsletter* summed up the 1990/91 season. Even at
this stage everyone could sense that there was something special in the air
and that the club's best days may well be just around the corner:

SAINTS BACK IN TOP FLIGHT

ST. MAUR'S (Rush)......... 1-7
LUCAN SARSFIELDS....... 0-7

IT WAS an Easter Sunday to remember for the Saints from Rush.

They received the golden ticket to re-enter senior football with a cherished victory in the Intermediate Football League final at Swords.

This time they'll hope their stay in the top grade will last longer than their last visit two years ago. But one thing is for sure — they'll search long and hard to find more sporting opponents than Lucan Sarsfields.

Lucan, who had a short journey in senior ranks themselves over ten years ago, lined the exit from the pitch at the end of the match to salute their opponents' triumph.

Easter Rising with a difference for Maurs

That's the kind of spirit that prevailed all afternoon in a duel that saw the refereeing of Joe Woods at it's most efficient. About 300 spectators didn't see much pretty football, but plenty of heart and courage.

St. Maur's were a worried crew at the interval. They led by a mere point, 1-2 to 0-4 after having the stiff breeze at their backs blowing from the pavilion end. They had recorded ten wides and had wasted abundant good possession that their more direct style created.

Any elegant craft came from Lucan, who moved the ball neatly in attack. They had every right to feel optimistic at the break, but then they saw St. Maur's produce a blistering start to the second period that laid the foundation for their success.

Still, Lucan had some very fine chances of taking the prize in that second half.

Excellent free-taker Donal Walsh brought a marvellous save from Alan Devine, and was then unfortunate to shoot wide from very close-in.

And Rory Leahy drove wide a minute from the close with a shot that many of the Lucan faithful thought was heading for the net.

They were rare opportunities gained against a very secure St. Maur's defence, who refused to panic under severe pressure as Lucan tried to force equality.

The game's only goal came after 19 minutes. Ian Mullett, like a fish in Lucan's hands, turned crisply from eight yards to fire in a wonderful effort off the post.

Mullett was dangerous any time he got the ball. In that crucial spell for St. Maur's following half-time, he led the attack brilliantly.

And two Gary Murphy frees in the first seven minutes of the resumption helped to confirm St. Maur's new-found conviction.

ST. MAUR'S (Rush) — Alan Devine; Paul Halpin, Dermot Bollard, Colm Leonard; John Moore, Charlie Monks, Brendan Newcomen; David Price, Joe McGuinness; Lary Halpin (0-2), Adrian Kelly, John Bollard; Eddie Kirk, Ian Mullett (1-3), Gary Murphy (0-2). Subs. — Joe Walsh for John Bollard (half-time); Malachy Bollard for Walsh (52 mins.). Mentors — Andy Donoghue, Brendan Harper, John Bollard. Wides — 15.

LUCAN SARSFIELDS — Ronan O'Flynn; Mick Kilduff, Alan O'Brien, Donal Griffin; Fergus Walsh, Colin Feely, Colm Kelly; Terry Hennessy, Damien McGowan (0-1); Terry Dignam, Noel Lally (0-2), Rory Leahy; Martin Heneghan, Fergus McNulty (0-1), Donal Walsh (0-3). Subs. — Roger Tobin for Heneghan (47 mins.); David Ryan for Dignam (56 mins.). Mentors — Tony Tobin, Mick Casey, Christy Leahy, Tim Donoghue. Wides — 7.

Referee: J. Woods (Clann Mhuire).

Inter football final report, 1991.

As we come to the end of another season we can look back on what was and what might have been. Our intermediate footballers were just a kick of a ball away from gaining senior status … Our under-21 footballers did us proud winning their section of the league … Our intermediate hurlers did reasonably well in their league and senior status could be on the cards here in another season or two.

In the juvenile section we fielded teams in every age group from under-11 to under-15, in the case of under-11 we had three teams, at under-12 we had two teams and at under-13 we had two teams. Although we did not win many leagues we did well in most sections, our under-14 footballers coming runners-up in their league and our under-15 hurlers coming runners-up in the shield. Our under-12 footballers did well in the ACC festival and our under-13 footballers kept the O'Sullivan Cup in the club for the second year running.

The following year the club made a giant leap forward in the underage ranks with breakthroughs at almost every grade. The club entered six teams in the south-east leagues and ended up with five sets of medals. For the first time in years, since the introduction of the underage coaching scheme in the eighties, the club also entered an under-10 team. They would go on to win their league undefeated, beating underage kingpins Ballyboden by 5-9 to 2-1 in their first game.

The club had flattened the third pitch in the 12th Lock by this time and a juvenile pitch was added to the facilities in the ground. The development meant that the club was now in a position to host a section of the under-14 hurling Féile na nGael for the first time, and the club's own team answered the call in winning all three of their group matches up in the 12th Lock.

The run saw them through to a semi-final in St Vincent's ground where they impressively saw off the challenge of southside giants Kilmacud Crokes, but the dream campaign came to a heartbreaking end in the final when they lost out to St Finian's of Swords in Parnell Park.

The year before, in 1991, the club had made two giant leaps into previously unexplored territory. Firstly, on the fundraising front, the club lotto, which to this day remains one of the club's most important sources of income, was created.

After a series of draws and other fundraisers that had delivered the 12th Lock grounds, the new clubhouse and dressing rooms, and the three fields the club now called home, the club lotto would become a lynchpin of the club's finances. The lotto began in September 1991, and Séamus Clandillon was involved from the beginning:

> It was first proposed by Paddy Kelly and was run each Sunday night by Paddy himself and the same weekly team of Anna Carton, Mick Mulhall, Seamus Kelly and Dan McCarthy.
>
> You had to select three numbers out of twenty-four at the beginning, and the cost was £1 per ticket. It was a serious commitment; they were there every week. Back then the tickets were actually printed in a local prison, and by 1992/93 there were extra teams added to look after it, and soon enough we had eight teams going.
>
> Over the years the members of the club, and indeed the general residents of Lucan, have been great supporters of the lotto, making it one of the most important fundraisers in the club. It's even got its social buzz now, and Sunday nights up in the club just wouldn't be the same without it.

Social initiatives would return to the forefront of the club's attentions in 1996 (having initially begun in the guise of a ladies committee back in the early 1980s) when the rejuvenated social committee was formed with a view to organising Saturday night dances. Seán Flynn was one of those involved:

Nuala Reidy, Maureen Doherty, Tommy Clyne, Peter Flannery, Eddie Mescall, Bob Dardis and Phil Cunningham would all have been on that committee with me. Dancing started off with the T.R. Dallas band on 12 October of that year I remember, and there was a cover charge of three pounds. This really was a great success, so the dancing continued for many years after that until the building of the new clubhouse.

We had so many different bands there over the years, The Imperial Imps, Johnny Peters and Billy Joyce from Lucan, Mary D'Arcy, Bourbon Street, Sonny Knowles and bands like that. People came from all over Leinster to hear their favourite band and enjoyed the hall and floor for the dancing. The club also held a very successful céilí on the last Friday night of each month around that time, but the biggest event the social committee organised was the New Year's Eve supper dance. It used to be sold out weeks in advance.

The other giant leap forward for the club was the birth of a fourth string to the Gaelic games bow in the form of ladies Gaelic football. The Dublin Ladies Board had only been set up in 1985, and in 1991 the time was right for Lucan to get involved. One of those early pioneering players, Tracey O'Brien, whose husband Fergal Walsh would go on to run the team for many years, recalls the early days of the ladies' game in the club:

I actually had my twenty-first in the club in 1990. I think it was the first function in the new hall. That was my first involvement with the club on a personal level, though my granddad [Jack O'Brien] had been chairman of the club for years and my brother Alan played for the intermediate team. Then the following year the ladies football section got up and running and I joined up then properly. I haven't been able to stay away from the place ever since.

When I started secondary school at St Joseph's, camogie would have been the big thing. Joan Fitzharris used to try and get the new girls coming to the school involved with that. At that stage if you were going to get involved in the GAA it would have been camogie. Then in 1991 the ladies football came about when Seán McCaffrey and a few others asked a few of us to come up and get involved.

Brigie Hurson and Phil Mescall would have been the main ones behind it when we got up there; they were the key people in getting the whole thing up and running. Denis Clifford would have been a central figure in the whole thing too. Denis managed us for the first year. He was fantastic. He kept it all going after that first year. None of us had ever played Gaelic football before.

Nora Keane would have been the goalie, and in our backline the total age would have been over 100 years. Antoinette Buggle, Brigie Hurson, Mary

Bresnan, Orla Kilduff – girls like that would have been there at the start. There were a couple of girls from Leixlip that came to play with us in the early years too, players like Orla Balfe, and Dickie Rock's niece Nicola. She was actually a Dublin player even at that stage.

We got to the semi-final of a senior championship in those early days. We were a handy enough team starting off, and that was a great achievement in our first year. It was always a hard sport to get people involved in; camogie would have been the big sport for girls. But we did really well all things considered.

Our first real taste of success was when we got to the final of the Junior Championship in 1996 in O'Toole Park. We were favourites going into that final because we were in a higher division, and we had beaten Parnells by 1-7 to 0-7 in the semi-final, but we got a bit carried away with ourselves and promptly got taken back down to earth by Naomh Barróg. They beat us by 4-10 to 3-9.

A report on that final in the 31 July edition of the *Evening Herald* told the story:

In their first season, Kilbarrack's Naomh Barróg clinched the Dublin Junior Ladies Football Championship crown in a cracking contest in O'Toole Park. Barróg, unbeaten all year and almost assured of the Division 3 title, led at the interval by 3-6 to 1-5 in a duel that produced some fabulous football from both sides.

Linda Keating, Julie McInerney and the highly impressive Colette Bolger scored Barróg's first-half goals, with the brilliant Lynn Coffey scoring Lucan's seventh-minute goal. Una Ní Mhuirí's goal on 37 minutes brought Lucan right back into contention, but Keating's close-in goal two minutes later proved extremely valuable for Barróg.

Division 2 side Lucan had more than enough opportunity to recover in that second period, shooting 10 wides in the process. But all were agreed that the quality of the hour was outstanding.

Even at this early stage, the future of ladies football in the club looked bright, with an under-16 team entered in 1996 for the first time. In just a few short years' time the combination of all these factors would provide the club with a magical year, and a run to the All-Ireland semi-final.

A special feature in the 23 December 1992 edition of the *Evening Herald*, under the byline of the evergreen Niall Scully, gave an insight into just where the club stood, looking into what would be an historic decade of achievement on and off the field:

The rain was coming down in torrents, almost enough to fill the River Griffeen in the village of Lucan in West Dublin. PRO of Lucan Sarsfields, Fergal Walsh, had the refreshments ready in his home. A pot of tea and biscuits enhanced the kitchen chat as a friendly black cat listened.

The residents need never hunger for information regarding the exploits of Lucan Sarsfields: the Parish Newsletter always holds a page for the club. It had plenty of good tidings recently; the Lucan ladies football team, in only their second season, gained promotion to the top division after finishing runners-up in Division 2. Lucan also advanced to the championship semi-final.

Nowadays the club caters for 800 members, serving 17 football teams, 14 hurling teams, 4 camogie teams, and the 1 squad in ladies football. All the hectic activity is overseen by the wisdom of chairman Paddy Kelly, and at the AGM this season a special committee was organised to foster the expansion of the juvenile ranks. The local schools have been extremely co-operative and no praise is too high for teacher Vincent O'Connor. The kids especially look forward to their trips to Croker for the big games.

The club has three adult football teams. A junior 7 side has been added this term. They fill a need for those players leaving the under-21 ranks who previously have been lost to the game. The junior 4 panel consists of a mixture of the enthusiasm of youth with experience, while Tony Tobin's under-21s, possessing a panel of 28, had made an excellent impression this season.

Lucan moved to the 12th Lock on the Newcastle Road a decade ago, and have two senior and one juvenile pitch there. The pavilion has recently been improved and tennis courts have been laid. The clubhouse provides a tremendous social outlet and its main hall can accommodate 200 people.

Like the footballers, the hurlers perform in the intermediate standard, and they reached the semi-final of the championship this season. Boss, Peter Flannery, has a young crew to work with, and they definitely have the potential to earn their key to senior status. Much work has been done at the younger age level with the sliotar and caman, and these efforts are now beginning to bloom.

Similar activity is being accomplished in the camogie section, which has grown with distinction over the past while. Beginners are presently being taught on Saturday mornings. Lucan have squads in the junior B, under-16, under-15 and under-13 grades.

Such a commitment to the youth of the locality takes a huge amount of cash to meet the bills. A members' draw helped to satisfy the coffers, but the major fundraiser is the annual golf classic. Sponsorship from the Spa Hotel has been a Godsend.

Lucan reflects with pleasure on winning the Junior Football Championship in 1976, and their elevation to the senior code, if only for a short term, in 1982. In 1966 the junior hurlers collected the junior B division, reaching the intermediate table in 1975. In 1984 the junior C camogie clan finished on top of the table, and in 1990 the junior Bs repeated that achievement.

As Fergal drained the teapot he remained in hopeful mood that more silverware would arrive at the club soon enough. The little black cat purred on, in total agreement of course.

The club's underage section was continuing to progress in great strides. In 1992, Pat Rooney made the county minor football team and Phil Lanigan made the minor hurlers. And at school level St Mary's won the Johnston, Mooney & O'Brien Cup. By 1993 then, things were really beginning to pick up.

The under-11 As won their football league undefeated, while the under-13 As won their league and a special competition. The under-21 footballers won their section of the league once again, as well as the Norton Cup. Three members of that team – Damien O'Brien, Fergus McNulty and David Ryan – were selected for the county team, with Damien also having progressed to the senior county panel by this stage.

On the hurling front, the under-10s and under-12s also brought home their respective league crowns, while St Mary's BNS once again tasted success at Croke Park in winning the Herald Cup, defeating Blanchardstown by 4-3 to 0-2. At under-21 level the club provided an unprecedented four players to the county team, in twins Phil and Don Lanigan, Derek Maher and John Mills. These four players would play a key role in the club's breakthrough year just a few seasons down the line.

The club's inter hurlers were all the while still knocking on the door. A fine tournament win at the St Peregrine's nine-a-side event, in which they'd beaten Na Fianna, Batterstown, Dunboyne and a very strong Confey side in the final, had confidence high going into the 1994 campaign.

It was to be another disappointing year for the team. After their best championship campaign in years, Lucan had defeated St Patrick's by 0-10 to 1-4 in the semi-final to book a date with Poppintree outfit Setanta in the final. Once again the team just came up agonisingly short, losing out narrowly. Their misery was compounded shortly afterwards when St Pat's avenged their championship defeat in the league final. The team was beginning to wonder if they would ever have their day in the sun.

On the football front, 1994 proved a turning point in the fortunes of Lucan Sarsfields. Mick Casey Jnr was part of the county's minor team that won the

Leinster championship title, losing out in All-Ireland semi-final to Galway later that year, while Damien O'Brien, Colm Kelly and Fergus McNulty's Dublin juniors also reached an All-Ireland semi-final, where they lost out to Kerry. The players were clearly there to make the jump to senior; the team just needed that little something extra to get them across the line.

In 1994, the team received a major boost when Jack Sheedy returned to the club from Garda, and in another huge step, All-Ireland winning Meath star Liam Hayes came on board as team trainer. In March 1994, the new era began with a first-round championship win over Craobh Chiaráin. The *Evening Herald*'s Declan O'Donoghue reported:

> As expected, Lucan Sarsfields saw off the Craobh Chiaráin challenge in the first round of the Intermediate Football Championship at Balgriffin, but it was a close call. While hurling will always be the priority in Donnycarney, the Craobh can play the big ball game sweetly too, and Lucan had many anxious moments before getting through on a 0-14 to 0-10 scoreline.
>
> Colm Kelly, John Mills, Fergus McNulty, Eugene Gorry and Damien O'Brien shone for the winners. A year ago, O'Brien seemed to be shaping up as one of Dublin's most promising forwards, but as work commitments mean that he can only train with the Dubs on Tuesday nights and never on a Thursday he has lost out.
>
> Yet he has a lot to offer, and it will be interesting to see how Lucan's talented and consistent Colm Kelly, who also caught the eye of the Dublin selectors last season, fares out in his new centre forward post.

It was a season of finding their feet under the new regime for the Lucan team. It would not quite be their year, but the foundations were in place and the bugs ironed out in time for the 1994/95 championship campaign that would herald the club's first county championship crown ever. The return of Tommy Carr from Ballymun Kickhams that same year would also provide a massive boost.

The history-making campaign began in earnest in November 1994 when the team saw off Ballyboden by 0-13 to 1-8 in a tense and tight battle, as reported in the *Echo* newspaper of 24 November:

> The stiff winter breeze blowing through O'Toole Park was a contributing factor to Ballyboden's downfall last Sunday morning in their tough Inter Championship clash against one of the competition's favourites, Liam Hayes's Lucan.

Lucan's Eugene Gorry sent most of the shivers up the spine of the local side – converting no less than seven points, as he judged the direction of the breeze again and again with unnerving accuracy. Dennis Donovan and Brian Byrnes had given 'Boden the lead not long into the game, and playing with the wind advantage they pressed down on their opponents and John Kavanagh added a superb third from just inside the half-way line.

Ballyboden were beginning to cruise, despite hard battling from the Lucan lads, led by Dublin stars Jack Sheedy and Tommy Carr and Gorry then scored three confident points in a row to draw the sides level, with Lucan beginning to find some shape. However, Byrnes and Donovan were far from finished and between them made it 0-5 to 0-3 in favour of Ballyboden.

Lucan responded with Gorry driving home his fourth from four frees. It seemed though, that luck was with Boden when Dennis Donovan was deemed to have been taken down in the Lucan box and substitute Mick Maher made light work of the spot kick converting past a flailing Seán Finnegan.

However, the match remained tight with excellent strikes from that man Gorry and Jack Sheedy keeping Lucan in sight of their tiring opponents. A bizarre and potential nasty incident between two opposing players and officials from the sideline saw referee Jim Turner banish both club's officials (except subs) to the spectator areas, however it proved to be an isolated incident in an otherwise thrilling game of football.

It was from then on that Lucan played with the conviction that was to win them the game. A hat-trick of glaring wides from Boden didn't help their cause and it was the unstoppable Gorry and the determination of Jack Sheedy who tightened up the score, with Colm Kelly putting the game beyond the reach of Ballyboden.

What lay in store in the months ahead was the greatest achievement in the club's then 109-year history. After having drawn the first final on a scoreline of 0-9 to 1-6, on Friday 2 June, in Fingallians' ground in Swords, Lucan Sarsfields defeated arch-enemies St Vincent's by 0-9 to 1-5 in a replay to send the club into the senior championship ranks.

It was a day most people in the club old enough to remember will never forget. And in many ways, the culmination of over a century's worth of effort. The *Echo*'s Stephen Leonard reported on the famous day in early June:

Lucan Sarsfields returned to the prestigious heights of senior football last Friday night in Swords when they earned a thrilling one-point win over the mighty St Vincent's in the championship title match. It had been a long time coming, thirteen years to be exact, but the Lucan men are back where they belong having long posed as a formidable force in the ranks of intermediate football.

Yet the northside giants went close to shattering Lucan's dreams in the final replay and assumed a one-point lead seconds after the throw-in, compliments of Seán Brady. Yet despite a spirited start by Vincent's, the Lucan backs remained composed and kept their opponents scoreless for the next seven minutes, in which time Sarsfields equalised through a Eugene Gorry free before Tommy Carr's point gave them a first-half lead.

Lucan's Jack Sheedy enjoyed a reasonable outing, emerging with two points to his credit. Yet the Dublin star will be disappointed with failing to increase this personal tally after being presented with three goal-scoring opportunities, the first of which travelled wide after five minutes before the superb goalkeeping of Vin's Graham Kinahan twice denied him a netting.

Although unable to muster up the big knock-out blows, Lucan still managed to open up a 0-6 to 0-3 lead by half time courtesy of points from Sheedy, Gorry and Fergus McNulty. It was a crucial three-point cushion for Sarsfields who began to lose their grip after the restart through a lack of execution that saw them hit seven wides in the second period while the northsiders squandered only two openings – mistakes which finally proved fatal.

Eamon Clancey reduced the deficit to a solitary point for the Saints when he fisted home Terry Jennings' long delivery from midfield for a 41st minute goal after hitting a point one minute after the break. Yet Lucan always stayed ahead through points from Damien O'Brien, Tom Carr and Sheedy, and even when Carl Meehan struck for Vincent's last point 10 minutes from time, Sarsfields always looked in control and well capable of holding strong at the back to clinch their most rewarding victory in years.

This fantastic triumph proved the culmination of the efforts of Lucan players past and present to see the team earn senior status, and if their fortunes here ever match the success engendered at intermediate level what is to stop Lucan Sarsfields from scaling the heights of glory in their new-found surroundings.

In a separate piece covering the celebrations that followed, the *Echo*'s Cian Murphy reported how 'Lucan celebrate Kelly's heroes':

By 9.30p.m. last Friday the pilgrimage now turned victory procession for Lucan's loyal band of supporters was now well on its way from Swords back across to the 12th Lock for the biggest (and longest running!) party their club-house has seen as they celebrated their team's win over St Vincent's.

Tears of relief and joy flowed as the club realised its dream in joining the senior football ranks. Never before in a championship final at intermediate – they had come close to league success twice before – nothing could have prepared them for the emotions released when Fergus McNulty led them to the Martyn Cup last Friday.

'It's a major achievement', commented club PRO Seán McCaffrey. 'It is very rewarding for the people running teams now that almost all of the team played juvenile football for Lucan.' Only Eugene Gorry and Damien McGowan hadn't played at juvenile level, making the win very satisfying for the club.

'There will be a great deal of old Lucan supporters like Joe Collins and Tom Malone, who are joint presidents of the club, who if you pinched them on Friday night wouldn't have believed it was true', said Seán of the feeling which had still to sink in for most people.

While a few weeks ago talk of Lucan doing the double was discounted, it is now a reality and according to Seán McCaffrey 'it is there for the taking'. Looking ahead to the future, the belief within the club is that there is a need for three or four more players on the panel as well as establishing a strong second team to back up Lucan's senior team as they enter the dog fight of Division 2.

The performances of recently promoted teams like St Mark's, St Jude's, St Olaf's and Trinity Gaels will give them hope and they will be no pushover. Lucan are now the 10th team for south county Dublin in senior football, thus establishing the area as a prime source of footballing talent. In the meantime though, it's congratulations on a job well done to mentors Paul Kelly, Liam Hayes, Mick Molly, Richie Crean and the team.

For Richie Crean, who had played on the Lucan team that had won the club's last championship at junior level in 1977, had played in an intermediate championship final in 1978, and had been part of the Lucan team that had been briefly promoted to the ranks of the senior football league in 1982, the win was one of the most special days he can remember:

The 1995 intermediate league and championship double was pretty special. In my mind, we were getting back to where we should be. There was great work done in the late '80s to get us to that point though. Huge work was put in by the likes of Tony Tobin and Seán Walsh, Christy Leahy and Paul Kelly and Mick Molloy and those lads pushing things along. So to finally have that breakthrough was great.

We haven't looked back since that time. If you look at that inter final back in 1978, we weren't beaten by much that day. And Crokes went on from there and didn't look back. I suppose that could have been us, but it just wasn't to be. Getting senior for a club of our size was just so important and we haven't taken a backward step since.

I think the 1995 team was a much younger team, with a great blend of experience with the likes of Tommy Carr and Jack Sheedy coming back in. We had two defined seasons from inter to senior after that too, and that certainly helped with driving on. The guts of that team was built in the late 80s with young fellas coming through.

I was with Navan O'Mahony's from 1987 to 1991. We won four championships in a row, but I transferred back to Lucan in 1991, and the structures that were there were just fantastic. We were knocking on the door in 1993 and 1994, being beaten by teams that would have gone on to win the thing. But eventually the door opened in 1995. It was the culmination of a huge amount of work. It was like 1981 in that in came off the back of years and years of striving.

Tom Carr also recalls that special day, although years away from the club (playing with Ballymun) meant that he didn't revel in the celebrations as much as most of his team mates:

I was in the later stages of my career, shall we say, in 1995, and Richie Crean and Jack Sheedy got on to me asking me would I not like to finish up my career where I'd started. They said they'd a good team, good enough to go senior. Jack had come back to Lucan in 1994, and he was constantly on to me about it all through the year. I was still playing with Dublin that year, but when I went off the Dublin panel the following year I said what the hell and decided to go back to Lucan, which I did in 1995.

I remember playing in that intermediate final in 1995, but I was living in Tullamore at the time and I used to travel up and down. Even straight after that final I was into the shower, hopped into the car and away on the road home, so I didn't even get to celebrate with the team. I was managing a hotel down there at the time. Looking back now, I feel a bit sorry about that. I knew that when they finally went senior they were good enough to stay there.

I remember the first year we were senior in the 1980s there wasn't a real feel in the club that we could stay up senior. But in 1995 it felt like a real community effort, like we were there to do a job. For me it was a case of job done. I played on for a few more years after that, but I made the decision when I moved to Mullingar that I'd leave Lucan and I played with the local club down here.

Carr, who would go on to manage the Dublin senior football team a few years later (with Crean as a selector) while still playing for the club (where Crean was manager), also remembers the early dynamics under manager Liam Hayes:

> Liam was a good manager. It was an unusual set-up in that we'd obviously bumped into one another on the pitch quite a fair bit over the previous ten years. I remember going out for the first few training sessions, and myself and Liam had never really had a social chat before that. There was a fair degree of suspicion I suppose; he was from another county and he was managing the home club, but I found him to be a very good football man and very level headed and good in the dressing room.

For returning Lucan man Jack Sheedy, the championship victory, with his own home club and with whom his father had acted as a selector for many years, was very special indeed:

> I had played with the Garda until 1994 when I came back to Lucan. Richie Crean came back as well and then we got Tommy back too in 1995. We won the league and championship that year and that was great.
>
> When we came back in, the work that had been done in the meantime was fantastic with the young lads coming through. You had the likes of Fergus McNulty, Damien O'Brien, Conor Bresnan, the Lanigans – there were great lads coming through. We had other outside lads like Eugene Gorry and Damien McGowan there too, so we had a better balance.
>
> Paul Kelly had a big influence on that team, and Liam Hayes was a key figure too. He was a good manager, though a bit different. Liam had his own style. Richie had a massive influence on the whole thing though. He struggled with injury towards the end of his career but he was hugely influential both on and off the field. To win the league was fantastic, but to go and win the championship and go back up senior was definitely my best day in the club.

For Sheedy, what was to be his best memory with the club was to be tainted a few days later by an injury that would not only effectively end his Dublin career, but would cost him an All-Ireland medal:

> I remember we won the final replay on a Friday night, and we partied on all through Friday night and Saturday. Dublin had a challenge game then on the Sunday down in Munalvey and I did my cruciate. That was not a fond memory for me.

That was in May, so I missed the whole season. We had just finished the league two or three weeks earlier. We played our first Leinster championship match a few weeks later. That's not something you can easily forget.

There were two courses of action. You either got surgery or you worked on weights. I went and worked on the weights, and I was back flying again. It wasn't strong enough though and it went again, and that was it then, over definitively. I was still involved with the panel and it was great, but it put a bit of a dampener on winning the championship with Lucan.

I still regard it as my best memory with Lucan though, winning that championship. I think what really made it special though was winning it with young lads that had come through the club.

Sheedy was denied his All-Ireland medal as the Dubs went on to defeat Tyrone in the final that September. But he still looks back fondly on a wonderful career with the Dubs in which he won an All-Star award in 1994 as a member of Lucan Sarsfields, and particularly the famous Leinster Championship clashes with Liam Hayes's Meath in the early '90s:

The Meath games in 1991 were special. I look back at the odd DVD every now and then. It's no comparison to football nowadays, but it was something very, very special. It created a lot of things. There was such a buzz about football after that, it was like living in a capsule.

Nobody thought anything like that would ever happen in football. Time stood still almost. It felt like being a professional footballer for those few weeks. It was ultimately very disappointing, especially having the last kick of the game in the fourth game.

I had done my hamstring about ten minutes before the end, but I was the only one left on the field who would have been regarded as a free-taker. To miss that kick was awful. I had it to tie it up, but obviously I missed and they went on to win it by a point. We got our revenge in 1995 though.

Though perhaps slightly overshadowed by the heroics of the championship campaign, Lucan had quietly gone about their business in waltzing almost unchallenged through the intermediate league. Winning fourteen of their fifteen games, and drawing the other one, Lucan easily claimed the league title to complete an amazing double.

With breath finally drawn on an amazing campaign, the team was honoured at a special victory dinner dance in the Spa Hotel in November. With senior status now secured in both league and championship, the club was finally where it had so long wanted to be – mixing it with the big boys of Dublin Gaelic football.

In 1996, the team would make the vital step of securing their senior status, consolidating their place in Division 2, finishing well up the table, and the following year the team finished joint second in the league.

In 1997, the team were beginning to grow into themselves at senior level, defeating St Margaret's in the championship in April of that year, with promising young players like Greg Hickey, David Herlihy, Mick Casey and Barry Whelan all beginning to break onto the team. And in 1998 another milestone was achieved when the club secured their place in Division 1. A feature on the club by Randall Scally in *Hogan Stand* magazine, October 1998, reported on the win that had seen the team reach the top table the week before:

> Lucan Sarsfields' meteoric rise through the ranks of Dublin football con-
> tinued on September 12 when the west county club clinched promotion to
> Division 1 of the Dublin Senior League courtesy of a resounding win over
> Naomh Barróg.
>
> Lucan could afford the luxury of needing to take just one point from the
> last two games against Naomh Barróg and St Patrick's Palmerstown. As it
> transpired, however, promotion to the premier division was secured before
> their final outing against St Pat's.
>
> This latest Sarsfields success story is what ambitious club members hope
> will be a stepping stone towards the club's ultimate goal, which is, of course,
> to annex a Dublin Senior Football Championship title.

That same year, under the management of Richie Crean, the team had made a valiant effort to do just that, but were beaten by the best team in Dublin, 1996 county champions St Sylvester's, after a replay. Then club secretary, Livinus Smith, recalled the 1998 campaign in that same *Hogan Stand* article:

> We were disappointed to lose to St Sylvester's, but at least we proved over the
> course of the two games that we are there or thereabouts. Winning promo-
> tion to Division 1 made up for that disappointment, however. We only lost
> one game (to Garda) during the campaign and with at least six under-21s in
> the team we should be an even stronger side next season.

That they most certainly were, and in the 1999 championship the team's mix of youth and experience had combined to give Lucan what Jack Sheedy, still playing for the club himself at the time, believes was the best Lucan Sarsfields football team ever, 'In 1999/2000, when we were beaten in the championship semi-final by Vincent's, I really felt we had the potential to go on and win a championship that year. That was probably as good a team as we ever had in Lucan. We beat a star-studded UCD team to get to that semi-final.'

All the same, the team had done exactly what it had set out to achieve. Going into the twenty-first century, Lucan Sarsfields were a senior football club. They weren't just making up the numbers. They were serious contenders.

While the joy the footballers had brought to the club in 1995 would never fade in most people's minds, neither would the memory of one of Lucan Sarsfields' greatest servants who passed away later that year.

Paddy Kelly had been a driving force behind almost every aspect of the club, from Scór to underage development at all codes, and in 1996 the club honoured his memory by presenting the Paddy Kelly Cup to the juvenile hurling board to compete for in Division 2 of the P.J. Troy under-14 hurling competition.

Fittingly, the club's underage hurlers were making history of their own around that time too. In 1995, the club's under-14 hurlers secured Lucan Sarsfields' first ever Féile na nGael title when they defeated Raheny in a thrilling Division 3 final in Parnell Park by 4-4 to 1-1.

The underage structures that had been put in place in the early nineties were beginning to come to fruition, and in 1996 the club went one better again to win the Division 2 Féile na nGael crown under Jim Quinn and Seán McCaffrey, thanks to victory over Kilmacud Crokes in the final in Parnell Park. For the first time in years, quality players with a habit of winning were beginning to come through the ranks, hungry to achieve at the highest grade. All they really needed was a senior team to aim for. Luckily, that would shortly follow.

In a giant leap forward, Lucan finally got a massive monkey off their backs in 1996 when the second team secured the club's first adult hurling silverware in over twenty years in the form of the Miller Shield. After so many years of losing final after final, the Lucan team had a steel that previous generations had perhaps lacked and possibly even the odd spot of luck that had deserted those before them. The next generation were beginning to make a name for themselves, with the team in what was effectively the breeding grounds for the club's intermediate team winning their section of the under-21 hurling league in 1996, but the Miller Shield win was a proper adult level breakthrough, a 4-9 to 3-6 win against Clanna Gael Fontenoys in that July final a turning point in the fortunes of Lucan's hurlers. The *Evening Herald*, and Niall Scully, take up the story:

Anna Carton accepts the Club Person of the Year award from Billy Gogarty in the 12th Lock, 1994.

Peadar Condron becomes the first inductee into the club's Hall of Fame in 1994, receiving the award from Mick Molloy (far left), Billy Gogarty (centre) and Don Dardis (right).

Wise old heads: Long-time club members Mick Molloy, Padraig McGarrigle, Don Dardis, Paddy Kelly, Hall of Fame inductee Peadar Condron and Billy Gogarty at the club's awards night in the 12ᵗʰ Lock in 1994.

The Lucan Under-12 football team that took on St Jude's in a local tournament in 1995.

Cumann Na Sáirséalaigh
Leamhcáin

LOTTO GROUPS FOR SUNDAY NIGHT LOTTO 1996/97

Group A	Group B	Group C	Group D
Seamus Clandillion(C)	Anna Carton(C)	Mick Mulhall(C)	Tom Clyne(C)
Seaghan O'Lanagain	Ray Murphy	Seamus Kelly	Maureen Clyne
Mary O'Lanagain	Joan Molloy	Dermot Russell	John O'Mahony
Tom Waldron	Mary Cunningham	Peter Horgan	Sally O'Mahony
		Lorraine Kellegher	Jim Kelly
			Mary Kelly

Group E	Group F	Group G	Group H
Billy Gogarty(C)	Livinus Smith(C)	Shay Hurson(C)	Sean McCaffrey(C)
Paul Gogarty	Tommy Smith	Brigid Hurson	Tony Clarke
Alan O'Brien	Albert Curran	Phil Mescall	Eoin Mullarkey
Fintan McCarthy	Hugh McGonigle	Don Dardis	Siobhan Mullarkey
Kevin Callaghan			Pat Glover

Above: Lotto teams, 1996/97.

Below: Lucan Sarsfields Under-13 hurling league Division 2 south winners, 1996: Tom Duff, Andrew Duff, David Geraghty, Stephen Walsh, Ciarán Curley, Jerome Twomey, Kevin Bielenberg, Peter Bielenberg, Ger Barrett, Philip Linton, Conor McKeon, Mark Neville, Declan Murphy, Joe Byrne. Front row: Paul Sloan, Shane Casey, Daragh Brennan, Aidan Graham, Joey Byrne, Padraig Ward, James Nealon, Timmy Bradley.

The good folk of Lucan celebrated last Saturday night as word reached the village that the local Sarsfields hurlers were bringing home the Miller Shield, their first trophy in almost twenty years. O'Toole Park was a joyous place for the Lucan faithful, who had endured the bad days with a smile. One of the biggest smiles of satisfaction belonged to mentor, Peter Flannery.

'The Corn Fogarty is the last thing we won, and that was in the late '70s', recalled Peter. 'The lads put in so much work to make this possible. And we really needed this victory. The only sad thing is that we had to beat Clans in the final, because, like us, they required a win to help their hurling development. Yet, despite our leads, Clans never died.'

Lucan led all the way. Inspired by their crafty captain, centre-forward Michael Griffin, Lucan had a thriving forward division that enjoyed a generous amount of possession. The Ringsend club came within four points of the victors on 51 minutes, and in the process dealt Lucan a mighty fright.

Lucan made the ideal start with a Griffin score inside three minutes. A minute later, only a wonderful Enda Hogan save from Liam Carton denied Lucan a second goal, with Ultan Tuite cracking the rebound off the post. Carton had better fortune on 20 minutes when Tuite's pass enabled him to crash home from close range making it 2-3 to 0-3 for Lucan. P.J. Vaughan, Carton and Tuite were causing all kinds of bother for the Dublin 4 defence, and it was no surprise that Lucan held the half-time advantage of 2-5 to 0-6.

Vaughan added the third goal three minutes into the second period with Carton's swift turn and strike bringing the fourth two moments later, 4-6 to 0-6 to Sarsfields. Lifted by a Michael Egan goal on 45 minutes, Clans, with 10 minutes left, saw Richie Hogan pounce to strike two goals in a minute, the second of which came from a free, leaving Clans just four points behind.

But Lucan were to readjust their seat belts and they pulled away to safety with points from Tuite and Ciarán McGrath. Clans did attempt another little revival, but the final whistle beat them.

The club was beginning to produce the talent. In 1997 the club's minor hurlers made a massive breakthrough when they pulled off the biggest shock of the year. Seaghan Ó Lanagáin, who had been involved with the team all the way up, recalls fondly that famous day in Knocklyon:

We had limited success over the years, but at minor level we got to two county semi-finals. The highlight of that was definitely the year we beat Ballyboden. They had won four minor titles on the trot and were going for their fifth but we beat them over in Pairc Uí Mhurchú in 1997.

We had virtually the same squad all the way through but we were boosted by a few of the under-16 lads that year in Seán Quinn and Tommy Somers who were huge additions. Unfortunately we got Kilmacud Crokes in the semi-final so there was no county title there.

That same under-16 team, which also featured other future county minor stars Joey Byrne and Daragh Brennan (who were both still under-15 at the time) amongst others, suffered heartache at the hands of a star-studded Ballyboden in the championship quarter-final in O'Toole Park. The sheer talent lined up against them that day shone through as Enda's, featuring current county stars Stephen Hiney and Conal Keaney amongst others, powered to a narrow win in a heated battle.

The Lucan side, under the management of Seán McCaffrey and Jim Quinn, would dust themselves off in time to secure the consolation prize when a win against Crumlin in the 12th Lock later that year would see them secure the club's first Division 1 county title at any age in any grade in the club's entire history. It was just the beginning of better things to come.

Left: Lucan's Under-21 hurlers celebrate in the 12th Lock after winning the under-21C hurling championship in Parnell Park in 1996.

Below: The Under-14 hurling team, with mentors Jim Quinn, Kevin Brennan and Joe Byrne, that were defeated in the Féile na nGael hurling final by Na Fianna in Parnell Park in 1997.

Above: The 1997 Lucan Sarsfields Intermediate hurling championship team in O'Toole Park.

Below: The Under-15 camogie team that won their league in 1997. Back row: Noel Flynn, Sarah Goulding, Aoife Concannon, Gillian Flannery, Cathy Wright, Elaine Galvin, Gráinne Ní Lanagáin, Patricia McGarrigle, Caroline Flynn. Front row: Joy Coyle, Róisín Hayden, Aoife Sheils, Catriona McGarrell, Imelda Smith, Sabrina Gibbons, Deirdre King, Aideen Casey.

Above: Minor footballers, 1998. Back row: Alan Hurson, Alan Barnes, Mick Moore, Kevin McGonigle, Brian Percy, Alan O'Neill, Tony Moulton, E. Flannery, Paul Casey, Fergus Gordon, B. Byrne, Gerry McGarry, Cronan Dooley. Front row: P. Curran, Shane Russell, Pierce O'Leary, E. McNulty, Fintan Clandillon, Eoin Ó Lanagáin, Donal Crowley, Tomas Cummins, D. Hickey, Mick Wallace.

Below: Junior B footballers, 1999.

The inter hurlers were quietly biding their time as they built towards an Intermediate Championship run of their own – winning the St Sylvester's tournament and losing to Naomh Mearnóg in the senior grade Keogh Cup final. One major addition to the panel, outside of the exciting crop of youngsters coming through, had come in the shape of former Tipperary captain Liam Bergin, who had recently moved into the local area. The club newsletter of February 1997 picked Liam out for special attention as part of its player profile section:

> Liam has the type of hurling pedigree that many would die for – two Munster Hurling Championship medals, a Munster Club Senior Championship, Munster minor and under-21 medals (in 1981 and 1983), and all that before he was 21 years old! He also managed to captain Tipperary's senior hurlers at 19 – the youngest ever!
>
> Seven years working in New York brought him no less than five New York Senior Championships, and upon his return to Dublin, Liam joined Ballyboden and played with them for three years before joining Lucan Sarsfields. It is hoped that Liam will add at least one more medal to his large collection – a Dublin Intermediate Hurling Championship medal.

The up-and-coming team now had a massive asset in a hurler with huge experience at the highest level and a record for succeeding in everything he put his hand to. The stage was set for a Lucan onslaught on the championship, and in 1998 the team received another monstrous addition when another former Tipperary captain, Declan Carr, returned to his home club to finish his career.

Declan, who had captained Tipperary to an All-Ireland in 1991 and had won an All-Star in 1989, recalls how it came about that ended up back in Lucan, at a time when his inter-county career was anything but finished:

> I remember 1996/97, I was out in San Francisco and my brother Tom came out to play a bit of golf and he brought John Mills Snr with him. I suppose John put it into my head to come home and that Lucan would love to have me back playing hurling with them and that's how it came about that I ended up finishing my career with the club.
>
> It was something that had been in my mind for a while, but I finally came home then in 1998. There would have been great men involved with the team at the time, the likes of Liam Carton and Peter Flannery and Mícheál Moylan. Liam Bergin would have been the core of the team.
>
> It was funny the way things worked out because I would have hurled

against Liam a fair bit down in Tipperary. We would have been the fiercest enemies on the hurling pitch in Tipp, but sure we ended up playing on the same side then up in Lucan.

It was great for me though, it really was like going home. I was faced with a decision coming home from America whether to go back and hurl for Holycross or to go back to Lucan. I was doing a bit of work in Dublin at the time, but I had a big call to make. Nicky [English] would have been involved with the Tipperary county team at the time so I asked him would my playing with an intermediate club team in Dublin have any effect on my chances of getting back on the Tipp senior team.

He said that given my past history with the county he didn't mind once

SCHOOLS SPORTS LATEST
ST JOSEPH'S WIN THE SENIOR CAMOGIE TITLE

ST JOSEPH'S College in Lucan won the Dublin Senior 'B' Camogie championship title on Wednesday.

This is the first year that the all-girls school has fielded Camogie teams — they now have a junior and a senior team.

The seniors defeated Loretto Beaufort on Wednesday afternoon in the 'B' league final at the Phoenix Park.

The final score was 2-2, 0-0. Audrey Murtagh (1-0), Juliene Helbert (1-0) and Niamh Farren (0-2).

The Lucan girls will not have much time to recover since they face a Leinster league quarter final Thursday against Kilcormack at Glenaulin, Palmerstown. *1999.*

• **Maynooth Post Primary U-14** football team defeated St Mary's Edenderry in the Leinster 'B' U14 semi-final by 4-9, 1-5 at Hawkfield, Newbridge, on Wednesday.

The Maynooth students now face Enniscorthy in the final. A date has yet to be fixed for that game.

• **Scoil Dara** beat St Mary's Edenderry by 4-11 to 0-7 in the North Leinster Junior Football semi-final play-off last Friday [22nd] at Cappagh.

Cill Dara scorers: John O'Donoghue (0-6), Aidan Foley (0-1), Ciaran Foley (0-1), Edward Hopkins (0-1), Paul Conneally (1-0), David Gannon (0-2), Ciaran Collins (1-0), Alan Foley (0-1), Ronan Walsh (1-0).

Junior Dublin League
St Joseph's College V Goldenbridge Inchicore - Won
St Joseph's College V Loreto High School Won
St Joseph's College V Colaiste Bhride - Won
St Joseph's College V St. Mark's - Lost

St Joseph's Senior B camogie title winners, 1999.

my performances on the field were up to scratch. I was only thirty-three at the time so I hadn't given up on playing with the county. I played the 1998/99 season and won a National League after beating Galway in the final while hurling with Lucan. I suppose in a way that gave Lucan a bit of a boost too to some degree, having some sort of profile. They were a great bunch of lads, and a very solid team with the lads we had in key positions.

Liam Bergin was there, Pat Doyle. I played midfield with Derek Maher most of the time, and the odd time with John Mills. It was an amazing team really, because it stayed largely the same over a period of about two or three years, but it was gradually growing stronger and stronger all the time. Lads like Eoin Ó Lanagáin, Cronan Dooley and Fintan Clandillon were coming through so we had a great mix.

The squad had been taken over by the management of Mícheál Moylan, Seaghan Ó Lanagáin, Liam Carton and Peter Flannery at this stage, and the early signs had been bright. The team won the Corn Fogarty, Corn Céitinn and Keogh Cups in 1998, and their steady progress finally culminated in an historic 1999 season.

It all began in April when the team hammered Clondalkin neighbours Round Towers by 4-10 to 2-6. Two of the club's youngest stars, Fintan and Tadhg Clandillon, who between them aged just over forty, combined to bang in three goals that day, while nineteen-year-old Eoin Ó Lanagáin came off the bench to grab the fourth.

From there the team marched into a hornet's nest to face Donnycarney big guns Craobh Chiaráin, and thanks to another two goals from Fintan Clandillon they emerged 2-9 to 2-7 victors. Old rivals Setanta awaited in the semi-final, and with Declan Carr amassing a personal haul of 1-7, Lucan emerged hugely impressive victors on a scoreline of 2-20 to 4-8. With history in the making, Kilmacud Crokes awaited the Lucan men in a date with destiny in Parnell Park on 9 July.

After an age of waiting, Lucan beat their southside rivals by 1-16 to 2-8 to secure their place in the senior ranks for the first time ever.

'I think we went forty games unbeaten or something like that,' Mícheál Moylan recalls. 'That was a tremendous time in the club's history.' Seaghan Ó Lanagáin adds:

In 1998 we won all four competitions bar the league and championship, and in 1999 then we won everything, the league and championship and the two cups we were eligible to play in. Declan Carr was a tremendous asset, and

Liam Bergin was outstanding not just on the field but on the coaching side of things. There was a great spirit in the hurlers in those days. We played thirty-four games in 1999 between the various competitions and we went unbeaten, so that was some year.

'We got to a stage where we felt we were invincible at intermediate level, and that all finally culminated with a championship in 1999,' Declan Carr remembers. 'I think we went thirty games or so unbeaten into 1999 when we won the league and championship.'

For Declan, on a personal note, another fond memory of his from around that time was getting to play a season of football with his brother Tommy before he retired. 'One of the biggest thrills I had coming back to Lucan was getting to play with Tom. Our paths had sort of gone separate ways after myself and the family moved back to Tipp in 1980,' Declan says:

Mick Downes was the manager of the Lucan footballers at the time when I went back, a very serious and intense guy when it came to football, but myself and Tom got the chance to play one season of football together before we both finished up. It was back to where it all started for us, because we began by playing football together at under-8 and under-12, so that was a really great way to finish.

My earliest memories of GAA are with Lucan and playing up in Dodsboro. So it was great to finish my career by winning something with Lucan. My good memories start and finish with Lucan Sarsfields.

With the club now senior league and championship in both hurling and football, the underage grades continuing to produce top-quality players for the future (the last success of the decade came when St Joseph's Convent School won the Senior B County Camogie Championship with victory over Loretto Beufort in the Phoenix Park with many of the future stars of the senior team involved), the club's attentions turned back to the clubhouse.

Going into the new millennium, it was decided that Lucan Sarsfields' recent success on the field should be mirrored with a fitting modern-day, state-of-the-art clubhouse. Shay Hurson took over as club chairman in 1999, and not long into the job his new executive committee began to seriously look at the club's facilities. Shay recalls of the time:

After being in the club for a few years I got involved with the executive and eventually I became chairman then in 1999. The club had an AGM when

CUMANN LUTHCHLEAS GAEL

**COISTE SOISEARACH
IOMANA
ATHA CLIATH**

1999

Intermediate Hurling Championship Final

Kilmacud Crokes V Lucan Sarsfields

at Parnell Park on
Friday 9th July at 7.30 p.m.
Réiteoir: G. Fitzpatrick (Raheny)

Junior "C" Championship Semi-Final

Clontarf V Whitehall Colmcille

at 6.15 p.m.
Réiteoir E. Mullarkey (Lucan Sarsfields)

Luach 50p   S. O'Lionán Runaí

Right: Intermediate hurling championship final programme, 1999.

Below: Intermediate hurling league and championship winners, 1999.

I was away on holidays and when I came back I found out that outgoing secretary Livinus Smith and chairman Billy Gogarty weren't continuing on.

I was asked to take on the role and I agreed to do so and I put together a good group of people to come with me on to the executive. Most of them were getting involved at this level for the first time. Gillian Ryan came on as secretary, and we put a whole new group together because I think people had got tired of the previous team that had been there for so long. We needed new faces.

In my first year we began looking at the clubhouse situation, and we eventually came up with the 3,000 ticket £100 draw, which was enormous at the time. No other club had ever sold that many tickets before for something like that. There was £300,000 taken in from it and the prize fund was up around the £100,000 mark.

We had good prizes and we had McCoy Motors on board. With the number of prizes that were there I think people really felt they had a chance and I think that added to the success of the thing. We had huge goodwill towards us at the time too. Tickets were sold all over the country for that draw.

Anna Carton took on the role of looking after the financial side of the whole thing, and there was a massive amount of paperwork and that involved. On the night of the draw itself we had a huge marquee up and it was a great night. The place was packed and we went on until the wee hours of the morning.

After that, we got a few quotations in and we eventually gave the work to Kingston Construction for two reasons. Firstly, they had priced the job reasonably okay, and secondly because they were people whose sons were playing with the club.

It was a huge undertaking. There was a lot of work involved in getting the lotto grants and filling out all the paperwork, but Donal Walsh, in particular, would have been great in that regard. There were so many people involved in getting the whole thing together, and I think the final price on the project was around £1.6m or so.

All that was left to do now was to build it.

PLAYERS OF THE ERA

Coaches involved with under-10 coaching scheme, 1990/91: Ray Barnes, Eamon Cullen, Albert Curran, Philip Dowling, Hugh McGonnigle, Seaghan Ó Lanagáin, Pat Mooney, Don Crowley, Eamon Nugent, Terry O'Neill, Tom Reynolds, Eamon Gartland, Martin Kelly, Dermot Russell, Hugh McNulty, Joe Dooley, Padraic Colleary, Joe Delaney.

Coaches involved with under-10 coaching scheme, 1991/92: Martin Walsh, Seaghan Ó Lanagáin, Mick Casey, John Flynn, Pat Mescall, Pat Mulhern, Barry Walsh, Michael Malone.

Intermediate football championship first round v. Ballyboden St Enda's, November 1994: S. Finnegan, T.J. Briody, J. Mills, A. O'Brien, F. McNulty, C. Kelly, D. Ryan, D. O'Brien, T. Dignam, C. Bresnan, T. Carr, N. Collins, M. Casey, J. Sheedy, E. Gorry.

Under-11 footballers, 1994: Patrick O'Connor, Brendan Curran, Pádraig Ward, Noel Flynn, David Geraghty, Ciarán Curley, Paul Nealon, Neil Holland, Stephen Walsh, Declan McManus, Joey Byrne, Brendan Russell, Paul Sloan, Gerard Barrett, Paul Flynn, Shane Casey.

Intermediate football championship final v. St Vincent's, June 1995: Ronan

O'Flynn, John Mills, Alan O'Brien, Donal Lanigan, David Ryan, Colm Kelly, T.J. Briody, Damien O'Brien, Tom Carr, Jack Sheedy, Damian McGowan, Fergus McNulty, Niall Collins, Eugene Gorry, Conor Bresnan, Philip Lanigan, Eanna Gowran.

Ladies football junior championship final team, 1996: Antoinette O'Shea, Gillian Ryan, Trudy Keogh, Maura McGrath, Maria Gunne, Tracey O'Brien, Maeve Maguire, Lynn Coffey, Una Ní Mhuirí, Gillian Mulqueen, Jackie O'Brien, Yvonne McHugh, Aileen Quinn, Siobhan Donachie, Margaret Ryan, Audrey Murtagh, Karine Bartelt.

Under-14 Division 2 Dublin Féile na nGael hurling title winners, 1996: Brian Quinn, Jerome Twomey, Ger Power, Sean Quinn, James Mulhern, Leonard Skelly, Richie Butler, Aiden McKelvey, Stephen Murphy, Cian Fleming, Terence Smith, Peter Bielenberg, Daragh Brennan, Aidan Glover, Joey Byrne, Kevin Roche, Aaron Dunne, Conor Healy, Ger Gleeson, Daire Reidy, Philip Linton, Andrew Duff.

Intermediate hurling Corn Fogarty winners, July 1996: Eoin Mullarkey, Conor Griffin, Martin Heneghan, John Egan, Stephen Farrell, Niall Gaffney, Paul Kelly, Ciarán McGrath, Brian Kelly, Alan Mockler, Michael Griffin, John Clancy, P.J. Vaughan, Liam Carton, Ultan Tuite, Cathal Corcoran, Vincent O'Connor.

Under-21C hurling championship winners, v. Scoil Uí Chonaill, 1996: Dermot Foley, Cathal Corcoran, Declan Mulhern, Conor Griffin, Ian Fitzgerald, Vincent Shanagher, Stephen Kelly, Paul Foley, Alan Mockler, Daniel Hickey, Tadhg Clandillon, Mark Crystal, Aidan O'Brien, Senan Clandillon, Paul Kelly, David Herlihy, Francis Kearns, John Doyle, Martin O'Halloran.

Senior football championship v. St Margaret's, April 1997: R. Doolan, D. Ryan, C. Kelly, J. Mills, A. O'Brien, F. McNulty, G. Hickey, K. McLoughlin, D. O'Brien, J. Sheedy, D. Herlihy, M. Casey, D. McGowan, E. Gorry, P. Lanigan, B. Whelan, M. Dardis.

Senior football championship v. St Sylvester's, July 1998: Alan Curtis, Barry Whelan, Colm Kelly, David Ryan, Mick Casey, Tom Carr, Colm Hickey, Conor Bresnan, Kevin McLoughlin, Rory Leahy, Jack Sheedy, David Herlihy, Damien O'Brien, Eugene Gorry, John Doyle, T.J. Briody, John Mills, Fergus McNulty, Greg Hickey, Fran O'Hare, Mark Dardis, Niall Collins, Tadhg Clandillon, Robert O'Sullivan.

Minor hurlers, 1998: Pierce O'Leary, Eoin Ó Lanagáin, Fintan Clandillon, David Hickey, Cronan Dooley, Alan Barnes, Tomás Cummins, Brendan McGarry, Gerard McGarry, Michael Moore, Barry Corcoran, Brian Percy, Tony Moulton, Alan O'Neill, Emmett Farrelly, Brian Byrne, Shane Russell, Paul Casey, Fergus Gordon.

Intermediate hurling championship final v. Kilmacud Crokes, July 1999: Vincent Shanagher, John Mills, Hugh McNally, Senan Clandillon, Neville Kelly, Pat Doyle, Cronan Dooley, Derek Maher, Declan Carr, Phil Lanigan, Liam Bergin, Tadhg Clandillon, Fintan Clandillon, Declan Kelly, Colm Sunderland, Liam Strong, Steven Farrell, Ciarán McGrath, Alan Mockler, Martin Burke, Lar Norris, Seán Quinn, Mick Griffin, Joe McDonagh, Eoin Ó Lanagáin, Alan O'Neill. Mentors: Liam Carton, Peter Flannery, Mícheál Moylan, Seaghan Ó Lanagáin.

SIX

2000-2011
THE BREAKTHROUGH YEARS

As the new millennium dawned, the social and economic context in which Lucan Sarsfields was operating was very different from the previous century. Lucan had been transformed from a quiet rural village to become a very large and still rapidly expanding suburb of Dublin. New housing estates and apartments were continuously appearing on the landscape and many new people were coming to live in the area.

The club was well used to people from all corners of Ireland coming to live in Lucan and getting involved. The club had always sought to welcome and encourage new people to join in; the combination of locals and 'blow ins' provided a very healthy and diverse mix. However, the new century brought further enrichment to the complex tapestry that constituted the club membership base, with the arrival in Lucan of many non-nationals from all parts of the world. This was just one of many changes the club experienced in the first decade of the new millennium, a decade that has been the club's most successful to date and has seen the club achieve breakthroughs on many fronts.

Among the areas of great progress was the development of new facilities. When the decade began, the blueprints for the new clubhouse were being heatedly discussed. Things had been progressing brilliantly on the fundraising side of things, with the main event, the Millennium Draw, proving a massive success, as Seamus Clandillon recalls:

It was the biggest draw in club history up to that point and it took place on 27 May 2000. Tickets were £100 and 3,000 of them were sold, thanks to a massive effort from within the club. There was everything from Land Cruisers and cars to exotic holidays and match tickets up as prizes. A massive crowd came up to the club for the draw that evening, and the local community really were unbelievable in the good will and support they gave the club.

With lotto funding also on its way, the next task was to decide just what form the new development would take. Gerry McAndrew was the man leading the club into the new decade, having been elected as chairman in late 1999, he recalls how the project eventually began to take shape:

The plans for the new clubhouse were being drawn up when I took over, and I remember one of the main discussion points at the time was whether we were going to put in a sports hall or not. There was huge debate over that. Confey had just built theirs so a lot of people were keen to match them. Another group argued that we should just worry about the clubhouse first. That's the way we went in the end.

The other point that was being argued about was the new hall which was actually pencilled in to be a little bit smaller than the old one had been, so there were concerns over that too and how many people we could fit in there.

There was going to be a big debt there no matter what we did, despite all the successful fundraising efforts that would have been going on at the time. People like Seán Walsh and Donal Walsh had done great work on the lotto funding, and there was great momentum there from Shay's last year as chairman on the fundraising side of things.

Gerry McNamara and Donal Griffin were leading the way on the actual design of the new building and the costings and all that side of things. I think it all worked out great in the end though, it was delivered as it had been designed if you look at the plans.

There were several different schools of thought as to where we should put the new building, in trying to keep as much space as possible for playing fields and the likes. I think it all worked out well in the end though.

We agonised over the number of dressing rooms to put in too, but I think we got that right as well. I think we spent more time deciding on the finish of the dressing room walls than we did on anything else over that few years believe it or not.

There was a lot discussion about the balcony too, but again I think it has worked well, and on balance I think most of the right decisions were taken.

The club's membership were kept apprised on proceedings with a brochure, entitled *Spirit of the New Century*, which was released in 2001 and which explained how:

In December 1999, the club, at a specially convened extraordinary general meeting, unanimously supported a proposal to build a new clubhouse at the 12th Lock.

This development will help the club maintain its position as Lucan's biggest sporting organisation and help provide all its players, members, sponsors and visitors with modern and comfortable facilities. In designing the clubhouse, the club's vision was to develop something that would be both practical and attractive. We think we have achieved this.

The new development consists of six dressing rooms, one referee's room, a gymnasium, meeting rooms, storage facilities, offices, lounge bar, function rooms, disabled facilities and a games room.

The cost of the new development is in excess of £1.3m and it is proposed to fund this by a combination of funds raised by the club, grants from the GAA and National Lottery and bank borrowings. The Millennium Draw has been completed and was great success with all tickets sold. This was achieved by the tremendous work of the members and with the support of the local community. It shows the determination and the ability of the club's members to complete the new development.

A few months later, planning permission came through for the new development, and an updated newsletter informed members of what the plans were from this point on. The 3,000-ticket Millennium Draw had raised a whopping £200,000. The club had been approved for a further £300,000 under the National Lottery Sports Capital Programme, and Life Memberships were to be offered in the final stage of fundraising. The dream was getting closer by the day.

The opening of the new clubhouse brought a new dimension to the social aspect of the club. It also presented a challenge to the executive to put in place the structures to successfully manage a bar on a full-time basis and to make it a successful commercial venture.

After successfully operating the old clubhouse bar, mainly on a voluntary basis, with weekend-night opening only, the club decided it was time to appoint a full-time bar manager to resource a seven nights and weekends operation. Hazel McLoughlin was initially appointed, prior to the big opening in June 2002, but had a relatively short tenure. The club reverted to running the bar in-house for a period, with great support from Liam Carton, Gerry McNamara, and Bridgie Hurson, while the search for a new manager continued.

That search concluded in April 2003, with the appointment of Liam Cuttle. Liam has commanded the space behind the bar for all of the eight years since then, while other regular bar staff in the period included Cathy

Club member and player Conor Griffin, who was killed in a car crash while on duty as a Garda at the turn of the century.

and Willie O'Neill, Kevin Cummins, Martina McGilloway, Tom Byrne, Fachtna 'Doc' Clandillon and Maeve McGuire.

In its relatively short few years the new clubhouse bar has become a social centre for the club and the community. It has been the scene of many celebrations of success, many reviews of near misses and harrowing defeats, awards nights, fundraisers, table quizzes, card playing, occasional pool and darts, family occasions, birthdays, christenings, communions, funerals, weddings, tonnes of ham sandwiches, committee meetings, many a Sunday night singsong, music, occasional dancing, hundreds of lotto draws, countless raffles, and frequent late night negotiations. It has also become a centre for the wider Lucan community, with a host of local organisations including schools, parents' associations, community groups, and other sports clubs running events there. It has served to strengthen the links between the club and the wider community and develop the inter-dependency between them.

Back in the year 2000, as the monstrous task to develop the new clubhouse began in earnest in the executive rooms, the club was also enjoying unprecedented success on the playing fields. There were twenty-eight teams in the club at all grades, and the hurlers and footballers were both playing senior championship. It was the club's underage section that would provide

Above: Junior Football League and Championship Winners, 2001.

Below: Fintan McCarthy (right in tracksuit) celebrates with his team mates after winning the Junior B Football Championship at Parnell Park in 2001. Fintan, who was a local Green Party Councillor, was tragically killed in a car crash in China in 2006 alongside his partner Sonya Rabbitte.

10th June 2000 Liffey Champion THE NEWSPAPER THAT CELEBRATES SPORT

Lucan Sarsfields GAA Club Millennium Draw Results

•1st Prize: Toyota Landcruiser Winner: Ben Conlan, Templeogue
Seller: Des Molloy
•2nd Prize: Toyota Corolla Winner: Gavin Mulligan, Ballyboughal
Seller: Michael Kilduff
•3rd Prize: Toyota Yaris: Pat Keane, Beech Park
Seller: Pat Keane
•4th Prize: Toyota Yaris: Sylvester Rowe, Navan
Seller: John Ryan
•5th Prize: Cash Bonanza £10,000: Christopher Doyle, Lucan
Seller: Sean Mc Caffrey
•6th Prize: Holiday of a Lifetime: Vil/Brigid Mulqueen
Seller: Shay Hurson
•7th Prize: Dream Kitchen: Dolores Collins, Lucan
Seller: Niall Collins
•8th Prize: Cash Bonanza

Magnificent draw comes to pass at Lucan Sarsfields GAA Club

Planned development receives £200,000 boost

OVER £200,000 was raised by Lucan Sarsfields GAA Club at its Millennium Club Draw which took place last Saturday week (27th May), writes DAVID LYNCH.

A total of 3,000 tickets, each priced at £100, were made available and all of them were sold.

The draw was co-ordinated by Ray Barnes, and Toyota car dealer Art McCoy was its sponsor.

It was estimated that up to 1,000 people attended the draw, for which a marquee had been erected by the club.

Its chairman, Shay Hurson welcomed the guests, who included Dublin County Chairman John Egan to the event.

The draw is an important part of the financial drive for the new club house. Building for this club house is planned to begin in September.

"This Millennium Draw is the first stage of a three-staged-plan to get the money for the new club house," said Mr Barnes.

will reach 50,000 within the huge amount of

to be a huge success with 3,000 tickets being sold in six months," said Cllr Paul Gogarty, a member of the club who was in the audience on the night.

The organisers of the draw wanted to give a special mention to Ann Carton, the former treasurer at the club who administered all aspects of the event.

Tony Hickey, the Assistant Garda Commisioner, won the top seller's prize on the night. He was also the scrutineer of the draw itself.

Ben Conlon from Templeogue won the first prize in the main draw.

This meant that Ben drove home from Lucan Sarsfields in a Toyota Land Cruiser.

The first four prizes in the draw were spon-

• Top sellers: (l-r) Ray Barnes Draw co-ordinator, Art McCoy (sponsor), and top ticket seller Tony Hickey (Asstitant Garda Commissioner).
Photos: Morgan Treacy.

very hopeful. We are

Above: Millennium Draw launch report (2000).

Below: Senior footballers line up for an early round of the league, April 2001. Back: Jack Sheedy, Paul Casey, Diarmuid Sheehy, Conor Bresnan, Colm Hickey, Noel McHugh, Fran O'Hare, Mick Miniter, Fergus McNulty. Front: Fergus Gordon, Stephen O'Shaughnessy, Ronan Doolin, Mick Casey, Stephen Corrigan, John Doyle, Barry Whelan.

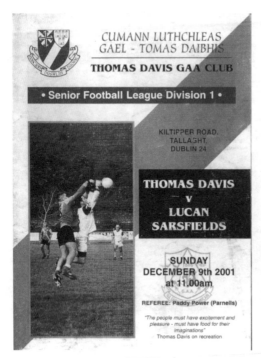

CUMANN LUTHCHLEAS
GAEL - TOMAS DAIBHIS

THOMAS DAVIS GAA CLUB

• Senior Football League Division 1 •

KILTIPPER ROAD,
TALLAGHT,
DUBLIN 24

THOMAS DAVIS
v
LUCAN
SARSFIELDS

SUNDAY
DECEMBER 9th 2001
at 11.00am

REFEREE: Paddy Power (Parnells)

"The people must have excitement and pleasure - must have food for their imaginations"
Thomas Davis on recreation

Left and below: Match programme, Senior Football Division 1 League final, 2001.

	Thomas Davis		Lucan Sarsfields
1 Cormac McCormac	**Thomas Davis**	1 Ronan Doolan	**Lucan Sarsfields**
2 Dean Fairbanks	PANEL	2 Stephen Shaughnessy	PANEL
3 Manus Breathnach		3 Diarmuid Sheehy	
4 David Farrelly		4 Colm Hickey	
5 Kevin Donavan (C)		5 Stephen Corrigan	
6 Paul Curran		6 Michael Casey (C)	
7 Gary Gilmartin		7 Paul Casey	
8 Pat Courtney		8 Kenny Wade	
9 Martin English		9 Fran O'Hare	
10 Eamon Cawley		10 Barry Whelan	
11 Kevin Lydon	Paul Nugent (Manager)	11 David Herlihy	Mick Kilduff (Manager)
12 Seamus Downey	Alan Byrne (Coach)	12 Niall McKiernan	Mick Downes (Coach)
13 Jimmy Owens		13 John Doyle	Donal Griffin (Selectors)
14 Philip Gray		14 Damien O'Brien	Mark Dardis
15 Shane Smith		15 Jack Sheedy	Mick Casey Snr.
16 Paddy Kavanagh		16 Alan Curtis (GK)	
17 James O'Connor		17 Brian Kavanagh	
18 Ciaran Farrelly		18 Aidan McKelvey	Sponsored by
19 John Benton		19 Conor Bresnan	THE LUCAN SPA HOTEL
20 Glen Farrelly	Visit out website at	20 Eoin McNulty	
21 Brian Kirby	thomasdavisgaa.com	21 Michael Moore	Club Patrons:
22 John Duffy		22 Darragh Reidy	KBA: Kieran Brady & Associates
23 John Dillon		23 Fergus McNulty	The Lucan Spa Hotel
24 Andy Dowdall		24 Thomas Cummins	Liffey Valley
25 Chris Lanny		25 Mick Miniter	Keane Windows
26 Brian Rowe		26 Paul Kelly	The Ulster Bank
		27 Fergus Gordon	EuroSpar
		28 Noel Flynn	Fort Lucan
		29 Noel McHugh	McCoy Motors
		30 Robert O'Sullivan	
		31 Ciaran O'Neill	Club Sponsors:
			Maplewood Homes
			Lark Developments
			Lucan Credit Union
			Bank of Ireland, Lucan
			CameraVision
			Nationwide Tiles
			Supervalu Palmerstown

Iomlán _____   Iomlán _____

Cúil _____   Cúil _____

Cúilíní _____   Cúilíní _____

Under-14 hurling Féile panel, 2001.

the first trophy of the new century though, when the under-14 footballers brought Division 1 gold back to Lucan Sarsfields.

The team completed an unprecedented double in an amazingly success-ful campaign at the very top grade. The 2000 club yearbook takes up the story of the glorious year for what was in essence the best underage football team the club had produced in 114 years of trying:

> Pride of place among Lucan Sarsfields' achievements during the Millennium year goes to our under-14 football team. They made club history by accom-plishing the unique double of winning Division 1 of the Dublin Féile and the Division 1 under-14 league title. Previously, no football team from the club had won a Division 1 title in the Féile or in any Dublin juvenile league.
>
> Lucan had great wins over all the teams in the league, most notably over St Vincent's, St Brigid's, Ballyboden St Enda's and St James's Gaels who were the strongest teams in the league. Lucan then renewed rivalry with the same teams in the Féile, playing their group games in Swords against Kilmacud Crokes, St Vincent's and Fingallians.
>
> The team emerged to reach a semi-final against favourites St James's Gaels. Goals from Gerry O'Brien and Ciarán Russell helped Lucan win an epic duel. The final against St Brigid's was played in wretched wet and windy conditions. There were unrestrained scenes of joy and celebrations after the match when the trophy was presented to captain Johnny McCaffrey.

The team went on to represent the club in the All-Ireland champion-ships, reaching the quarter-final stages before being narrowly beaten by St Lawrence's of Kildare. That same crop of players, too, were destined for even greater things.

Elsewhere, at underage level, the club's under-9, -10, -11 and -12 foot-ballers and under-11 and -12 hurlers all secured medals in the Dublin juvenile leagues. The senior hurlers consolidated their place in the senior ranks, narrowly missing out on promotion to Division 1. Defeat to Naomh Mearnóg in a Senior B Championship playoff ended their year, but the signs were growing increasingly bright for the future.

Derek Maher and Fintan Clandillon had spent the year on the county senior panel. Tadhg Clandillon had been nominated for a Blue Star award and had joined Neville Kelly and Pat Doyle on the Dublin intermediates. Cronan Dooley, Eoin Ó Lanagáin, Darragh Cunnigham, Brian Fagan and Fintan Clandillon had all played for the county under-21s, and Seán Quinn and Joey Byrne lined out for the county's minors.

The talent was most certainly beginning to emerge, and the signs looked good for the decade ahead, though the year was also tainted with sadness at the loss of club-man Conor Griffin who was tragically killed in a car acci-dent while on duty in his role as a Garda. Conor had played under-21 and junior hurling with the club.

The ladies section, meanwhile, was continuing to prosper; the intermedi-ate footballers suffered heartbreak in the county final, while the camogie team secured the Junior B county title, winning thirteen of their fourteen games.

The senior footballers had secured their place in the top flight of Dublin football, and under Mick Kilduff and trainer Mick Downes were getting better and better with every passing day.

While the victorious under-14s were bringing much-needed sil-verware to the club's footballing fraternity, four of the club's best young stars were busy making history of their own. Ciarán O'Neill, Aidan McKelvey, Stephen O'Shaughnessy and Anthony Norton, students at Lucan Community College, all lined out for the Dublin Vocational Schools team as they defeated Tyrone in the All-Ireland final at Croke Park in May 2000. The production line was beginning to do its job, and the club could sense that something big might just be around the corner at last.

Two other top-quality players coming through the ranks at the time were future Dublin senior football captain Paul Casey and his older brother, Mick Jnr, who had recently made his senior debut for the county. The Casey family enjoyed a very special day out in August 2000, when Mick Snr, who had been a stalwart with the Lucan football team for years since moving to Dublin from Kerry, and the club's senior footballers, travelled the Casey's old backyard to take on Skellig Rangers.

The Kerryman newspaper reported on the game, and the return of one of their favourite sons, amongst a host of connections shared between the two clubs:

> Skellig Rangers played host to Dublin club Lucan Sarsields in a very enter-taining game and one the home team found very beneficial. The Rangers had the best of the first-half exchanges, but the visitors got to terms with the local side's style of play and ran out winners by three points.
>
> The Lucan team had many connections from Portmagee playing with the team. The Griffins – Ger, Brian, Timothy and Kevin are sons of Nualinn Griffin (*née* O'Sullivan). There were two Wallaces, Michael and Maurice, involved, who are sons of Mary Bridget Wallace (*née* O'Sullivan). The four Casey brothers were Michael, Alan, Shane and Paul, who were joined on the field of play by their father Michael, who also scored a point for the Dublin club.
>
> Michael Casey Snr played with the Rangers for the closing moments and it was great to see one of our former stars finishing the game with the green and gold of the Rangers. At one stage there were seven Caseys on the pitch, with John and Jonathan playing for the Rangers.

The 2001 season ahead would bring an even more special day for Mick Casey Snr, as he, along with fellow mentors Jim McCarthy, Dermot Russell, Cormac Gordon and Frankie Farrell, would bring the Junior B football championship back to the club.

After having spent the previous twelve months unbeaten – and having secured championship wins over Trinity Gaels, St Sylvester's, Ballyboden St Enda's and Fingallians – the team travelled to Parnell Park on 29 July to take on St Kevin's/Killian's in the county decider.

It was Lucan's first junior football final appearance in twenty-four years, and in the end the Sarsfields side completely outclassed their opposition, emerging 1-17 to 3-3 winners, thanks largely to the scoring prowess of Mark Behan, who kicked nine points. The team would go on to win the league, completing a remarkable double for the club, and another major boost to the football section.

On 17 June 2002, the special day arrived when, after months and years of toil on behalf of the committee, the brand new clubhouse opened its doors for the first time, just in time to celebrate the club's first Leinster championship success.

The ladies footballers had been working away for years in search of a Dublin Junior Championship victory, but they would embark on a season of previously unparalleled success in winning the Leinster Junior Ladies Football Championship to boot. Tracey O'Brien reflects on an historic year for the ladies' game in the club, and the path they had taken to achieve their ultimate goal:

> In the year 2000 we had our first big day out since 1996 when we got to the intermediate final. We were well beaten by Kilmacud Crokes that day. They had only formed as a team in 1996, and, amazingly, their first competitive game had actually been against us. We had murdered them that day, but then four years later, sure they were the queens of Dublin football by that stage.
>
> We had a bit of a problem in 2001. About seven or eight of us went to play with St Brigid's just to keep playing. The team had pretty much fallen apart here and we just wanted to make sure we still had a core of girls there so as that we could come back to Lucan the following year. Round Towers wanted us to play with them that year, but that would have been a bit too much with the local rivalry.
>
> Then, in 2002, Fergal [Walsh] came back on board and we had the best team I ever would have played on. We had girls like Angela Gallagher who had come in and younger players coming through like Sinéad Ní Lanagáin, Caroline Geraghty and Orlaith McKelvey. That year we won the Junior League and Championship double and we reached the Leinster final.
>
> We beat St Sylvester's in the Dublin county final that year. They were a great team, and they would have had Sinéad Aherne playing for them. She would have been a star even as far back as then.
>
> We played the semi-final of the Leinster Championship up in the club. The scoreboard had just been installed and there were crowds we'd never seen before up at it. I remember we were seven points down just five minutes in, and there were people who had just arrived that turned around and headed off again.
>
> We ended up turning it around though and we won by three points. We went on to beat Valleymount, a team from Wicklow, in the final up in Confey. We went on to Roscommon then to play a quarter-final and we won that, and we found ourselves in an All-Ireland semi-final against a team from Tipperary, Cappawhite, in the 12th Lock.
>
> The long hard season really caught up with us at that point though. We were actually favourites going into that game. The talk had been that Lucan

were going to win it, but we just didn't perform on the day. They beat us, but they didn't actually go on to win it. They lost to a team from Monaghan, Tyholland, in the final, a team that actually had a mother and three daughters on it.

It really was a fantastic year, and that was definitely the best group of players we ever had. To win a league and championship and a Leinster title was amazing, but the support in the club that year was really fantastic. The clubhouse had just opened, so it was an amazing year.

In 2003, we were intermediate and we won that. We played Sylvester's again that year, and there had been a bit of a grudge between us since that junior final. That was a very strange game. The ref didn't play the full amount of time in the first half so we went over to him at half time. He said that we'd agreed to end it early because the Champions League final was on that evening.

So, of course, we appealed that whole thing and the match got replayed and we murdered them altogether. In 2004, we were back in the senior ranks again, but in some ways we were a little bit sorry to go up so quickly. I think we could have done with another year at intermediate level.

We got to the semi-final of the senior championship in 2004, but we were down to face Ballyboden. There was only ever going to be one winner. In 2005, we got to another semi-final against, Na Fianna, but things sort of fell away after that. People came and went and other girls were getting that bit older. There weren't too many young girls coming through at that stage. It's funny the way it ebbs and flows. Na Fianna would have been one of our biggest rivals starting off and now they're senior; they won a senior championship a couple of years ago.

And then you look at one of the bigger clubs for ladies football back then, Olaf's, they don't even field a team anymore. Portobello even, they would have been the stars of the ladies game for years at the start, but they went a few years without even having a team, though they've started to get things together again now. So I think, overall, as a club, we've actually done really well to still be where we are.

We had some great people involved with us over the years. Fergal, obviously enough, and Donal Griffin too would have been great. Donal Walsh would have helped out over the years and Colm Hickey, Gerry Mescall. Tom Lynch from Meath and Neil McKelvey would have all been terrific.

We had a huge number of players involved with Dublin over the years too. In more recent years we would have had players like Patricia Gordon, Angela Gallagher, Anna McGillacudy and Elena Griffin playing for the county.

We probably would have liked to have had more players on county teams, but I think we've done pretty well overall. There's a great crop of young players coming through, players like Marie Moynihan and Katie McCormack, who have All-Ireland medals underage, and Sarah Moloney even more recently.

It's twenty years this year [2011] since it all began, so hopefully we'll come again as a club. There are plenty more young players coming through now than we ever would have had, so we're certainly going in the right direction.

Back to 2002, and not many people could have predicted just what a huge year it would be for Lucan Sarsfields. While the ladies footballers were bringing previously unseen crowds and glory to the club, their counterparts in the camogie section were busy making history of their own.

The team reached both the Junior league and championship finals, losing a heartbreaking championship final to Raheny in almost pitch-black conditions in Naomh Mearnóg. Under the management of Noel and Betty Flynn, their efforts had been enough to secure their promotion to the intermediate ranks, and in 2003 they would follow up by going one better again, winning that year's Intermediate Camogie Championship in thrilling style. The *Liffey Champion* reported on the game under the headline

Camogie team – Junior League and Championship finalists, 2002. Back: Lynn Flannery, Aideen Casey, Siobhan Ryan, Julie McGinley, Ailish McGarrigle, Marian Flynn, Edele O'Brien, Caroline Flynn, Patricia McGarrigle, Roisín Hayden, Caitríona Byrne, Marian Freeman. Front: Gillian Flannery, Gráinne Ní Lanagáin, Emer Keenan, Audrey Murtagh, Frankie Andrews, Caitríona Doyle, Ann Ward, Heidi Doyle, Vivienne Ralph, Margaret Ryan.

Lucan Sarsfields Bar Rota Oct/01 - Feb/02

No.	PHONE	NAME	DAY	DATE	DATE	DATE
1	6282448	T, KEOGH				
	6241927	M.O'LANAGHAIN	FRI	26-Oct-01	7-Dec-01	18-Jan-02
2	6282084	M. MALONE				
	6249036	M. ROCHE	SAT	27-Oct-01	8-Dec-01	19-Jan-0S
3	6243661	MARK SMYTH				
	6241039	TONY DONOGHUE	SUN	28-Oct-01	9-Dec-01	20-Jan-02
	TEAM		TUE	30/T10	11/T16	22/T13
4	086 6299331	G.O'SHAUGHNESSY				
	6241025	G.McANDREW	FRI	2-Nov-01	14-Dec-01	25-Jan-02
5	6241928	P. TOBIN				
	6241331	JOE WHITE	SAT	3-Nov-01	15-Dec-01	26-Jan-02
6	6249211	F.DELANEY				
	6241833	M. DOHERTY	SUN	4-Nov-01	16-Dec-01	27-Jan-00
	TEAM		TUE	6/T11	18/T17	29/T14
7	6241324	C. O'NEILL				
	6241324	W. O'NEILL	FRI	9-Nov-01	21-Dec-01	1-Feb-02
8	086 6299331	A,O'SHAUGHNESSY				
	6282145	L. CARTON	SAT	10-Nov-01	22-Dec-01	2-Feb-02
9	6282020	B HURSON				
	6282020	S. HURSON	SUN	11-Nov-01	23-Dec-01	3-Feb-02
	TEAM		TUE	13/T12	25/T18	5/T15
10	6281771	M. FLANNERY				
	6240088	J McGANN				
	6240088	P. McGANN	FRI	16-Nov-01	28-Dec-01	8-Feb-02
11	087 2359321	A. HURSON				
	6240662	S. O'BRIEN	SAT	17-Nov-01	29-Dec-01	9-Feb-02
12	6241305	F. Mc CARTHY				
	6210230	M. FINN	SUN	18-Nov-01	30-Dec-01	10-Feb-02
	TEAM		TUE	20/T1	1/T4	12/T7
13	6241296	BRENDAN KNEAFSY				
	6241928	D.TOBIN	FRI	23-Nov-01	4-Jan-02	15-Feb-02
14	6282284	JOE MULQUEEN				
	628226?	PAUL Mc CABE	SAT	24-Nov-01	5-Jan-02	16-Feb-02
15	6240802	GERRY BELLEW				
	6280743	WALTER CRUMMY	SUN	25-Nov-01	6-Jan-02	17-Feb-02
	TEAM		TUE	27/T2	8/T5	19/T8
16	6214770	J. EGAN				
	6281839	M CLAFFEY	FRI	30-Nov-01	11-Jan-02	22-Feb-02
17	6249451	N. CARRABINI				
	???????	M. KELLY	SAT	1-Dec-01	12-Jan-02	23-Feb-02
18	0876364181	T SEALEY				
	6241331	A WHITE	SUN	2-Dec-01	13-Jan-02	24-Feb-02
	TEAM		TUE	4/T3	15/T6	26/T9

Remember if you do not work your night someone else has to.
Club Tele. No. 01 6240744

Bar rota, 2002.

Clubhouse under construction, 2002.

Club chairman Gerry McAndrew shows Tánaiste Mary Harney around the new clubhouse in the 12th Lock in April 2002.

Cumann Peil Gael na mBan
AIB ALL IRELAND JUNIOR CLUB SEMI FINAL

CAPPAWHITE
V
LUCAN SARSFIELDS

Sunday 10th November 2002
Lucan
2.00pm

Cumann Peil Gael na mBan
AIB Junior All-Ireland Quarter Final

St Mary's (Roscommon)
V
Lucan Sarsfields

Sunday 27th October 2002
Tulsk
2.00pm

Above and below: Ladies football programmes, 2002.

Whats going on in Lucan Sarsfields !

Sat 21st Sept-Jumping Johnny Peters

Sat 28th Sept- Kathy Nugent Cabaret (booking early advised-tickets in Clubhouse)

Sun 29th Sept- Family Fun Day in 12th Lock

4th October -Electric Lemon(fresh from Witness)

11th Oct-Charity Golf outing (Special Olympics)-Hollystown GC

Oct 29th-Trip to the Dogs (Harolds X)

The Club would like to thank Tom Waldron-Lucan Insurance Consultants for his generous sponsorship of this programme.

Leinster Ladies Junior Football Championship-Semi- Final

Lucan Sarsfields (Dublin)
V
Taghmon/Camross
(Wexford)

Venue-12th Lock , Lucan-4.30
21 Sept 2002

Lucan Sarsfields would like to warmly welcome all supporters on this great day
www.Lucansarsfields.ie

Lucan Sarsfields

1. Anne O Shaughnessy
2. Caroline Geraghty
3. Gillian Ryan (Capt)
4. Maeve Maguire
5. Sinead O Lanagáin
6. Tracey O Brien
7. Orla McKelvey
8. Patricia Gordon
9. Elena Griffin
10. Angela Gallagher
11. Jackie Quinn
12. Anna McGillicuddy
13. Gillian Mulqueen
14. Sinead Coffey
15. Regina Power

Aoife McKelvey,Una Ni Mhuiri, Catriona McGrath,Siobhan Casey,Linda Tapley,
Maria McGrath, Ailish McGarrigle, Barbara Wynne,Lucia Gavin,
Mary Roche,Aoíbhin Collins,Heidi Mahon,Alison Hickey, Aileen Quinn, Grainne
Masterson, Annette Flynn

Management- Fergal Walsh , Tom Lynch

Lucan Sarsfields was founded in 1886 and opened its new Clubhouse in 2002.
Lucan Sarsfields have qualified for the semi-final by beaten the Laois Champions
Park Rathiniski by 2 points in the first round and by comprehensively defeating the
Bennykerry Tinryland of Carlow in the quarterfinal. They won the Dublin Junior
Championship this year after many heartbreaks by defeating St Sylvesters. This is
Fergal Walsh's 11 year managing the team and he seems keen to equal Sean
Boylans record years of management!

Taghmon / Camross

Panel
Mary Doyle,Sinead Fox,Grace O Sullivan,
Sinead O Gorman,Sarah O Brien, Avril Nolan,

Sinead Kearns,Mary O Gorman,Noelle Gough (Capt),
Aine Breen,Aisling McNamara,Aileen Power,

Noirin Doyle,Sharon Kennedy,Leanne O Brien
Mary Grennan,Anne Marie Baniffe,Selina Nolan

Edwina Colfer,Orna Foley,Marion Foley
Laura Colfer,Marianne Carroll,Cathy Colfer

Ruth Colfer,Mairead McDaid,Gilla Laffaan McDonald
Amanda Bridges,Anne Curran

Manager -Denis Nolan
Selectors- Donie O Brien, Timmy Sullivan
Coach- Benny Grannell

Taghmon/ Camross was founded in 1969 with the amalgamation of two
older clubs
Taghmon (Football) and Camross (Hurling). They have recently (2001)
opened a new Clubhouse and in 2001 won the AIB Wexford Club of the Year.

Ladies football programme, 2002.

Senior hurlers, 2002: Seaghan Ó Lanagáin, Liam Carton, Brian Fagan, Eoin Ó Lanagáin,
Joey Byrne, Tadhg Clandillon, Ciaran McGrath, Jerome Twomey, Vinny Shanagher,
Anthony Nolan, Declan Carr, Tommy Somers, Derek Maher, Colm Sunderland, Darragh
Cunningham, Pat Doyle, Micheal Moylan. Front row: Fintan Clandillon, John Mills, Sean
Quinn, Alan Mockler, Phil Lanigan, Neville Kelly, Senan Clandillon, Stevie Farrell, Liam
Bergin, Brendan McGarry, Gerry McGarry, Alan O'Neill.

Senior status for Lucan Sarsfields camogie team

LUCAN SARSFIELDS camogie team (above) sensationally gained senior status recently in a pulsating Intermediate Championship final against St Marks.

It was the club's first year in the Intermediate ranks and the win, while a narrow one (Lucan 2-6 St Marks 3-2), was richly deserved.

St Marks controlled the first half and were well worth their half-time lead.

Lucan then turned on the style but, despite being on top in the second half, they found themselves six points down with seven minutes to play after another goal by St Marks late in the game.

Then, with Lucan laying siege to the St Marks goal, they scored two sensa-tional goals in the last four minutes.

This Lucan team lost three finals at Junior Grade last year so this day was especially memorable to the team and their mentors.

Three years ago the girls were play-ing Junior B and now, with practically the same panel, they have gained senior status for the club.

This achievement means Lucan Sarsfields have reached senior status in football, hurling and camogie.

The club's lady footballers — last year's Leinster Junior Champions — need to win their last league match to go senior also.

Scorers in that memorable camogie final were Margaret Ryan (1-3), Niamh Russell (1-0), Edel O'Brien (0-1), Roisin Hayden (0-1) and Grainne

Ui Lanagain (0-1).

LUCAN: Marie Darcy, Ellis McGarrigle, Sinead Ni Lanagain, Lynn Flannery, Marian Flynn, Grainne Ni Lanagain, Louise Beirne, Vivienne Ralph, Nuala O'Grady, Margaret Ryan, Roisin Hayden, Eadain Casey, Marie Maclochlainn, Emer Keenan, Niamh Russell, Edel O'Brien, Caroline Flynn, Gillian Flannery, Marian Freeman, Mary Roche, Imelda Smith, Nicola White, Patricia McGarrigle, Julie McGinley, Catriona Doyle.

● Mentors Needed – Girls Camogie and Football:
If you want to see your children pro-vided with these facilities at Lucan Sarsfields, it is time to commit to help-ing out with a team. Contact Fergal (football) 01 6240676 or Betty (camo-gie) 01 6241358.

Camogie goes Senior. Report in the *Liffey Champion*, 2003.

'Senior Status For Lucan Sarsfields Camogie team':

Lucan Sarsfields' camogie team sensationally gained senior status recently in a pulsating Intermediate Championship final against St Mark's. It was the club's first year in the intermediate ranks and the win, while a narrow one (2-6 to 3-2) was richly deserved.

St Mark's controlled the first half and were well worth their half-time lead. Lucan then turned on the style, but despite being on top in the second half, found themselves six points down with seven minutes to go after another goal by St Mark's late in the game.

Then, with Lucan laying siege to the St Mark's goal, they scored two sen-sational goals in the last four minutes. This Lucan team lost three finals at junior grade last year so this day was especially memorable to the team and their mentors. Three years ago the team were playing Junior B, and now, with practically the same panel, they have gained senior status for the club.

This achievement means Lucan Sarsfields have reached senior status in football, hurling and camogie. The club's lady footballers – last year's Leinster Junior Champions – need to win their last league match to go senior also. Scorers in this memorable camogie final were Margaret Ryan (1-3), Niamh Russell (1-0), Edel O'Brien (0-1), Róisín Hayden (0-1) and Gráinne Ní Lanagáin (0-1).

Seaghan Ó Lanagáin was also involved in camogie in the club over the years, and particularly in the early noughties, as he recalls:

> I would have been involved in one way or another with the camogie section through my daughters Gráinne and Sinéad. Gráinne played for Dublin growing up at under-14 and under-16 level, but we would have had only one team in the club so the younger girls would have been playing at adult level at the time too.
>
> We had a successful few years before the younger girls really came through. We went from senior B2 to senior B1, but we didn't have the strength and depth we have now or we will have in the years to come. I think the future is very bright now.
>
> But for what we had I think we were very successful. Unlike football or hurling, we didn't attract too many outsiders. They were a great bunch to be involved with though, and I think the future of camogie in the club is very, very bright.

While the club's ladies section was enjoying its most successful ever year, the hurlers were doing their best to secure a breakthrough of their own. In 2002, the under-21 hurlers, under the management of Seán McCaffrey, reached the club's first ever A grade county championship final at any level.

It had been an epic campaign in which the Lucan men had successfully seen off the best in Dublin, only to be denied a first ever top-flight championship for Lucan Sarsfields by a group of non-Dubliners playing under the DIT banner.

The students, who boasted a plethora of inter-county superstars and who had beaten the club's under-21s in the previous year's semi-final, emerged victorious with six points to spare. It was a bitter blow to a team that had already proven itself to be the best in the capital, but the manner in which the Lucan men had reached the county decider had been a massive fillip for the club.

The April 2003 Lucan Sarsfields Update Newsletter hailed how the team had given a 'great boost to Lucan hurling':

> Lucan's under-21 hurlers had an excellent league and championship campaign. They progressed to the semi-final of the league where they went out to Na Fianna. It was in the championship, however, that they really had a great season.
>
> The gallant bid for a first A championship in the club's history began against Kilmacud Crokes. Despite a late comeback by Crokes, we prevailed on a scoreline of 0-12 to 3-2. We were drawn against Ballyboden St Enda's in the quarter-final. A tense match at the 12th Lock, with a goal from a free from Boden bringing the match to a replay. In another hard-fought encounter in which the

Under-21 hurling team that lost the 2002 A County Championship final to DIT in Blunden Drive in early 2003, the first Lucan team to ever reach a top-grade final in modern times: Andrew Duff, Brian Bergin, Sean Quinn, Ger Power, Kevin O'Reilly, Ciaran O'Neill, Cian Fleming, Alan O'Neill, Ger Gleeson, Tommy Somers, James Mulhern, Keith Brennan, Jerome Twomey, Joey Byrne, Paddy Mulhern. Front row: Matthew McCaffrey, Damien Mitchell, Dave Corrigan, Brendan McGarry, Aaron Dunne, Ger Twohig, Aidan Glover, Johnny McCaffrey, Kevin Roche, Daire Reidy, Daragh Brennan, Pierce O'Leary.

Lucan ladies footballers celebrate winning the Leinster Junior Championship in Confey after defeating Valleymount of Wicklow in the final, 2002.

Lucan Sarsfields captain Kevin O'Reilly lifts the Under-15B title in O'Toole Park in 2002.

The panel of sports stars that attended a special charity fundraising 'Night of the Stars' evening in the 12th Lock.

Left: Lucan captain Daire O'Connor celebrates with the Junior football team after they secured the Junior A Football Championship in O'Toole Park in 2003.

Below: The club honour their county representatives at a cermony in the 12th Lock. Back row: Fergus Gordon (on behalf of his sister Patricia), Johnny McCaffrey, Sujon Alamgir, Sinead Ní Lanagáin, Angela Gallagher, Katie McCormack, Paul McGann (Chairman), Stephen O'Shaugnessey, Paul Casey, Dave Cullen. Front row: Mairí Ní Mhuineacháin, Owen Quinn, Kevin O'Reilly, Peter Callaghan, Garry Coleman, Elena Griffin.

Willie Coleman, Martin Mockler, Joe Byrne and Bernard Callaghan celebrate with the 2005 Minor A Hurling Championship trophy in the clubhouse after the team's historic first A championship victory.

The minor hurlers of 2005 celebrate their historic first A Championship win for the club.

Liam Ryan, winner of the 2006 Club Person of the Year Award, featured with former winner Alice Whyte.

Above: The Under-21 footballers celebrate their historic first A football championship victory for the club in Russell Park over Kilmacud Crokes, 2006.

Below: The camogie team of Scoil Mhuire GNS, captained by Ailise Dowling, celebrate the second of the three-in-a-row Cumann na mBunscoileanna Division 1 titles following their victory over Scoil Mearnóg at Parnell Park in 2007 .

Lucan and Dublin Under-21 hurling captain Johnny McCaffrey goes eye to eye with Galway skipper Kevin Hynes before the Under-21 All-Ireland final of 2007.

Opposite above: The club's first ever All-Ireland winning Féile Division 1 camogie team celebrate their historic victory over Mullagh of Galway in Portlaoise, 2008.

Opposite below: The 2008 All-Ireland Féile Division 1 Championship winning team take a lap of honour in Croke Park after their breakthrough success.

Former American Football star Dhani Jones, who trained with Lucan as part of his television series in 2008, in action in his one and only game of hurling in the 12th Lock.

Above: All-Ireland Camogie Féile winners, 2008. Back row: Ciara Sheehan, Grace Mulhern, Rachael Kenny, Niamh Williams, Ailise Dowling, Lucy Mulligan, Gráinne Rochford, Laura Morrissey, Sarah Courtney, Ailish O'Grady, Siobhan Grimes, Tara Keenan, Laura Murtagh. Front row: Lynsey Jordan, Claire Rigney, Ailbhe Ryan, Aoife Dodrill, Sarah Muldoon, Anne Marie Courtney, Orla Beagan, Kate Whyte, Shannon Clarke, Alison Twomey.

Below: The 2008 Under-14 Féile na nGael winners celebrate in Parnell Park in May.

The St Mary's BNS Senior team that secured the Under-13 Dublin schools title in 2008.

The teams take the field for the first ever 'Battle of the Parishes' between St Mary's and Esker in the 12th Lock in 2009.

The Lucan Sarsfields Senior football team that won the 2010 St Vincent de Paul Cup in Parnell Park with victory over St Sylvester's. Back row: David Herlihy, Brendan O'Neill, Noel Flynn, David Kealy, Tommy Brennan, Peter Callaghan, James O'Niell, Daniel Gallagher, Andy Kirwan, James Curran, Brian Collopy, Mark Twomey. Front row: John Doyle, Mick Kirwan, Johnny McCormack, Declan O'Shaughnessy, Brendan Gallagher, Mick Casey, Ciaran O'Neill, Keith Moran, Fergus Gordon, Ciaran McHugh.

Above: Lucan Sarsfields' Dublin stars David Quinn (left) and Peter Kelly are honoured to mark Dublin's success in the Leinster Under-21 Hurling Championship, 2010.

Below: Gerry McNamara throws in the ball to re-open the 12th Lock pitch after redevelopment in 2010.

Above: The 2010 All-Ireland winning Lucan Sarsfields Féile na nGael Division 1 camogie team. Back row: Niamh Byrne, Jenny Ryan, Amy Gorman, Laura Morrissey, Rachael Leonard, Maeve Ward, Aoife Clancy, Rhona Downes, Aoife Greene, Dayna Barry, Tara Farmer, Charlotte Rooney, Niamh Power, Eimear Murray. Front row: Sarah Boland, Orla Moloney, Ciara Casey, Orla Beagan, Aoife Flynn, Anne Marie Courtney, Amber O'Connor, Ruth Mulligan, Cisca Devereux, Amy Conroy.

Below: Lucan Under-21 footballers celebrate winning the club's second Under-21 A football championship with a win over Na Fianna in Parnell Park in February 2011 in the final of the 2010 championship.

GAA President Christy Cooney attends the 12th Lock for a special tree-planting ceremony as part of the club's 125th-anniversary celebrations in March 2011.

The club's nursery stops for a photograph in 2011 on the club's new all-weather facility.

President Mary McAleese attends a special function in the clubhouse in January 2011 to mark the club's 125th Anniversary Year.

Dublin Under-21 Football Champions visit the football and hurling nursery at 12th Lock, February 2011. John McCormack, Colm Larkin, Ollie Collins, Andy Kirwin (Captain) and Ciaran McHugh meet the future players when they bring the cup to the nursery.

The Lucan Sarsfields team that won the club's first ever adult camogie A Championship when securing the 2010 Minor Camogie Championship with victory over arch rivals St Vincent's at Craobh Chiaráin, 26 March 2011.

Dublin captain Johnny McCaffrey (right) and Peter Kelly (left) with the Dr Croke Cup after the Allianz Hurling League Division 1 Final, Dublin v. Kilkenny at Croke Park, 1 May 2011. (©Martina McGilloway/iLivephotos)

Juvenile camogie player Caroline McKeown, who was tragically killed in an accident in 2002. Lucan schools now compete for the Caroline McKeown Cup, dedicated to her memory.

character of the team was tested, we came out on top in a 0-10 to 0-9 thriller.

We travelled across the city to the fine hurling pitches of Pairc Uí Thuathail for the semi-final against Craobh Chiaráin. Before a big Lucan support, we went through to the final after a 2-11 to 2-7 win. DIT were our final opponents.

DIT, powered by several county stars, prevailed by six points before a huge Lucan crowd again at Pairc Uí Thuathail. Disappointment at the end but a fabulous campaign which brought big Lucan support to matches and that must bode well for the future of Lucan hurling.

Back on the football front, 2002 was also a special year for two of Lucan's emerging stars. Paul Casey and Stephen O'Shaughnessy both picked up Leinster medals at senior level with the Dubs, while Paul was also part of the Leinster championship winning under-21 team. The year would end in disappointment for him when he captained Dublin to defeat in the All-Ireland final, but it would also end in utter heartbreak for both men, and for the club's senior footballers.

After years of knocking on the door, Lucan had begun the previous 2001 season with high hopes that a major breakthrough was just around the corner. Under the stewardship of Mick Downes and Mick Kilduff, the Lucan men powered their way into a first ever Division 1 league final appearance against Thomas Davis, and a place in the last four of the Dublin Senior Football Championship. It was a familiar story, as Lucan suffered heartache, losing both games; the first to Davis in Kiltipper Road, and the latter, by a single point, in agonising fashion at the hands of Na Fianna.

But, as 2002 began, there was still optimism in the air. The team would finish the league campaign mid-table, but the focus was on the Dublin Championship. Again, the team would fall at the second last, losing another enthralling semi-final in heartbreaking fashion. Team mentor Mick Casey summed up the 2002 campaign in his report to the AGM in July 2003:

> After a very successful 2001 campaign, reaching the Division 1 league final and the championship semi-final, hopes were high that we could progress that little bit extra and achieve our major goal of winning a senior trophy for the club.
>
> Unfortunately this did not happen. We suffered heartbreak again at the semi-final stage of the championship, unlucky to lose to St Vincent's by one point in a game played in terrible weather conditions in Parnell Park.
>
> A highlight of our championship campaign was our first-round three-game marathon with our near neighbours St Mary's of Saggart. Our Division 1 league campaign was somewhat inconsistent, mixing some brilliant performances with mediocre ones and finishing eventually in mid-table.
>
> The end of the 2002 campaign saw our manager Mick Kilduff stand down after a hugely successful period at the senior helm. Under his leadership the team achieved Division 1 status and became serious league and championship contenders. A special word of thanks to the players and Mick Downes [team trainer] for the huge effort, commitment and dedication throughout the year

Under-21 hurlers, 2002: Andrew Duff, Tommy Somers, Sean Quinn, Ciaran O'Neiil, Jerome Twomey, James Mulhern, Alan O'Neill, Aaron Dunne, Brendan McGarry, Dave Corrigan, Johnny McCaffrey, Aidan Glover, Kevin Roche, Daragh Brennan, Daire Reidy.

Left: Lucan's 2003 Dublin Under-16 hurling representatives Kevin O'Reilly, Mick May and Johnny McCaffrey.

Above: Members of Club Executive and Development Committee make a presentation to Minister Mary Harney at the Clubhouse Opening in 2003. Left to right: Ray Barnes, Mick Roche, Liam Reidy, Gerry McAndrew (Chairman), Ailish McGarrigle, Paul Stapleton, Minster Harney TD, Betty Flynn, Shay Hurson, Gerry McNamara, Sean Walsh.

in competing to the highest standards in one of the most competitive leagues and championships in the country.

Jack Sheedy, who was still a prominent player at the time despite approaching his fortieth birthday, remembers the 'near and yet so far' nature of the club's senior football campaigns in the early part of the decade – an era when Lucan had, arguably, the best team the club had ever assembled. Jack would go on to take the reins for the ensuing few years, and in 2004 the team would reach the Division 1 league final after a stirling regular season campaign. Just as in 2001, however, the element of luck the team so badly

The ECHO, Thursday, September 4, 2003

Lucan crush Mark's dreams

TRAILING by six points with eight minutes to go, Lucan Sarsfields pulled off a stunning revival to snatch the Intermediate Camogie Championship crown at the expense of Saint Mark's last Sunday.

Lucan 2-6
St Mark's 3-2

Two goals in the closing minutes from Edel O'Brien and Margaret Ryan helped the Lucan girls to a 2-6 to 3-2 win at Kiltipper Road.

Mark's, who had dominated the game for so long, looked to be on their way to securing the title when Amy Murphy, Janet Fennell and Sharon Russell scored vital goals.

The Springfield girls enjoyed good spells of possession but Lucan

Lucan Sarsfields secured the Intermediate Camogie title for the very first time on Sunday at Kiltipper Road.

always stayed in contention thanks to brave performances from Lynn Flannery and Margaret Ryan in defence.

However in a frantic finale, goals from O'Brien and Ryan guided Lucan Sarsfields to a dramatic win.

"It was a fantastic victory," said a delighted Lucan manager Noel Flynn.

"We only went up to intermediate this year and to win the title at the first attempt is a great achievement. We were beaten in three finals last year and it's great that we have gone all the way this year," he added.

Back row. (L to R): Finnola O'Grady, Gillian Flannery, Marian Flynn, Noel Flynn (Manager), Louise Beirne, Stephen Beacon (Trainer), Eadaein Casey, Betty Flynn, Marie Darcy, Imelda Smith, Roisín Hayden, Emer Keenan, Marian Freeman, Sean Flynn.

Front row. (L to R): Edel O'Brien, Lynn Flannery, Mary Roche, Sinéad Ni Lanagain, Eilis Mc Garrigle, Marie Mac Lochlainn, Nicola White, Caroline Flynn, Niamh Russell, Vivienne Ralph, Grainne Ni Lanagain, Margaret Ryan.

Above: Inter Camogie final report *Echo*, 2003.

Left: Chairman Paul McGann presents the 2003 Club Person of Year Award to Kathleen Roche.

Above: Lucan Sarsfields GAA Clubhouse.

Below: Aerial view of the club grounds with the new clubhouse, 2003.

Above: Under-11B, football, league runners-up, 2003.

Left: Under-16 hurling team that lost to Ballyboden in the 2003 A county final: Paddy Brennan, Stephen Power, Aaron Doonan, Eoin McCarthy, Kevin Smith, Peter Callaghan, Kevin O'Reilly, Peter Kelly, Owen Quinn, Garry Coleman, Shane O'Neill, Adam Lester. Front row: Cathal Rochford, Andrew Mockler, Naoise Fleming, Eamon Cummiskey, David Quinn, Gearoid Brennan, Niall Gleeson, Mick May, Johnny McCaffrey, Aidan Roche, John Byrne.

needed to get across the line evaded them on the big day.

A win over reigning county champions Kilmacud Crokes in the semi-final had seen Sheedy's men enter the O'Toole Park Christmas-time decider in a confident mood. However, bitter local rivals St Mary's proved too good on a dark day for the club in front of a massive crowd in Crumlin. Sheedy, who would captain the Ireland over-40s to a victory over Australia in the 12th Lock in October 2004, recalls:

> When we were beaten in the championship semi-final by Vincent's, I really felt we had the potential to go on and win a championship that year. That was probably as good a team as we ever had in Lucan. We beat a star-studded

UCD team to get to that semi-final.

I took over as manager from Mick Downes for a couple of years. We couldn't really find anybody else. It was a great experience, but in hindsight I think it was probably the wrong thing to do at the time because I still wanted to play football.

I finished playing in 2006, probably ten years too late in most people's minds. I loved playing with the club though, and seeing young lads coming through and developing. It would be my one big thing as a manager that there's a personal touch there. I think it helps young lads to integrate better and to understand the game better.

Managing is a full-time job and you just can't do both at that level because there's so much attached to the role. That all meant that fellas didn't get what they needed, so I think it came a bit too soon.

My big thing was to get Richie [Crean] in as manager. I remember being over in his house talking about it, and he says to me, 'Why don't you do it? If you do it, I'll help you out.' We didn't go backwards or anything, but we could have achieved a little bit more maybe. I don't think we had a championship-winning team at that stage though.

I got involved with the inters after that. To be involved with your own club is always a great experience. I probably enjoyed my football more in the last three or four years than I ever had before.

The official opening of the brand new clubhouse finally arrived on 5 May 2003. Tánaiste Mary Harney and newly elected GAA President Seán Kelly performed the official duties on a massive occasion for the club, while the Dublin senior football team took on Cavan in a friendly game. It was a red-letter weekend of celebrations for Lucan Sarsfields, and a proud day for chairman Gerry McAndrew, who had led the project from late 1999 until its day of fruition almost four years later:

It really was a great occasion for the club. It was an entire weekend's worth of celebrations effectively – we had a marquee put up and we had Dickie Rock and other well-known artists up to play. There were gale force winds I remember that weekend, and we had some nightmare trying to keep the marquee from blowing away. Gerry McNamara had his work cut out trying to keep the thing in place.

Gerry was such a huge contributor to the project – and indeed any project we undertook. He was on site with the builders throughout the whole process and he really put some amount of work in. I think we took in €11,000 on the first night it was opened, which was pretty phenomenal. That certainly exceeded all expectations for us.

There was a great sense of optimism in the club at that time. We got to two senior football semi-finals around then. That was the closest we'd come as far as senior success on the field went, and we haven't reached a county football semi-final since.

I suppose the focus was on the clubhouse works from an executive point of view, especially during the year of the actual build. The executive was meeting on a weekly basis throughout that year, and all the various subcommittees focused on the building works.

The club produced a special commemorative programme for the occasion in which Gerry summed up how far the club had come, and how that optimism he spoke of was manifesting itself:

Lucan Sarsfields GAA Club has a long a proud history dating back almost to the foundation of the association. The opening of this tremendous new clubhouse represents a further major milestone in that history. This clubhouse provides facilities for our players and members that are on a par with any other GAA club or indeed any other sports organisation. It is a facility that we can rightly be proud of when entertaining visiting teams or friends and relations.

The recent survey of the Dublin GAA clubs conducted as part of the juvenile restructuring proposals places Lucan Sarsfields in the top ten of Dublin clubs as regards the performance of juvenile teams. This clubhouse takes us into a similar position as regards the quality of our facilities.

While the clubhouse is a tremendous achievement, the success of any GAA club must be measured by the number of teams fielded by the club and the level of commitment and participation by the players involved with all those teams. On this front the club has gone from strength to strength with now having thirty-eight teams playing on a regular basis. I look forward to the success and growth of the club over the coming years.

With the clubhouse built, the club now had to worry about paying for it. A note in that same commemorative brochure laid out the sheer measure of the task that lay in store in the years ahead:

The clubhouse and associated ground works is expected to cost €2.3m and has been funded to date by bank borrowings (€1m), National Lottery funds (€680,000), funding from central council (€25,000) and funds raised by Lucan Sarsfields (€595,000).

We now have a very large asset in our clubhouse but also a very large debt outstanding which we must start making capital repayments on from June 2003. We may also need to reduce this debt quickly if we want to proceed with further developments such as all-weather pitches and additional land purchases. With this in mind, we need all members to support our major sources of income, namely our club lotto, golf classics, poker classics, family fun days and our Christmas draws.

The Christmas draws had been a huge success since having been revamped by Kathleen Roche in 2001, and to this day they continue to provide a massively important source of income to the club.

Raffles had been run by the club's social committee up until the end of the 1990s, and brought in some badly needed funds, as well as adding a sense of anticipation and fun to the Saturday night of the raffle itself.

The concept of the Christmas raffle changed dramatically in 2001 however. Kathleen had seen, through the years, the different style of raffle that clubs such as Confey and St Mary's of Leixlip had been running, and believed that Lucan had the potential to do likewise. These raffles were on a much bigger scale that those run by the club up until that point, but under the new scheme the value of prizes on offer would be increased dramatically, and (unlike the Confey and St Mary's draws) all prizes would be sponsored. While there was no particular target for ticket sales in 2001, sales of 2,000 were certainly aspired to. This number was reached with two weeks to go, and a second run of tickets had to be printed. The draw was a terrific success, with 3,819 tickets sold in the end, raising almost €25,000.

After that initial success, Kathleen continued to run the Christmas Draw for eight years in all until 2008. In 2009, after the club had hosted a major €100 draw for the new all-weather pitches, there was a smaller Christmas Draw organised, with the ever-present Seamus Clandillon to the fore. The draw returned with a vengeance under a new committee in 2010, when it yielded over €38,000 and confirmed yet again the superb fundraising capability of Lucan Sarsfields. In total, since 1998, the Christmas draws have raised almost €350,000 for the club. Kathleen attributes the success to the great support from all club members, and some exceptional individual contributions:

Bernie Geheran played a major role, especially in the early years of the draw, and her down-to-earth, never-take-no-for-an-answer approach certainly enhanced the draw in many ways. Gerry McNamara was an invaluable supporter, who came good year after year, particularly in securing sponsorship from his many business connections. Cathy O'Neill was both a great sponsor and an active promoter of the draw, as were John Dalton and Jack Butler. Seamus Clandillon was always available to do anything that was required, and the role he and his wife Niamh played on the night of the draw in maintaining control over tickets that came in at the last minute contributed significantly to the professionalism of the draw itself. Alice Whyte and Josephine Donohue gave huge help all through the years, sorting tickets and money while Cormac Gordon ensured that all was above board in the drawing of tickets and recording of winners. There were some great individual ticket-sellers, among them Donal Walsh, Hugh McNulty, Dave Corrigan, Ray Barnes, Joe Whyte, Mick and Therese Malone, Noel and Betty Flynn, and John Egan. Those two great sellers of weekly lotto tickets, Tom Duff and Tommy McCormack, also contributed hugely, as did Bill Ryan and Niall Carabini. The Christmas Draw will undoubtedly continue to be a mainstay of club funding into the future.

June 2003 saw another special occasion for the club when the Ireland Special Olympics Team came to visit. Lucan was one of the host towns for Team Ireland and Lucan Sarsfields Clubhouse was used as their base for the start and culmination of their week's events. This helped to build a strong relationship between the club and the local Special Olympics organisation, Lucan Hedgehogs, which exists to this day.

Back on the field, at that time the footballers were pushing for senior honours. The ladies section was winning all around them, and the underage hurlers were closing in on a long-overdue A championship. The senior hurlers meanwhile, had, by the mid-part of the decade, moved to within striking distance of a senior B league and championship.

M.J. Ryan had been appointed as the new senior manager at the start of the 2004 campaign, and with his fresh impetus, supported by the knowledge of long-serving club men Mícheál Moylan, Seaghan Ó Lanagáin, Liam Carton and Seamus Clandillon, Lucan made a run to both the league and championship finals.

After opening the campaign with wins over Plunkett's, St Brigid's, Naomh Mearnóg, Good Counsel and Cuala, Lucan went on to defeat Commercials, St Mark's, Naomh Fionnbarra and St Jude's in the space of just twelve days to book themselves a place in both the championship semi-final and league final.

Having secured maximum points from their eleven league and championship clashes over the course of the season, Lucan went into their semi-final clash, with beaten 2004 A championship finalists St Brigid's, in top form. They cruised to a 0-21 to 1-5 win thanks to 0-12 from the stick of Daragh Brennan, and a month later went into the Parnell Park decider to face local rivals Commercials.

The big occasion got to the young Lucan team, however, and they were beaten by 0-12 to 3-6 in a game they could very well have won. The season was not completely gone though, and M.J. Ryan and his management team got the side up off the ground to face St Jude's in the league in early December.

It was to be another bitterly disappointing day for the Lucan men though, succumbing by two points in the end to a side that had finished six points adrift of Lucan in the league table. It was a rough end to a season that had promised so much, but there was some light at the end of the tunnel in some of the young stars beginning to emerge. Micheal Moylan remembers it as a season that could really have delivered so much more:

> We lost to Commercials in a hotly contested match in 2004. It was a real pity we didn't win that. We had plenty of chances to win it. We lost the league final then to Jude's, having won every match in the group stages. That was a tough old season.
>
> From the team that lost the senior B final Johnny McCaffrey was exceptional. He played wing back that day, even though he was very young, and it was obvious in that match in Parnell Park the talent that was there.
>
> People were asking me about him afterwards and asking who he was. He was only a minor at the time, and that was a very physical match but he really came of age that day. He put down a marker that day and I'm not a bit surprised to see him develop into the hurler he is today.

'We had good success for a couple of years,' fellow selector Seaghan Ó Lanagáin added, 'but we lost two finals one year, the championship to Commercials and the league to St Jude's. It's like anything else though, making the breakthrough is the hardest thing.'

No matter how disappointing the outcomes may have been on finals day, Lucan had secured two major goals along the way. In 2005, the club would be playing in Division 1 of the adult senior hurling league for the very first time, and the Dublin Senior A Hurling championship.

Elsewhere, the club's intermediate footballers were also enjoying a decade to savour. In 2003, under the stewardship of Mick Malone, Noel Buggy, Mick Kilduff, Hugh McNulty and manager Fergus McNulty, the team went on a rampage through the Dublin football scene, winning both

Above: Intermediate football league winners, 2004. Back row: Padraig McGarrigle, Fergus McNulty, Ray, Brian Redmond, Tadhg Clandillon, Shane Casey, Cyril Buggie, Anto Norton, Niall McNulty, Ciaran Fahy, Michael Moore, Shane Russell, Fintan Clandillon, Eoin McNulty, Noel Buggie. Front row: Mick Minitor, Ronan Doolan, Alan O'Neill, Mick Kirwin, Dave Hickey, Barry Kelly, Johnny Brennan, Daire O'Connor, Eoin Dunne, Peter Duff, Ciaran Malone, Darren Creen.

Left: Match programme for Ireland v. Australia in Over 40s International Rules played at the 12th Lock in 2004. The Ireland team included Lucan veterans Jack Sheedy and Gerry Mescall.

the Division 5 league and the Junior A football championship. Noel Buggy reflected on his team's success halfway through the 2004 campaign in his report to the AGM:

> This time last year we were playing Junior A Division 5 and doing very well. We subsequently went on to win the league and then the championship, which promoted the team to the intermediate league and championship. At the start of the season the team are now playing in Division 4, and to date we are top of that league.

A few months later, and rather incredibly in just their first season in the intermediate ranks, the team would go on to win the league title once again. Even more amazingly, perhaps, was that they managed the feat in undefeated style, beating Good Counsel in their last game of the season to finish atop the pile by four points. Division 3 football would follow in 2005. These really were the best of times for football in the club, with Lucan's own Kevin Moran also having been named Dublin minor football captain for the 2004 season.

Things were changing for the club in other respects also. Having long enjoyed a monopoly on the youth of the village, a new show rolled into town in 2003 with the establishment of the Westmanstown Gaels juvenile club. For the first time ever, there was a genuine rival seeking to attract the youth of Lucan away from the Sarsfields club.

Plans for the appointment of a juvenile development officer were already in place, and by September 2004, Lorcan O'Toole had been appointed as the club's first Games Promotions Officer (GPO).

The club was also responding to its changing environment in other respects. The Lucan area was experiencing a very large increase in the number of people from different nationalities and different ethnic backgrounds in those years. The club sought to attract and encourage membership from its increasingly cultural diverse community and in 2005 it produced a multi-lingual promotional brochure to target all the members of ethnic minorities in the schools of Lucan between the age of seven and twelve with a view to getting them involved in Gaelic games with the club. The brochure was produced in six different languages – Polish, Russian, Romanian, Cantonese, Urdu and English. This initiative was massively successful and the number of non-national children involved in the club increased by almost 100 per cent in the twelve-month period following its launch.

Subsequently, in April 2008, Sarsfields hosted a Social Inclusion Day in conjunction with the Camogie Association. This was the first of its type in the country and was a tremendous success. Girls from different ethnic, cultural and social backgrounds from eight local schools (Scoil Mhuire in Woodview, Gaelscoil Naomh Phádraig, Lucan Educate Together, Archbishop Ryan Senior School, Archbishop Ryan Junior School, St Thomas NS in Esker, Scoil Mhuire NS and Scoil Áine) were invited to participate in a fun-based camogie blitz. Over 130 girls took part on the day and in total represented twenty-seven different countries which was all part of the Camán Camán Let's Stick Together programme in celebration of the European Year of Intercultural Dialogue. The event was attended by the President of the Camogie Association, Liz Howard, as well as a number of public representatives, who were all keen to be associated with the scheme.

Following the success of this initiative, the club was featured in a TV documentary about multiracial social inclusion in sport. The programme featured coverage of a large number of non-national children participating in the Lucan Sarsfields Summer Camp in August 2008.

Back in 2005, the year had commenced on a sad note with the death of Seamus Morris in February. Morris, who passed away at just forty-four, had been a star footballer in his day with Wicklow and his original club side Tinahely, and had also been a part of the 1995 All-Ireland winning Kilmacud Crokes team. He had subsequently moved to Lucan as a teacher in Scoil Áine and got involved with Lucan Sarsfields juvenile football. He had been involved with the club's under-13A football side since they had been under-9, and in June 2005 a series of special memorial games were organised in the 12th Lock in his honour. The 1995 Dublin team were slated to take on the 1995 Crokes team, while a visiting side from Tinahely took on Lucan. It was an emotional day for many in the club, and a fitting memorial to a man who had given so much to the games of the Gael. The day's activities raised a whopping €17,000 for St Luke's Hospital.

There had also been great sadness among the hurling section of the club in particular with the tragic death of Hugh 'Rupo' McNally in the early part of the year.

Fortunes changed and spirits lifted, however, and later in that year of 2005 the first major breakthrough finally arrived. It had been 120 years in the offing, but after decades and decades of blood, sweat and tears, the first A county championship of any description would finally find its way back to the 12th Lock. Led gamely by captain Johnny McCaffrey, and county stars Peter Callaghan, Kevin O'Reilly, Owen Quinn and Gary Coleman, Lucan finally had the breakthrough the club so badly needed when the minor hurlers secured the county A championship title.

The winning of the championship had been set as the team's main objective after having been heartbroken at the loss of the 2003 under-16 A county final to Ballyboden, and they got their mission under way with challenge wins over Ballinteer St John's and Kilmessan. The tone for the year had been set in March, when the side got their league campaign off to the perfect start thanks to a seven-point win over county kingpins and arch rivals Ballyboden.

Wins over Erin's Isle, St Vincent's, St Brigid's, Round Towers and Craobh Chiaráin followed, before the team got their championship campaign under way in September with a win over a disappointing Chiaráin's side. Straight into a championship semi-final, Lucan accounted for the challenge of Kilmacud Crokes and the stage was set for an epic battle against old nemesis Ballyboden in the county final. There was no stopping Lucan though, and after over a century's wait for the first A championship, the breakthrough had finally arrived.

It had been an amazing year for McCaffrey, Coleman, Callaghan, Quinn and O'Reilly in particular, as all five players had also been a part of the Dublin minor hurling team that had secured the Leinster championship title for the first time since 1983. McCaffrey captained the side that defeated red-hot favourites Kilkenny in a thriller before going on to defeat Offaly in the semi-final and Wexford in the Leinster final. Tipperary would eventually put paid to Dublin's All-Ireland dream, but the win had represented a massive achievement for the small ball game in the capital.

It was a crazily busy year for many of the club's underage stars. McCaffrey had also captained the county footballers that year, but a first-round loss to Laois ended their season prematurely. Back at club level, the footballers were soon on their way to completing a minor championship football and hurling double, making amends for the heartbreak of losing the minor A football county final to neighbours Round Towers the year before by bringing home the B championship crown.

Under the captaincy of Brendan Gallagher and a management team that included Paul McGann and Ger Gleeson, the year had started disappointingly with an early defeat to Fingallians in the league. However, the ship was soon settled with a succession of wins over Round Towers, Ballinteer, St Patrick's and Craobh Chiaráin, and by the time the minor B football championship opener had rolled around, Lucan had all guns blazing.

A nervy 2-9 to 1-10 win over Raheny set the ball in motion, and after a 2-8 to 1-4 quarter-final win over Templeogue and a 1-18 to 0-6 hammering of Trinity Gaels, Lucan found themselves just sixty minutes away from clinching an amazing double.

County final opponents Naomh Olaf would provide the team's stiffest task to date. After a thrilling final, Lucan needed two late points to force a replay the following week in O'Toole Park, but a blitzing second-half display saw them to a 0-9 to 1-3 win and an historic double entered into the record books.

Club secretary Paul Stapleton summed up the incredible twelve months the club had enjoyed in his annual report to the February 2006 AGM:

2005 was an eventful year for the club and an historic one in many respects. Pride of place goes to the minor hurlers who achieved an historic breakthrough for the club, bringing back a first ever A championship title. The minor footballers then followed up with the B championship to complete a remarkable double.

Ladies football programme, 2005.

JUNIOR D FINAL
St. Annes

1. CELINE McDONALD

2. SARAH KINSELLA   3. BERNIE McCARTHY   4. ROSIE GALLAGHER

5. KATIE HEMPENSTALL   6. CATRIONA PHELAN   7. SHONA DOYLE

8. CLAIRE DONAGHEY   9. SINEAD DEEGAN

10. ROSEEN BRADY   11. ELAINE FLEMING   12. EMMA BYRNE

13. AUDREY QUINN   14. SHARON COFFEY   15. AISLING DUNNE

Substitutes:
16. JENNIFER ARMSTRONG; 17. CATHERINE McKEEVER; 18. KATIE CATHOOLE
19. NICOLE FARRELLY; 20. YVONNE HAYDEN; 21. MARY JANE McKEEVER;
22. ANTOINETTE DEMPSEY.

JUNIOR D FINAL
Lucan Sarsfields

1. MAEVE MAGUIRE

2. IMELDA SMITH   3. CLIONA O'DONNELL   4. COLLEEN GALLAGHER

5. LINDA TAPLEY   6. HANNAH MULDOWNEY   7. KAREN KENNY

8. CATHERINE KEANE   9. SIOBHAN O'NEILL

10. LORRAINE MORAN   11. ELAINE TWOMEY   12. EMER BRUNNELL

13. JENNY CASSERLY   14. HEIDI MAHON (C)   15. DEIRDRE RUSSELL

Substitutes:
16. SIOBHAN AMBROSE; 17. MARY ROCHE; 18. MARY BRANNIGAN;
19. LORRAINE O'NEILL; 20. SINEAD O'NEILL; 21. SIOBHAN CASEY;
22. AISHLING PARSONS; 23. ANN MARIE LILLIS.

Manager: TOM CASSERLY

Mentors: ED O'BRIEN, MAEVE MAGUIRE,
FEARGAL WALSH

Ladies football programme inside, 2005.

The level of representation on Dublin teams was also a remarkable feature of the year. We had fifteen people involved with Dublin championship teams, from senior to under-14, with many winning Leinster titles while two of our under-14 girls, Marie Moynihan and Katie McCormack, brought All-Ireland medals back to Lucan.

Johnny McCaffrey captaining the Dublin minor hurlers to a Leinster title and Stephen O'Shaughnessy's All-Star nomination were particularly notable individual achievements, but all our representatives performed extremely well and put Lucan Sarsfields on the map at a national level like never before.

2005 will also go down as a milestone year for camogie in the club. The development of camogie at juvenile level in the past year has been phenomenal with great success achieved and huge numbers now playing. We will be fielding ten underage camogie teams in 2006 which is a remarkable change from where we were a couple of years ago when we struggled to field one or even two teams. This revolution has been led by Liam Ryan, with great support from a huge number of other mentors and parents.

Another notable success of the 2005 season had come thanks to the senior footballers' St Vincent de Paul Cup victory. A win over Kilmacud Crokes in the semi-final and St Vincent's in the final saw the team bring back the first ever trophy at senior grade. It was the end of an era in many ways in the

Lucan players Stephen O'Shaughnessy and Paul Casey, who were regular members of the Dublin Senior football team during the 2000s, pictured with the Leinster Championship Cup.

Minor Hurling Championship Winners, 2005. Back: Niall Gaffney, Martin Mockler, Dave Corrigan, Philip Corcoran, Owen Quinn, Gearóid Brennan, Paddy Brennan, Cathal Rochford, Eamonn Comaskey, Peter Callaghan, Peter Carroll, Peter Kelly, Aaron Doonan, Andrew Mockler, Shane O'Neill, John Egan, Willie Coleman, Mick Roche. Front: John Byrne, Niall Gleeson, Mick May, Alan Whyte, Eoin McCarthy, Johnny McCaffrey, David Quinn, Kevin O'Reilly, Aidan Roche, Naoise Fleming, Gary Coleman, Robert Smith, Seán Egan.

club though, and a changing of the guard ensued at year's end.

Jack Sheedy and his management team stepped down at the end of the year, M.J. Ryan called it a day with the senior hurlers, Fergal Walsh handed over the reins of the ladies senior footballers, Fergus McNulty stepped down from over the intermediate footballers and Noel and Betty Flynn relinquished their positions with the senior camogie team. The club also mourned the passing of stalwarts Kevin Duke and Tony Strong over the course of the year.

The year had also seen the successful development of the new Paddy Kelly Memorial Hurling Alley, and though things were on the up and up overall, they were tough times financially for the club. The Christmas Draw, fun day, lotto and golf classic had proven their usual successes, but the secretary went on to lament the lack of support the club was receiving from members in certain areas:

> We had some disappointments off the field. The club did not have a good year commercially, and the continued decline in the support being given by members to the club bar and club events is disappointing. We had to cancel our dinner dance due to lack of support from members. This was a significant disappointment and embarrassment for the club and reflects the general apathy that prevails at present towards certain aspects of the club.

With the memory of the club's first adult A championship (minor hurling 2005) still fresh in the hearts and minds of long-suffering Lucan folk, the

2006 season began with much optimism as they looked to the future, no longer suffering from the mental scars of the failures of the past.

The senior hurlers and footballers both began the year under 'new' management, as such. In reality, however, Seán McCaffrey (hurling) and Mick Kilduff (football) were actually beginning their second stints at the helm of the club's respective first teams.

The hurlers, buoyed on in particular by the success of the 2005 club minors, had an entirely new management team with, Kevin Brennan being joined on the sidelines by Kilkenny men Willie Coogan and John Dermody. Both had been heavily involved in Dublin's Leinster minor success the year before, and the team soon got down to business.

It was a slow building process, and 2006 would serve more as a platform than a breakthrough season. The foundations were being laid and with a top crop of young players coming through the future looked bright. One of those young stars, Johnny McCaffrey, though only just out of minor, brought the club's first Interprovincial Railway Cup medal back to the club that year too, starring for Leinster in their win over Connacht.

Another notable success was recorded in May of that year when another three of the club's successful minor team from the previous year won All-Ireland Colleges medals with Dublin Colleges. Peter Callaghan, Mick May and Gary Coleman were part of the Dublin Colleges team that brought a first ever Senior Colleges All-Ireland title to Dublin, when they defeated a fancied St Flannan's team, coached by former Clare great Jamesie O'Connor, at Dr Cullen Park. Peter Callaghan probably has the unique distinction of being the only Lucan Sarsfields player to play a full All-Ireland final in hurling at the highest grade and collect a winner's medal.

The talent was certainly beginning to emerge throughout the club, and midway through the year the latest batch of youngsters stuck their hands up for attention. The under-13 hurlers became the latest team to make club history, securing the club's first juvenile A hurling title with victory in the P.J. Troy Cup Division 1 final. Of that successful team, eight players went on to play for the West Dublin Development Squad: Oisín McCabe, Chris Crummy, Seán McClelland, David Bellew, Matthew McCaffrey, Shane Claffey, Shane Donohue and Emmett Ó Conghaile.

The club's hurlers were knocking on the door in the adult grades as well. The 2005 under-21 championship wasn't run off until early 2006, where a nine-point haul from Kevin O'Reilly couldn't prevent the team losing out to Ballyboden by 1-16 to 0-15 in the first round. However, there was a marked improvement in the 2006 under-21 campaign which began in October.

A 0-13 to 0-5 win over St Brigid's in Russell Park got the season under way, and a sparkling 0-12 to 0-4 win over near neighbours Round Towers in the 12th Lock a month later saw the team through to a county semi-final.

Croabh Chiaráin provided the opposition in Clonshaugh two weeks later, and, after a truly epic tussle in front of a massive crowd, the sides could not be separated in extra time and were forced to a replay in Russell Park four days later.

Kevin O'Reilly had starred for the Lucan men in the first drawn game, notching up twelve points along the way, and he was again to the fore under the lights in Blanchardstown. There was heartbreak in store for Lucan yet again though – and once more after extra time – as Craobh emerged winners of an epically contested replay.

The senior footballers were enjoying a solid first year under their new management team, which now included Fergus McNulty, Donal Griffin, Conor Bresnan, Brian Redmond, Noel Buggie and Thomas Birch.

A wonderful league run had seen the team finish in joint fifth place, tied with arch rivals St Mary's of Saggart. The two sides battled it out in a play-off to see who would advance to the league semi-final, but after an epic battle it was the Saggart men who emerged on top, thanks to a dramatic late goal. Lucan had a chance to snatch victory from the jaws of defeat right at the death, but were denied by the post.

The championship had actually been a big jump forward for the team in many people's minds. There was certainly no shame in the team's second-round loss to eventual champions UCD, and from there Lucan progressed on through the back-door system. Victories over Thomas Davis and Raheny helped Lucan into the last eight, but that was as far as they would go, losing out 0-11 to 0-8 at the hands of Kilmacud Crokes in a game that was actually televised live on Setanta Sports.

The football section of the club were desperate for a trophy to cement their ever-improving efforts. In the latter part of 2006, finally, that magical day for Lucan Sarsfields arrived in the form of the first ever A football championship crown, the under-21 footballers the team providing the watershed moment.

Manager Alan Curtis and his team, ably assisted on the sidelines by Brendan Gallagher Snr and the guts of the senior football management team, began the season with wins over Skerries Harps and St Brigid's. Lucan had come back from seven points down with seven minutes left to defeat the Blanchardstown men.

Before they knew it, Lucan found themselves in a first under-21 county football final, but with an uphill battle against the cream of the county at the grade. Kilmacud Crokes entered the final as red-hot favourites, and they showed why they were so hotly fancied as they built a 0-6 to 0-2 half-time lead.

A gutsy fight back saw the Sarsfields men get back to within a point as normal time elapsed, before a stunning finish from wing back Peter Callaghan sent the Lucan line into raptures and the county final into extra time.

Crokes rushed into yet another lead as extra time kicked on, but points from Gallagher brothers Bren and Dan brought Lucan back to the verge of victory before Peter Kelly secured the club's first A football title with the game's only goal late on.

Club secretary Paul Stapleton noted in his annual report that:

> The under-21 Football Championship success was achieved within 12 months of securing our first A hurling title. After 118 barren years in terms of A championships, a minor hurling title in 2005, followed by an under-21 football title in 2006, suggests that we are making progress as a club. We have players who are winners and who want to win more. It also shows that we can successfully combine hurling and football and, in my view, we should continue in that vein and pursue greater success in both codes.

Indeed, many of the 2006 football championship winners had also been on the successful minor hurling title team in 2005, in the form of David Quinn, Peter Kelly, Johnny McCaffrey, Peter Callaghan, Mick May and Niall Gleeson. The dual stars of the future were emerging.

In 2006, the hurling alley, named in honour of former chairman Paddy Kelly, was officially unveiled. While this latest addition to the club's facilities was being unveiled, plans had already been made for a more significant addition, an all-weather playing pitch. The new all-weather facility, which was eventually completed in December 2009 and officially opened by An Taoiseach Brian Cowen in January 2010, was already in gestation back in 2006 and took a total of five years to reach culmination.

Back in February 2005, following a debate at the AGM, then chairman Paul McGann established a subcommittee to review and develop proposals for an all-weather pitch in response to a growing realisation that the club's playing facilities were not adequate to cater for the ever-increasing numbers in the club, and that following the completion of the new clubhouse in 2002, the focus of the next stage of the club's development needed to be on playing facilities. The shortage of adequate winter training facilities was very acute, so this was identified as a priority.

Seamus Morris programme, 2005.

The subcommittee, which included Michael O'Grady, Niall Carabini, Fergus Gordon and Ken Robinson, completed their work during that year and reported back with some options in the autumn. In November 2005, the executive called a special general meeting to seek support for a proposal to proceed with the development of a 6,000 square metre all-weather pitch on the site of the training pitch at a cost of €500,000.

The meeting was quite divisive, with strong support for a number of alternative options being touted and the result was a resounding defeat for the executive's proposal. It was a difficult night, and few would have predicted then that the initiative, begun by Paul McGann in February 2005, would eventually come to fruition five years later.

Mick Roche became Chairman in 2006 and set an objective of finding a way to develop playing facilities. Discussions with South Dublin County Council were initiated to see if they might be open to the development of the council lands at Grange (opposite Fossett's Circus). There had been several tentative discussions about that site previously that never came to anything, but this latest initiative quickly bore fruit and agreement in principle was reached with South Dublin County Council.

In September 2006, just ten months after the previous proposal was

Above: Division 1 camogie league winners, Under-12, 2006.

Below: Peter Callaghan and parents Marie and Bernard with the All-Ireland Senior A Colleges trophy, 2006.

soundly defeated, the executive called another special general meeting to consider an all-weather pitch proposal. This time the proposal was to develop a full-size pitch at Grange for a cost of €1.25m. It received the support of almost all the members. It looked like a major step forward in playing facilities was about to be taken.

Fate intervened however, when the Grange project was thwarted, initially by a legal dispute and then by the economy. The legal dispute related to the Tallaght Stadium Project and had nothing to do with Lucan Sarsfields, but South Dublin County Council were not willing to enter into long-term lease arrangements with any clubs until the issue was resolved.

By the time those issues were resolved it was already too late. The building boom was come and gone and the economy was faltering, and South Dublin County Council were unable to progress with the initial development of the Grange site which was required to allow the club to install the all-weather pitch. South Dublin County Council had planned the initial development of the site in conjunction with the next phase of the Adamstown development, but both remain stalled to this day.

Subsequently, the 2008 AGM saw Paul Stapleton replace Mick Roche as chairman and many new faces appeared on the club executive. Once it had become clear that the Grange option could not be progressed, the new committee turned their minds to other options, and the original 2005 proposal was again on the table. A plan was developed which included an all-weather pitch on the old training pitch as originally envisaged, and the upgrade of the senior pitch with floodlights, drainage and irrigation and a sand-based surface. This package, budgeted at €1.1m, was put to the members at the 2009 AGM and got almost unanimous support.

A project team lead by vice-chairman Seán Ó Conghaile was quickly mobilised to progress delivery. Gerry McNamara was once again on board and Seamus Fagan was the third member of the team. In parallel, a fundraising drive was launched, with treasurer Eoghan Williams very much to the fore, successfully securing loan approval from Ulster Bank, along with grant aid from the National Lottery and the GAA Leinster Council.

A €100 Club Development Draw was launched in June 2009 and held in October of that year, realising €340,000 in proceeds and a profit of €250,000. This was co-ordinated by a team that included Mark Smith, Ben Murphy, Diarmuid Dawson, Dave Byrne, Eamon Cuggy, Dara Keher, Niall Carabini and many others. However, as secretary Derek Quilligan recalled in his annual report in February 2010, the fundraising project had been rescued from the brink by a late, late surge from within the club:

Five days before the night of the All-Weather Development Draw, consideration was given to postponing the draw as we were unlikely to make the necessary ticket sales. What happened over the next few days was extraordinary. Every section of the club rallied to produce a flow of tickets into the club that became a flood on the night of the draw. We finished up selling 3,400 tickets, raising €100,000 in less than a week and raising almost €250,000 in all. We look forward to the completion of Phase Two of the project later in the year.

Meanwhile, Ó Conghaile and his team were progressing the project plans in tandem with the fundraising. Work commenced on site in September 2009 and the pitch was completed in December. It was officially opening by An Taoiseach Brian Cowen on 31 January 2010, almost five years to the day from when Paul McGann initiated the concept at the 2005 AGM. After five years of gestation, some procrastination, a little frustration and a lot of perspiration, the club finally had a modern all-weather facility. It was another giant leap into the future for the club.

Back in 2006, there had been sadness for the club with the sudden deaths of former Junior B football championship medal winner Fintan McCarthy and his partner Sonya Rabbitte in a tragic car crash in China, while other long-serving clubmen Philip Coffee, Christy O'Grady and Tony Price also passed away.

These were changing times for the GAA generally. In 2007, Croke Park was opened up to rugby and soccer internationals, and the Gaelic Players Association was growing ever more influential, as exemplified by the strike of the Cork hurlers that same year. The increased number of inter-county games was beginning to have a serious impact on club competitions all over the country, and, as a result, games were either delayed or abandoned and some competitions not even completed at all.

Lucan could do little other than get their heads down and get on with the business at hand, and no team did that with more aplomb in 2007 than the club's minor hurlers.

With most of the 2005 minor A championship winning team having moved on beyond the age group, Lucan entered the B competition. After two draws and a win in the round robin stages, Lucan progressed from the group in second place to book a date with Erin's Isle in the last four. A late Barry Torsney goal, added to an eight-point haul from David Quinn, saw Lucan emerge as 3-11 to 3-7 victors, and a date in the final against St Oliver Plunkett's/Eoghan Ruadh lay in store.

Goals from Alan Whyte, Sujon Alamgir, and two from David Quinn fired

Lucan to a 4-5 to 1-9 win at Parnell Park, after a battling display against dogged opposition. Peter Kelly had been a rock in the half-back line in that decider, and his brilliant year also consisted of leading the county's minor hurlers to an All-Ireland semi-final appearance after scoring a point in the Dubs' thrilling 2-14 to 1-10 Leinster Minor Hurling Championship win over Kilkenny in the Leinster final.

Despite the fact that this was the B championship, hurling in the club was clearly on the up and up, and no more so than at senior level. Seán McCaffrey and his team began their second year in charge with vast improvements immediately evident all round. League wins against Naomh Mearnóg, St Vincent's, Faughs and Cuala had confidence high in the camp, and challenge matches and Leinster League games against the likes of St Martin's and Young Irelands of Kilkenny meant Lucan were improving with every day out.

By September, the team was in flying form, and a huge psychological boost arrived in their opening championship outing when they secured a first-ever senior championship win over county big guns Craobh Chiaráin, by 2-13 to 1-8, in Craobh's own backyard of Parnell Park.

Wins over a South Dublin regional team and Faughs followed, leaving Lucan top of the group, and a date with St Brigid's in the last eight secured. Whereas the big day had often got to the senior team in the past, there was no such wilting this time around, and a brilliant display saw Lucan emerge 1-13 to 0-11 and into a county semi-final for the first time ever.

Awaiting them there was the star-studded blue and white of Ballyboden St Enda's. In the end, the weight of having played five championship games in the space of forty days proved too much for Lucan to handle, and Enda's emerged 4-12 to 0-13 winners. Though disappointed, the heads were far from dropped in the Lucan dressing room. This had been the club's best ever championship performance, and there would be more good news for the small ball game before the year was out.

Johnny McCaffrey, who had captained the county to Leinster minor success in 2005, was joined by Barry Aird, Peter Callaghan and Kevin O'Reilly as the county's under-21s repeated their provincial success of two years previously, with Johnny again as captain. An All-Ireland semi-final win over Derry a few weeks later saw the Dubs into a first ever All-Ireland under-21 hurling final, only for Galway to end the dream at the final hurdle, despite Peter Callaghan holding superstar Joe Canning to a single point from play. It had been yet another sterling year for Lucan Sarsfields' hurlers, and before the year was out, another trip to an A county championship final would be secured.

Stiofán Ó Conghaile, Gerry McNamara and Ollie Mann at the launch of the Club Development Draw in June 2009.

Lucan began their 2007 under-21 A hurling championship campaign with a win away to St Brigid's when a late Paddy Brennan goal saw Lucan home by the minimum – 1-7 to 1-6. O'Toole's were accounted for in Blunden Drive by 0-8 to 0-4 in the quarter-final, and a tricky trip to Cuala awaited in the last four.

Lucan was not to be denied in a second championship semi-final in the space of three months though, and a David Quinn goal ensured the team yet another appearance in a county final. Unfortunately, due to lack of progress on the other side of the draw, Lucan would be forced to wait over a year before getting the chance to compete in that county final – a game that would not be played in the end until 14 December 2008.

The senior footballers, meanwhile, took a step back from their 2006 progress, exiting the championship tamely at the hands of Division 2 side Whitehall Colmcilles, though a mid-table finish at least kept the side in the top flight. The under-15 footballers provided the only piece of silverware for the football fraternity in the club in 2007, defeating Castleknock by 3-11 to 2-8 in the B championship final in the Naul.

The Dublin 15 side would gain an element of revenge in the under-14 A hurling Féile semi-final though, narrowly defeating an injury-ravaged Lucan side in the semi-final. That same Castleknock team would go on to win the All-Ireland A Féile title later in the year, so as the form book went, Lucan were certainly playing right up there with the big boys when it came to producing talented young hurlers.

It was a mixed year overall, but a hugely successful one for the underage camogie section in particular, which was enjoying a renaissance of unheralded proportions after four years of nursery coaching and development within the club. Liam Ryan was leading the charge and in the space of a few short years, Lucan would go on to become the leading lights in the ladies game underage, not only in Dublin, but all over the country.

Former club chairman Gerry McAndrew says:

The development of camogie in this club has been exceptional in the last decade really. While there are a huge number of very committed people involved in that section of the club, it really all started with one man, when Liam Ryan just decided that this was the way it was going to go. He built the structures that made it all happen, and the underage section's two All-Ireland titles really are probably the most substantial on-field successes of the last ten years.

As Liam himself recalls, it had all come about by accident:

My daughter Ailbhe was always very interested in sport, and I think she was in senior infants when we got her going on the camogie. There are probably five or six girls that got started around that time that all have All-Ireland medals now after starting on that same day.

In about 2002, when those girls were about five or six, we noticed a boys' nursery hurling session going on up in Willsbrook. Joe Whyte used to bring his daughter Kate up to the boys' nursery where he was coaching – she would have been about eight months older than our girls – and she'd be the only girl up there.

I arrived up with a few more girls the following week, and after a few weeks up there we realised we had about five or six girls who were keen. We sort of thought that if we could get another five or six girls up and involved we'd have a team. We sent the girls away then and told them to bring a friend up with them the following week and that was the beginnings of it.

I remember seeing a document coming out from the club around that time where the chairman was saying how camogie had fallen away in the club. There had been a good team under Deirdre Russell – they would have been about under-16 at the time – but the problem was that nothing was coming behind it.

The policy aim the club had at the time was that, within five years, by 2008, there would be teams at under-12, under-14 and under-16. I remember thinking to myself at the time about how Lucan ticked a lot of boxes in what we could achieve; there was money there, a strong population, and at the time there was nothing there for girls to do at all. There was only stage school really, there was no ladies soccer team or anything like that really.

I remember thinking then too that there must have been a lot of young girls out there looking for something to do. We really didn't know how it would go down, whether camogie was just a dying thing or what the story was, because I'd never really been involved with it before.

I'd been involved with the Camogie Féile team in Clara that won the All-Ireland in 1992, but that was the country and a lot of those girls' brothers would have played hurling and the likes. So we had no idea how this was going to go down in Lucan.

I remember the first time we played a couple of matches, against Good Counsel and Erin's Isle – sure we were terrorised. We got an under-12 team up and going then, where we would have roped in the likes of Marie Moynihan and Niamh Nolan. But it was tough going at the start because a lot of these girls were only picking up a stick for the first time at 11 or 12. They were the first girls really, they would have been born in 1991 or 1992.

We started in 2003, but we really got going properly in 2004 and entered a few leagues. It was very slow going though, I don't think we won an A title until 2007. We won a few bits and pieces at Division 2 and 3 in 2005 and 2006, but in 2007 the under-11 team won the first A title. They went on to win the All-Ireland Féile then last year [2010].

It took four years before we really began to make progress. I don't know if I really had an overall plan in mind for the whole thing when we started this first, but I did decide early on that I wouldn't get involved in the running of any particular team and that I would try and stay back and take a long-term view.

Luckily enough Joe Whyte was there to take my daughter's team, and that I'd try and find managers for all the other teams. That has worked because we were always learning. I never believed in an uneven system where you might have a strong team at one age and weak team at another. I always felt that if you were organising it properly that you should have every year more or less the same results. Sort of like the Leaving Cert. And if you did have one particularly bad year you'd know you'd gone wrong somewhere or that something wasn't right in a set-up. That's always been the philosophy to try and even everything out, and I think that has worked. Funny enough, we thought this year's [2011] Féile team might have been weaker than previous years but they are after doing great work and they look now like they could be as good as any other team we ever had.

That structure has indeed worked and many great things would follow for camogie before the end of the decade. The under-12s had defeated St Vincent's in an epic Division 1 league final in 2006 to get the top-grade trophy haul off to a start, but in 2007 the first championship would finally arrive. And in the three years since, the camogie section have gone on to win two All-Ireland Féiles (in 2008 and 2010) and numerous county A championship titles.

It was an epic turnaround for a section of the club that had all but been extinct just a few years earlier. And the man largely responsible for initiating the renaissance, Liam Ryan, reflected with great pride on the success of the underage game and the breakthrough that ultimately led to national successes:

Our first really big success was a Division 1 under-12 A league title in 2006. We went over to play St Vincent's in their place, and up until that point they would always have looked on us with complete disdain. Vinny's had won something like nine under-16 championships in a row and had practically been in the final at every grade every year.

They had beaten us well in the league in Lucan earlier in the year, but they lost some other game over the course of the summer so it all came down to this one game and we beat them by two points or so.

The organisation of the whole thing was important at that time too. I think we had 120 people on two buses going to Croke Park for the All-Ireland Camogie Final that afternoon after the game. So we arrived over there with two double-decker buses full of people. We filled the sidelines and then we beat them. It was an unbelievable match.

That was the day the Vinny's v. Lucan rivalry began. I suppose we over-celebrated a bit, but it was the first time we'd won anything I suppose.

The first A championship came along in 2007 with Frank Greene's team and they've mopped up the championships ever since then all the way along. They've won championships every year since, last year [2010] we won the under-12, under-14 and under-16 championships as well as a clatter of B championships.

We won our first Féile in 2007 with Lorna Cullen (Quilligan) and Dave Byrne at the helm when they won Division 2. That was a good team actually. It was a mix of older and younger girls and I remember they beat a good Brigid's team in that final.

In 2008 everything went according to plan. The Féile team had lost everything coming up and weren't going that well, but Laura Murtagh came over from the football and that changed everything. She became the captain – indeed she's still the captain of that team – and she was a major factor in actually winning the All-Ireland that year.

We hosted the Dublin Féile that year and everything went well. I remember the County Board were giving out that it was too well organised; sure I remember Dave Keenan had boxes of fruit in every dressing room.

What I remember most of all, I suppose, is beating Vinny's by two points in our crucial group game. We hung on grimly in that game and ended up topping the group and avoiding Plunkett's in the semi-final. Plunkett's beat Vinny's in the semi but they didn't perform in the final and we won it out.

It was on then to the All-Ireland Féile. That competition was not without controversy and the club and team were in the national media spotlight throughout, largely down to a serious issue over the vetting of families hosting players for the national Féile. In the weeks before the All-Ireland finals, the Lucan team management and parents had called into question the Féile na nGael's policy of hosting young girls in family homes. A compromise was eventually reached but the media spotlight remained on Lucan throughout the competition. Within twelve months, the GAA responded to the negative publicity it received on the back of the Lucan Sarsfields controversy and implemented mandatory vetting for Féile host families, and indeed throughout the association.

Despite the controversy, the team headed down to Freshford in search of an All-Ireland to add to their first ever Dublin A crown with Martina McGilloway, Dave Keenan, Eoghan Williams, Antonio Sejean and Liam Ryan at the reins of the team. Liam takes up the story:

We took on Freshford – who had won ten or twelve senior Kilkenny cam-ogie championships at the time – and we beat them. I think they were really stunned. We went on and won an epic semi-final in Borris-in-Ossory in a summer thunder and lightning storm and then went on to the All-Ireland final.

The final was up the road in Portlaoise the next day and we were rat-tled with nerves. We were like a different team. Thankfully, the other team, Mullagh from Galway, seemed to be suffering as badly and we pulled away in the second half and won by four points. It was a marvellous day.

I think when we won our second All-Ireland two years later in 2010 we were much better prepared. There was a bigger crowd at that final in Ennis than there had been two years before in Portlaoise, and everything was bril-liantly organised. It's all a learning curve.

That second All-Ireland Féile camogie title in three years was achieved under the management of Frank Greene, Seamus Power, Kevin Morrissey and Antonio Sejean. Liam Ryan attributes much of the success in camogie to unseen work done by unsung heroes such as Sejean, Ester Keenan and many many others, 'Esther, our County Board Rep, Camogie Registrar, unofficial photographer and supplies the soup all winter long.' He also sees the schools as a vital part of the jigsaw:

> The schools camogie scene was vitally important in the building of a camogie culture in Lucan. The Lucan schools camogie competitions – the Caroline McKeown Cup and the Elaine Kelly Cup – are the bedrock upon which Dublin and All-Ireland successes are built.
>
> In 2006, 2007 and 2008 many of the Lucan Sarsfields camogie girls had been playing for Scoil Mhuire GNS when the school won an unprecedented three-in-a-row Cumann na mBunscol Division One titles on some famous days in Croke Park and Parnell Park. It felt like coming home when we brought the All-Ireland trophy on a tour of the thirteen Lucan primary schools in the week after the 2010 final.

The boys' section of the club, though slowly beginning to amass the A championships in recent years, certainly had a battle on their hands to keep up with the girls. The establishment of a juvenile ladies football nursery in 2008 also meant that the next generation of female club stars is just as likely to be dual.

The club was building from the ground up. In 2007, Adamstown Gaels GAA Club came into existence, and with Westmanstown Gaels by now well established in the area, the battle was on for the youth of the Lucan area. In early 2008, Johnny McCaffrey, by now an established inter-county hurling star, took over as the club's Games Promotion Officer (GPO). It was a positive move and a boost, not just to the club but to the entire GAA in the area, to have a home-grown superstar in the midst of the youth of the town.

The GPO has primarily worked to promote the games in the local schools and bring new players into the club nursery section. The nursery section has grown and developed through recent years with people like Lisa Tuite, Liam Mulhall and others leading the way today, building on the work done by Ronan O'Flynn in the middle part of the decade, and back to Paul McGann and Gerry McAndrew who were to the fore at the end of the nineties. The juvenile section in general has been well served by many very committed administrators during these years of rapid growth, including Josephine Donohue, Alice Whyte, Pat O'Keefe, Frank Fleming and Mark Smith, with Anne Jones and more recently Lorna Murtagh much to the fore in juvenile ladies football.

Back in 2007, the social element of the club was also continuing to prosper, and more medals made their way back to Lucan when Scór teams at adult and juvenile level secured county titles (John O'Keeffe, Ben Egan and Sean Clancy bringing home the Scór na nÓg Tráth na gCeist). This was one of many Scór successes in the decade, as the Irish cultural activities really came to the fore in the club, lead by two stalwarts from Inis Óirr, Seán agus Stiofán Ó Conghaile.

The family fun day, which was launched on Ryder Cup weekend in 2006, was growing exponentially by the year, the club's table quizzes were flying along, and summer camps were becoming a mainstay of the Lucan Sarsfields summer as attendances continued to grow each year. Lucan was growing bigger by the day, and the club was growing with it. By the end of 2010 there were 1,767 members of Lucan Sarsfields GAA Club.

There were changes at the top as the 2008 season began, most notably with Mick Kilduff stepping down from the senior football management position to be replaced by Mick Bohan, who officially took the reins in December 2007. His first season in charge got off to a fine start with a St Vincent de Paul Cup win over Thomas Davis. However, the same opposition would turn things around later in the year to defeat the Lucan men at the semi-final stage. The league brought some encouraging wins, most notably a ten-point victory over All-Ireland champions St Vincent's, but the campaign ended with defeat to Trinity Gaels and a mid-table finish. The championship brought more disappointment.

Wins over Fingallians and St Anne's in the team's first two group games set up an all-or-nothing clash with a star-studded Oliver Plunkett's. Despite a gargantuan effort against a side that would go on to lose the county final in a replay, Lucan were bettered by 0-13 to 0-12 and headed instead for the newly introduced Senior B Football Championship.

Their B campaign began brightly, with wins against Raheny, St Jude's and Round Towers, and by the end of November the team had won through to a final against St Sylvester's. The season ended on a sour note with a two-point defeat at the hands of the Malahide men, but it had been a bright year overall for a young team still absorbing the 2006 under-21 A county champions.

The 2008 senior camogie team, under-14 hurlers, junior ladies footballers and under-13B footballers succeeded where the senior footballers had failed though, bringing trophies back to the club after successful campaigns.

The senior camogie side, under a management team that included Seaghan Ó Lanagáin and Tadhg Clandillon, suffered disappointment in the senior B championship, losing out to Naomh Bríd in the quarter-finals, but they made up for that by winning the Division 3 title by a point from St Vincent's and Portobello. Marie Moynihan represented the club on the county under-16 team, while Audrey Murtagh led the way for the Dublin Senior B team, winning the Player of the Year award at the end of the season.

The under-14 hurlers secured the Division 2 Féile title with a win over St Vincent's, eventually going on to reach an All-Ireland quarter-final where they lost to Slaughtneil of Derry by two points in Shinrone, County Offaly. It was the team's only defeat over the course of their twenty-three-game season.

The ladies junior footballers, in just their fourth year as a team, followed up league and cup wins the previous season with a comprehensive D championship win in 2008, defeating Clann Mhuire in the county final in August. This was the third championship final appearance in three years for the team, with minors and under-16s to the fore, as well as stalwarts like Anne O'Shaughnessy. The club was beginning to rebuild for the future.

The under-13B footballers, meanwhile, enjoyed the distinction of becoming the first B team in club history to win a championship. They defeated Whitehall in the C championship final.

Back at adult level, the senior hurlers were edging ever closer to that elusive championship breakthrough. Once again, however, their progress would be halted by that same big blue and white coloured road block. For the second year in a row, Lucan reached the county semi-final only to be beaten in the last four by Ballyboden St Enda's. It was, by now, becoming trying. But progress was being made.

Wins over Dublin North West, St Jude's and Crumlin saw Lucan top their group unbeaten, and they headed to O'Toole Park to take on O'Toole's in the last eight. A gutsy performance on a tough day saw Lucan to a 0-13 to 0-12 win, and a place in the semi-finals for the second year in a row was secured. A huge crowd flocked to Parnell Park for the rematch with Ballyboden.

After trailing by a single point at the break, Lucan hit the front with a timely goal from Kevin O'Reilly. The massive Lucan crowd began to believe that this could finally be the club's day, but a string of crucial mistakes in the dying embers saw Boden come from behind to eke out a five-point win. Lucan was six points closer to the breakthrough, but the big win still eluded the team.

The players were clearly there though. Johnny McCaffrey, Tommy Somers and Aidan Roche all picked up Blue Star awards for their efforts, while four players made the county panel. There was a sense, not just in Lucan but in the minds of the teams that had seen their progress in recent years, that Sarsfields were coming into their own.

If any more evidence were needed, it arrived in early 2009, though not before another heartbreaking day in late December 2008 for the club's hurlers. The under-21 hurlers, rather amazingly, a full year on to the day since reaching the 2007 A championship final, were fixed to take on Ballyboden in the decider on 14 December 2008. The ridiculously long lay off had been too much for the team though, and a more game-hardened Ballyboden emerged victorious on a scoreline of 1-17 to 1-12, despite a haul of 1-6 from Kevin O'Reilly.

Even more bizarrely, the 2008 championship campaign had begun the month before the completion of the 2007 competition. Lucan had secured a bye past Ballyboden in the first round, before going on to defeat a game Cuala side in the next round by 1-17 to 0-13 in the 12th Lock. Kilmacud Crokes awaited in the championship semi-final. After a somewhat nervy display away in Stilorgan, shipping two late goals, Lucan emerged 1-12 to 2-6 winners to book a date in their second county final in the space of six weeks. Na Fianna awaited. Finally played on 31 January 2009, an absolute thriller ensued in Russell Park.

Trailing by 0-7 to 0-4 at the break, Lucan were up against it. But they dug deep and reduced the deficit shortly after the restart. A ding-dong battle ensued until the final few minutes, when Na Fianna hit the front with a hotly disputed goal. With time ticking away, Lucan was awarded a free just outside the twenty-one and Kevin O'Reilly stepped up to blast a top-spin screamer to the back of the Na Fianna net. Extra time followed.

Lucan got the better of the early exchanges in the first half of extra time, pulling away thanks to points from O'Reilly and Aidan Roche. Na Fianna battled on gamely, but Lucan was not to be denied for the second time in less than two months, and they hung on to secure a 1-14 to 1-13 win.

It was a special triumph for team manager Sean McCaffrey, who had been involved with the defeated finalists in the same competition in both 2002 and 2007, and who had been a key figure in driving the club forward to demand and achieve success at the highest level. The 2008 under-21 hurling title was the club's third A championship crown, and a first at under-21 in hurling, adding to the under-21 football crown of 2006 and the minor hurling title of 2005. These were glorious times for Lucan Sarsfields GAA Club.

They were also sad days for the club in those years, with the loss of two of the club's most committed and influential figures. Long-time club men Billy Gogarty (former chairman) and Joe Collins (former club president) passed away. Both had given huge service to the club as players, mentors, officials and leaders. The only solace was that the two great club stalwarts had lived to see the club finally win an A championship.

There had also been an extremely exciting occasion in May 2008 with the visit of former American Football star Dhani Jones as part of a documentary series. Jones, a former linebacker with the Cincinnati Bengals, was making a new television series called *Tackling the Globe* in which he went to various countries around the world to try the native sport. Jones and his TV company entourage brought a great buzz and excitement to the club during this visit,

Lucan Sarsfields and Dublin Under-21 hurling captain Johnny McCaffrey (centre holding cup) celebrates after the Dubs defeated Offaly in the Leinster Under-21 final, July 2007. Johnny was joined on the panel by Lucan's Barry Aird, Peter Callaghan and Kevin O'Reilly.

with hurling legend D.J. Carey among those who came to the club to help coach Dhani. The visit attracted national media attention and the club featured prominently on TV, radio and press that week.

With 2009 having got off to a blistering A championship-winning start, more success duly followed throughout the year, with sixteen more trophies winging their way back to the club, from under-10 hurling all the way up to junior ladies football.

The under-16 hurlers had high hopes of repeating the A championship success of the under-21s later in the year, but they agonisingly lost a county final epic to the old enemy Ballyboden St Enda's. They bounced back from the heartbreak of that defeat with a Division 1 league final win, bringing the top-flight trophy back to the club for the first time since 1998 under the management of Gerry Bellew, Seán Ó Conghaile, Cronan Dooley and Fintan Clandillon, and finishing the year having tasted defeat only twice – to Na Fianna in the league and Ballyboden in the championship final.

It was an extraordinary year for the under-12 division in the club too. The hurlers won three top-grade trophies in an amazing season, starting the year off by winning the Division 1 Cup over Kilmacud Crokes, before going on to beat St Mark's in the final of the Camaint and seeing off St Martin's of Kilkenny and Offaly's Coolderry to win the Leinster League.

Not to be outdone, the footballers comprehensively won the Division 1 South League and Cup competitions. The club had for years aspired to winning Division 1 titles at underage level, and after years of progress with the nursery, things were finally beginning to come to fruition.

The minor footballers, under the management of Declan Torsney, meanwhile, savoured a B championship final win over Ballinteer St John's after

Dublin Ladies Football Junior 'E' Championship Final
O'Toole Park. 7.00 pm Tuesday 4th September 2007

Lucan Sarsfields

1
Maeve Maguire (Capt.)

2
enny Barry

3
Cliona McDonald

4
Imelda Smith

5
atie Dillon

6
Hannah Muldowney

7
Niamh Malone

8
Lorraine Moran

9
Katie McCormack

10
iaine Twomey

11
Siobhan O'Neill

12
Leanne Behan

13
enny Casserly

14
Breege Greenan

15
Helena O'Toole

ubstitutions:

16.	Lisa Heavey
17.	Caoimhe Moran
18.	Orla O'Toole
19.	Michelle Mulvihill
20.	Deirdre Dee
21.	Tracey Burke
22.	Aisling O'Farrell
23.	Suzanne Curran
24.	Kirsty McLoughlin
25.	Carol Byrne

lub Colours:	Green & Black
Mentors:	Tom Casserly
	Ed O'Brien
Referee:	Lee Moroney

Dublin Ladies Football Junior E Championship Final O'Toole Park Tuesday 4th September 2007

Naomh Fionnbarra
v
Lucan Sarsfields

Referee: Lee Moroney

Throw-In: 7.00 pm

Above: Ladies football programme, 2007.

Below: Under-14 Féile hurlers, 2007.

Fachtna 'Doc' Clandillon entertaining the members late at night in the clubhouse in 2008. Doc now lives and works in Nepal, where he set up a charity called nagarhope to help the under-privileged children there.

having been defeated in the league final, and the ladies' Junior footballers continued their amazing run with a second championship in two years.

This time it was the C championship competition, beating Ballinteer by 3-7 to 1-9. Unfortunately, the team would struggle in 2010 and would eventually be disbanded after just a few games. But the establishment of a Gaelic4Mothers team in the club, under an initiative of the Ladies Gaelic Football Association of Ireland, offered a new outlet for ladies football in the club.

Elsewhere, the senior footballers claimed their most impressive win to date under new boss Mick Bohan, when they defeated reigning All-Ireland champions Kilmacud Crokes in the first round of the championship. It was a much-needed boost.

Wins over St Mark's and Raheny followed, but the team's championship run came to an end when they were drawn to face Ballyboden St Enda's in the fourth round. Boden would go on to win the competition outright. Clearly things were beginning to progress towards the ultimate goal.

The league campaign had begun with a home win over Na Fianna, and ended with an element of revenge thanks to a win over recently crowned county champions Ballyboden. The team finished mid-table, but perhaps the most interesting aspect of the team's final game had been the fact that it was the first ever played under floodlights at the 12th Lock.

The senior hurlers must have by now been wondering just what they had to do to take a similar jump forward. For the third year in a row, the team exited the championship at the semi-final stage. This time it was Craobh Chiaráin who inflicted the fatal blow, by a single point.

The team fought bravely on in the league, however, and wins over

Left: Mary Harney opening the hurling alley, 2008.
Right: Former chairman Paddy Kelly, to whom the Hurling Alley is dedicated.

Below: Junior ladies footballers, 2008.

O'Toole's, Faughs, Kilmacud Crokes, Crumlin, Naomh Fionnbarra, St Jude's and Ballyboden B, securing Lucan their highest ever placing in a senior league, in second place at the end of the regular season. The reward was a first ever appearance in a senior league final, and an away date with team's nemesis, Ballyboden St Enda's.

It was the same old story for a by now manically frustrated Lucan team. Two Boden goals either side of half-time knocked the stuffing out of the Sarsfields, and, in the end, they were left to rue a 3-10 to 1-9 defeat in a game they really could, and perhaps should, have won.

For once it wasn't all doom and gloom though. Victories over Cú Chulainn's of Antrim, Glenealy of Wicklow, Clonakenny of Tipperary and Meelick Eyrecourt in the final secured the Kevin's eleven-a-side tournament, a long overdue trophy for the long-suffering hurlers of the club.

Lucan are simply 'D' best
Sarsfields secure championship for the first time

LUCAN Sarsfields junior ladies football team had plenty to cheer about in Balgriffin on Sunday when they claimed the Junior 'D' Championship title.

It was a case of third time lucky for the Lucan girls who lost in two previous finals in the last four years.

The Lucan girls were full value for their victory with their forward line delivering big performances to clock up a couple of fine scores.

LUCAN 7-9
CLANN MHUIRE ...2-10

The scoreline may suggest a one-sided match, but Clann Mhuire did have their moments in the first half and indeed got off to a better start.

The northsiders controlled the opening eight minutes scoring two points before Sarsfields settled and hit back with a spectacular goal through Leanne Mahon.

Lucan's lead was short lived as Mhuire responded immediately with a goal to move into a six point cushion.

One of the key moment arrived mid-way through the half when Lucan's veteran keeper Ann O'Shaughnessy, who is mother of Dubs star Stephen, pulled off a superb save to deny Mhuire a nine point cushion.

Lucan grew in confidence after this and finished the half strongly with Niamh

Nolan, Elaine Twomey, Siobhan O'Neill and Behan registering scores to leave it 3-7 to 1-8 in their favour at the break.

The second half saw the Naul side do their best to break down Lucan, but with Cliona McDonald, Michelle Kelly and Amy Martin standing out, there was no way through.

Clann Mhuire could only manage to score a goal and two points as Lucan picked off the scores with ease.

Twomey added another goal in the second half while Elaine Moran, Siobhan O'Neill and Behan tagged on further scores.

It was a great achievement for the Lucan management team of Tom Casserley, Ed

O'Brien and Brian Prendergast.

"We are delighted for the girls'," remarked Lucan mentor Tom Casserley.

"We had to work hard for this win and the team worked hard in the second half to get the scores," he added.

LUCAN SARSFIELDS: A O'Shaughnessy, T Burke, C

McDonald, M Kelly, K Dillon, H Muldonwey, N Malone, N Nolan, E Downes, L Heavey, S O'Neill, L Behan, E Twomey, L Moran, H O'Toole. Subs: A Martin for Muldowney, L Murtagh for Burke, E Cooney for Heavey, I Smith for O'Toole, A O'Farrell for Twomey.

The Lucan team that won the Junior 'D' Final while (inset) the team celebrate at the final whistle.

Ladies football report, *Echo*, 2008.

All-weather pitch, work in progress, 2009.

Top: Ladies football Féile team, 2009.
Middle: Senior hurler and local teacher Cronan Dooley with children attending Social Inclusion Day, 2008.
Bottom: Under-12 girls footballers, 2008.

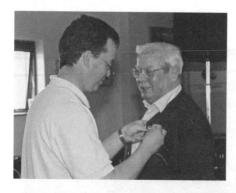

Left: Chairman Paul Stapleton appointing Don Dardis as Club President on Lá na gClub, May 2009.

Below: Ladies football Junior C Championship winners, 2009.

The year ended on a happy note too, when the team secured the title of Etihad Best Club Under the Sun and won themselves a trip to Abu Dhabi for a week of training with Tipperary legend Nicky English. Blue Star awards for Johnny McCaffrey and Peter Kelly rounded out a successful year for the team, and they would go into 2010 season with hope springing eternal that the elusive county final appearance might finally be on the horizon.

The year 2010 was to be one of major achievement for the club. The juvenile camogie section enjoyed another amazing year, winning a second All-Ireland Division 1 Camogie Féile, and Division County titles at under-12, -14, -16 and minor level, while the club's intermediate camogie team enjoyed a successful run of their own in winning the league and championship double under the management of Gerry O'Grady, Keith Brennan, Liam Martin and Willie Ruane.

The inter team played sixteen matches in total and finished the season undefeated, seeing off the challenge of Trinity Gaels in the county final in August. They then added the league title with victory over Clanna Gael in October, rounding off a sensational year. And, perhaps even more encouragingly, this promotion coincided with the arrival of the first stream of All-Ireland Féile winners.

The under-16s completed their amazing juvenile careers in 2010 in fitting style, defeating old rivals St Vincent's by 3-6 to 0-9 in the county final; in the process securing their third championship in a row after wins at under-14 and under-15 level, to add to their Dublin and All-Ireland Féile titles. The club had never seen their like.

The senior camogie team, meanwhile, reached the semi-final of the Leinster League, lost in the league final, and lost out in the quarter-final of the championship to Skerries by a point in a tense battle. It was a disappointing end to the year, but the future had never looked brighter for adult camogie in Lucan Sarsfields.

The club's underage hurlers continued their success in their respective leagues, with the under-10s winning their league and the Division 1 Camaint title. The under-14 and under-15 hurlers won promotion to Division 1 and Division 2 respectively, with the under-15s being unlucky not to pick up a championship win also. Brian Flynn's charges were narrowly pipped by Faughs in the final.

The minor hurlers also enjoyed a solid year, if disappointed at not having secured the silverware they so badly desired. The team competed in Division 1 and took part in the A championship. The league campaign had begun in ideal fashion with a quality win over eventual county champions Kilmacud Crokes. Wins over Castleknock and St Vincent's followed, but the team eventually finished the year in mid-table.

The championship began with a seriously tough task in the form of a trip to face favourites St Jude's. But the team put in their best performance of the year to emerge victors before moving on to face Ballyboden in their

Ladies Junior Football Championship winners, 2009.

Scór Cast, 2009. Left to right, back: Michael O'Grady, Donal Downes, Brian Flynn, Eoin Mullarkey, Sean Flynn. Front: Stiofán Ó Conghaile, Seamus Clandillon, Helen Ryan.

second group game. St Enda's saw off the Lucan challenge with a couple of points to spare, and the team's season came to an end with defeat to old rivals Castleknock. There was plenty of talent coming through the ranks though, with four of the team earning representative honours with the county.

The senior hurlers, with hopes higher than ever that the breakthrough was on its way, kicked off the year with a series of Boland Cup games before settling in to the Leinster League campaign. The team got off to a flier in the competition, and after wins over Marshallstown, Borris-in-Ossory, Ringtown of Westmeath and Geraldine O'Hanrahans of New Ross in the semi-final, Lucan found themselves in a final against Shamrocks of Wexford.

The game took place in Nowlan Park prior to the Leinster Senior Hurling Championship quarter-final meeting of Galway and Wexford, but in the end the Model County side scrambled to a 2-11 to 2-7 win, despite a contribution of 1-6 from Tommy Somers.

All the same, the scene was set for a big charge. The championship system had been changed for the umpteenth time ahead of the 2010 season and with two groups of six now the format, Lucan were drawn to face Craobh Chiaráin, Cuala, St Jude's, Crumlin and St Brigid's.

With the tricky prospect of five games ahead, Lucan defeated a strong Craobh side in the 12th Lock by 2-15 to 1-10. The stunning win was followed by an away win over Cuala, and at this point Lucan looked set to top the group and earn themselves a more favourable quarter-final draw.

However, on a disappointing night in Tymon Park, St Jude's pulled off a massive upset, beating Lucan by 2-14 to 2-9. A win over Crumlin in the team's next game in Newcastle six weeks later made sure of a place in the quarter-finals, but a very disappointing loss at the hands of St Brigid's in the final round robin game meant the team would be forced to take the scenic route.

Little did they know, however, just how treacherous that route would turn out to be. Due to a series of surprise results in the other group, Lucan would once again be drawn to face Ballyboden St Enda's for the third time in four years in the knockout stages.

Having lost the previous three county semi-finals by eleven, five and one point respectively, Lucan left themselves with it all to do against the reigning champions, trailing by 0-11 to 0-6 at the break. Boden pulled away in the second half, and with ten minutes remaining Lucan found themselves six points down.

With the painful memories of the last three seasons spurring the side ever onwards, Lucan battled on gamely to record the last five scores of the game. It wasn't enough though, and for the third time in four seasons, Ballyboden had knocked Lucan out of the Dublin championship. On every one of those occasions, however, Enda's would go on to win the county title. The gap was closing.

The team's league form had been just as impressive, finishing third in the table and needing to beat Ballyboden to earn a shot at Craobh in the county decider. Not for the first time, however, Boden came good on home soil in Sancta Maria and Lucan had ended another tremendously promising campaign with an empty trophy cabinet.

Lucan went in search of consolation though, also under the senior management, when the under-21 campaign began a month later. St Jude's provided the opposition in Tymon Park, and after a truly epic battle the sides could not be separated. Due to fading light, no extra time was played and a replay pencilled in. That replay did not finally take place until February 2011, and after another tight battle the hunger of the Templeogue men won through and Lucan had finished the 2010 season with nothing to show for their efforts.

One massively bright light that had emerged from the season, though, was the development of Peter Kelly. The former Leinster minor championship medal winner added an under-21 Leinster medal to his collection after the Dubs defeated Kilkenny in the semi-final and Wexford in Parnell Park in the provincial decider, before exiting at the hands of Galway in the All-Ireland semi-final. He also picked up the Young Hurler of the Year award for his tremendous season with the county at under-21 and senior grades.

David Quinn had also been a part of that Dublin under-21 hurling team – but that success was only a small part of the dream year 2010 had in store for him. Quinn, along with Colm Larkin, also won Leinster and All-Ireland honours with Dublin under-21 footballers and further success was to follow with the club later in the year.

With the club's hurlers still knocking on the door in search of that simple stroke of luck they needed to turn their ever-more frustrating fortunes around, the club's footballers were in search of a similar dose of good fortune. Things, on paper at least, did not look bad for the state of the big ball game in the club at adult level. The minors, under-21s and seniors were all competing in Division 1, while the club's second adult team were gamely in the hunt for promotion back to Division 3, and the third football team realistically hoping for promotion back to Division 8.

The third adult team – the Junior As – had for years competed in Division 7 and were keen to secure their way halfway back to where they feel they rightly belong. After a campaign that saw them secure twelve wins and a draw from fourteen league games, they achieved their ambition in October with plenty to spare over St Anne's in their final league game.

With four players on the county panel, meanwhile, the club's minors had hopes of putting together a serious league and championship challenge. They got their season off to a bright start with league wins over St Vincent's and Clontarf, but would eventually finish outside of the money due largely to a defeat at the hands of Ballymun and a draw with Ballinteer.

The draw for the championship saw the team down to face St Vincent's, Erin's Isle and Thomas Davis. A narrow one-point loss away to Vinny's in the opener and a subsequent defeat to Thomas Davis meant that not even a win over Isles in the final game had been enough to see them through to the knockout stages. It was a disappointing end to the year, but with many of the team's stars eligible again in 2011, the future remained full of promise.

While the Junior As were busy earning promotion, the intermediate footballers were embarking on a stunning campaign through the minefield that was Division 4 of the Dublin adult football league.

The team had begun their Intermediate Football Championship campaign in hugely impressive style with a win over Division 3 side Garristown, but Division 2 outfit Cuala proved a bridge too far in the second round. The second-chance saloon came in the form of St Vincent's, but after missing two penalties, the Gods frowned upon Lucan in extra-time of a thriller, as Vinny's emerged the narrowest of victors.

It mattered little in the grand scheme of things to the management team of Ger Gleeson and Mike Nolan; the main goal for the year was promotion to the third flight of Dublin adult football. Ideally, the team would have liked to have done so by winning the league outright, but there was to be no stopping the high-flying Ballyboughal, who won their first fourteen games in a row to secure the league title.

Two teams went up though, and Lucan were still in with a shout of grabbing a place in the top five and securing a bash at the playoffs. They were left in need of a win against the champions Ballyboughal in their final game to

Above left: Club members Alan McCarthy, Josephine Donohue, Ollie Mann, Dara Keher and Colette Condon prepare a Time Capsule which was buried at the 12th Lock on Lá na gClub, May 2009, celebrating the GAA's 125th Anniversary.

Above right: Club members Liam Carton, Seaghan Ó Lanagáin and Peter Flannery review some memorabilia on Lá na gClub, May 2009, celebrating the GAA's 125th Anniversary.

Below: The 'Mama Mias!' Gaelic4Mothers panel, 2009.
Bottom: Adult camogie players, 2009.

Under-21 football team who defeated Na Fianna to win the A Championship Final
at Parnell Park in 2010.

do just that, and it seemed the odds were against them. However, with the
return of former senior stars and Dublin senior hurlers Johnny McCaffrey
and Peter Kelly, they found a way to get it done, eventually emerging convincing seven-point winners.

Lucan were drawn to face St Pat's of Donabate in the playoff semi-finals,
and after another solid performance they won through by 2-12 to 2-6
thanks to a late insurance goal from Niall Gleeson. The final game of the
season followed on 14 November, and after a tight battle in the 12th Lock,
Lucan emerged victorious once more on a 1-8 to 1-5 scoreline over St
Brigid's to achieve their ultimate aim of promotion to Division 3.

The senior footballers, meanwhile, got their season off to the perfect start
with a fine league win over Na Fianna. However, a miserable run of results
followed, and the low point of senior football in the club for many years
arrived mid-way through the year when the team conceded a walkover to
St Vincent's in the league. It was a low point, but the team turned things
around and soon set about embarking on their finest run in many years in
the top flight.

From May to September the team went unbeaten in all competitions.
The run included league wins over Fingal Ravens, St Mary's, St Jude's,
Trinity Gaels and St Oliver Plunkett's. But not least prominent in that run
was a 1-10 to 0-10 victory over St Sylvester's in the St Vincent de Paul Cup
final in Parnell Park on July 16 – the club securing a first senior football
trophy since a 2005 win in the same competition.

That run of form throughout the summer had Lucan in fine fettle head-

Club stalwart Kevin Condron who passed away in 2010, pictured with son-in-law and former club player and mentor John Grimes.

ing into their championship opener against Clontarf in Russell Park. After a solid win against the northside outfit, Lucan took on Raheny in the second round in Newcastle and looked impressive in seeing them off, as their momentum carried the team to another win over Fingal Ravens. All that led to a place in the quarter-final, and a date in O'Toole Park with an Oliver Plunkett's team featuring 2010 Footballer of the Year Bernard Brogan amongst a host of other county stars.

It all proved too much for the Lucan men, who completely collapsed in the second half after a bright start, and as Plunkett's pulled away with a string of counter-attack goals, Lucan knew their last remaining hope of silverware would come in the league.

A win over Parnells in the 12th Lock a few weeks later, and a subsequent victory over Thomas Davis, secured Lucan a home semi-final and date with an ever-improving St Jude's side. In the end, however, Lucan fell well short of the mark and their season, which at one point had promised so very much, had ended in serious disappointment.

As the club's 125th anniversary began to loom large on the horizon, there was one final hope of securing an A football championship title. And once again, the magic for the club would come from the under-21 grade.

With the intermediate football management team of Ger Gleeson and Mike Nolan, along with Brendan Gallagher at the reins, Lucan began their A championship campaign with a tricky assignment away to Skerries Harps. After a tough battle in terrible conditions on the northside, Lucan emerged hard-earned winners. There were whispers, but no one dared remind those

Taoiseach Brian Cowen officially opens the new all-weather pitch, January 2010.

Lucan Sarsfields President presents award to Duff

TOM Duff received the 'Volunteer of the Year' award from Lucan Sarsfields President Don Dardis on Sunday night (9th May), at the 12th Lock.

Tom, who originally hails from Laois but is a long time Lucan resident and member of Lucan Sarsfields, received the honour for his relentless work at selling weekly lotto tickets for the 12th Lock outfit.

A car mechanic by trade, Tom never held a position on the Executive Committee of the club but he did manage numerous underage teams in the past. In fact, his two sons donned the colours of Sarsfields, Peter for the club's footballers while Andy was at on stage the captain of the senior hurling team before opting to travel the world.

President of Lucan Sarsfields, Don Dardis, explained that the award was fully deserved.

"Tom is a major seller of tickets for our lotto," he stated.

"He deserved the award because financially the

Lucan Sarsfields President, Don Dardis (left) presents the 'Volunteer of the Year' award to Tom Duff at the 12th Lock last Sunday night.

club needs the lotto to keep itself going."

Lucan Sarsfields Public Relations Officer, Gary Beagan, also outlined why Tom clinched the gong.

"He is one of the biggest lotto sellers in the club and he received the award in recognition of his contribution to helping the club raise much needed

finances," stated Beagan.

"He goes down to Lucan village every weekend, into Courtney's and Kenny's, and he usually sells around 30 booklets. He is a huge seller. He does unbelievable work every weekend.

"It is a thankless job but in the current economic climate it is a very important job."

Tom Duff award article, 2010.

Senior hurlers pictured in Abu Dhabi in 2010, following Lucan Sarsfields winning the Best Club Under the Sun Award in 2009.

involved, aloud at least, how the last time this championship had been won Skerries had been the team dispatched in the opening round.

The first of those obstacles came in the shape of a fancied St Oliver Plunkett's side away in Martin Savage Park. A titanic battle ensued on a beautiful day for football, and county under-21 stars Peter Kelly and David Quinn shone as Lucan emerged impressive victors. Lucan had now earned a home semi-final encounter – but an encounter with championship favourites Kilmacud Crokes.

Crokes came to the 12th Lock expecting to win, but without their senior stars, who were busy preparing for a club All-Ireland semi-final against Crossmaglen. With their own county stars, and the impressive Dermot Gallagher and Stephen Garbutt, Lucan had match winners of their own. After a thrilling clash in front a huge crowd in the 12th Lock, Lucan emerged victorious, as dreams now turned to securing a fourth A grade championship, and a second under-21 football county crown.

The day finally arrived on 9 February in Parnell Park, as Na Fianna came into the game, once again, as raging favourites amongst the neutral to lift the county crown. The Mobhi men expected a tight and intense battle, but with the wind and rain howling, no one on hand could have imagined just what a treat they would have in store. One of the finest games of football played in Parnell Park in recent years, and certainly one of the best football games Lucan have ever been involved in, ensued to the delight of the hundreds of supporters huddled in the stands.

After an epic tussle, Lucan, led by county stars Peter Kelly and David Quinn, and with emerging stars like Stephen Garbutt, Dermot Gallagher, Matthew McCaffrey and Keith Moran to the fore, shocked the county with an amazing victory, coming from seven points down at one stage to win the game by two points.

A pair of Na Fianna goals inside a two minute burst had Lucan struggling with twenty-eight minutes gone in the first half. But a David Quinn bullet

Members of Lucan Sarsfields Social Initiative Group visit Croke Park in April 2011.

and a string of inspirational long-range points from Peter Kelly reeled the gap in to just one point at the interval.

Like the semi-final against Kilmacud Crokes, Lucan finished the stronger, out-scoring the Glasnevin side 1-5 to 0-2 down the closing stretch, capped by Lawrence Alia's forty-ninth-minute goal to give them the lead for the first time of a pulsating final amid sodden and mucky conditions.

It left Lucan a point ahead, one which they stretched to three a couple of minutes into injury time. Na Fianna threw one last attack forward, one which saw the crossbar rattled but it bounced up and over for just a single. It was the second last kick of the night, the last being the resultant kick-out which ushered in the final whistle, confirming Lucan as 2-13 to 2-11 winners on the night.

Ger Gleeson hailed his team's fighting spirit when he spoke to the *Lucan Gazette* immediately after the game. 'I'm just delighted, shocked a bit,' Ger said as he was swarmed by his players and crowds of delighted Lucan support-ers on the pitch in Parnell Park:

> It's unbelievable, but again we came back in the second half. We just didn't turn up for the first 15 minutes, we might have shown them a bit too much respect but the character of our lads to never give up and come back from the dead like that is absolutely fantastic. We lost to them [Na Fianna] at minor but they are a great side and a great club so we wish them well for the future and will definitely go on to senior success with that group so hope-fully we can compete with them.

It was the club's fourth A county title in five years, and with the anniversary celebrations about to get under way, it was an ideal way to round things off. Amazingly, David Quinn and Peter Kelly possessed all four of those county medals.

The under-21 championship looked like the the final crowning success of the 2010 season but just a few weeks later, the emerging camogie queens of the county had the final say.

On 26 March, in Craobh Chiaráin's ground in Clonshaugh, Dave Byrne's minor camogie starlets took to the field to face bitter rivals St Vincent's in the 2010 county A championship final. It was the first opportunity for the emerging camogie section to secure a top-flight championship at adult level. Needless to say, they didn't disappoint.

Goals from Ali Twomey and Sarah Courtney fired the Lucan girls to a 3-3 to 0-5 lead at half time, but with a gale force wind in their backs in the second half, coach Fintan Clandillon knew that Vincent's would come out fighting after the restart. That they duly did and with just a few minutes to go Lucan trailed by two points. However, with inspirational captain Laura Murtagh leading by example, and Kate Whyte pulling off some brilliant saves in the Lucan goal, this was a game the Lucan girls were determined not to leave behind. In injury time, with their season on the line, Lucan pulled victory from the jaws of defeat.

An Ali Twomey free rebounded back out off the upright, and the ball fell to Tara Keenan who stroked the sliotar home to the back of the Vinny's net. Lucan's large travelling support went ballistic, and a sealing free from Twomey put the game beyond the Marino girls as Lucan held on to win an epic by 4-4 to 2-8.

It was a fifth adult A championship title for the club, and a first in camogie. It was also the first time Lucan had ever won two championships in the same year, the minor camogie adding to the under-21 A football championship that had been won just a few weeks before. A very fitting introduction to the club's 125th anniversary year.

The 125th anniversary celebrations began in January 2011 with the visit of President Mary McAleese. Her visit to the 12th Lock was to mark the club's milestone anniversary and to launch the club's participation in the GAA's new Social Initiative programme. The Social Initiative was the brainchild of the President and her husband Dr Martin McAleese, who identified a growing problem of social isolation of older men. Lucan Sarsfields were selected as one of the Dublin clubs to pilot the initiative and it has already been a great success, with many former members and indeed men from the wider Lucan community getting involved in a series of events and trips. For the club, it is a very appropriate way to recognise the contribution of people who gave so much over the years, and particularly apt in the year of the 125th anniversary.

The visit by Uachtarán na hEireann was a very special occasion for the club. Another memorable occasion followed in March 2011, when GAA President Christy Cooney came to the 12th Lock for a special tree-planting ceremony to mark the club's 125th year in existence.

Another major honour came Lucan Sarsfields' way that month when Paul Casey was named as interim Dublin senior football captain. Later that same month, the club's brightest hurling prospect and former Leinster under-21 and minor hurling championship winning captain Johnny McCaffrey was named by Dublin boss Anthony Daly as the captain of the capital's senior hurling team for 2011. That proved to be an inspired choice as, little over a month later, McCaffrey captained Dublin to win the National Hurling League title for the first time in seventy-two years. Lucan were also represented on that team by Peter Kelly. It was a tremendous achievement for Johnny and Peter, and a source of great pride for the club, as the Dr Croke Cup was celebrated in style at the 12th Lock that evening. Further success arrived the following day, as the club's under-14 footballers won the Division 2 Féile title. These successes, in different codes on the national and local stage on successive days, are a measure of the progress made by the club since its formation 125 years previously.

So with the first 125 years of Lucan Sarsfields GAA Club now winding to a close, the club is very much to the fore in all aspects of GAA activity and as a central part of the Lucan community. The future has never looked brighter and, while new challenges undoubtably lie ahead and many goals remain to be achieved, the club is well positioned to look forward in hope and confidence. The club has a proud history, but it is the players and members of today and of the next generations that will write the next chapters. The contribution of those gone before them will ensure that the best is yet to come.

PLAYERS OF THE ERA

Under-9 footballers, 2000/01: A. Dunphy, K. O'Toole, T. Jackman, N. Brehon, P. Dowling, G. Markey, S. O'Brien, S. Stapleton, B. O'Toole, C. O'Neill, L. McClelland, S. Clancy, S. McClelland, A. Parsons, O. Ennis, J. Morris, J. Maher, M. McCaffrey, E. Gray, D. Geheran, J. Manley, A. Conboy, A. Cunningham, D. Byrne.

Under-9 footballers, 1999/2000: Blain Curtis, Stephen Garbutt, Paul Dowling, Simon O'Keeffe, Graham Foley, Glen O'Neill, Declan Weldon, Thomas Jackman, Simon Collins, Colin Murphy, Conor Murphy, Matthew Grant, Alan Parsons, Conor Mongey, Richard Fox, David Courtney, Stephen Curtis, Seán Mulhern, Barry Torsney, Niall Smith, Shane Connolly, Tomás Collander, Rob McNulty and Neal Morrin.

Under-11 hurlers, 2000: Niall Byrne, Brendan Canning, Eoghan Carabini, Ollie Collins, Conor Downes, Seán Durkan, Gareth Hamilton, Dean Hickey, Peter Kelly, David Keogh, Colm Larkin, Joe McErlean, Liam McErlean, Chris O'Connell, Ciarán Roche, Neil Ryan, Alan Whyte.

Under-12 footballers and hurlers, 2000: Rory Mongey, Thomas Fitzpatrick, Aaron Curtis, Samuel Parsons, Ciarán Harte, Peter Carroll, Patrick Moore, Stephen McDonald, Michael Donnelly, Andrew Hope, Alan Croke, Patrick Brennan, Blazio Sempebwa, Niall Gleeson, Michael May, Owen Hughes, Christopher Wright, David Warren, Alan Barrett, Anthony McDonnell, Robert Smyth, Aidan Roche, Seán McGann, John Byrne, Barry Geheran, Naoise Fleming, Michael McInerney, Gearoid Brennan, Seán Kelly, Garry Norton.

Under-13 footballers, 1999/2000: Paul Walsh, Robert Fitzharris, Kevin O'Reilly, Peter Callaghan, Darren Parsons, Stephen Reilly, Darryl Norris, Seán Keane, Garry Coleman, Eamonn Comaskey, Ciarán Donohue, Aaron Doonan, Eoghan Foley, Daniel Howard, Eoin McCarthy, Shane O'Neill, Micheal Muldoon, Stephen Reilly, Colm Stafford, Brendan Gallagher.

Under-13 camogie team, 2000: Aisling O'Carroll, Laura McDonough, C. McStay, C. Casey, Amanda Corcoran, Lorraine O'Neill, Meadhbh Murphy, L. Moody, C. Kirwan, Claire O'Brien, Katie McDonogh, A. Dunphy, Nichola O'Sullivan, Hannah Muldowney, Ciara Meehan, Anne Briody, Róisín O'Grady, Sinéad Keane, Emma McGann, Grace Dowling, Ellen Mongan, Sandra Keenan, Jade Knowles, Ann-Louise Mongan.

Under-13 hurling, 2000: Stephen Reilly, E. McCarthy, Stephen Power, Seán McGann, Shane O'Neill, Aaron Doonan, Gary Manning, Kevin O'Reilly, Peter Callaghan, David Byrne, Darren Anderson, Lorcan O'Connor-Ward, Seán Keane, Niall Guy, Aidan Roche, Adam Lester, Andrew Mockler, Gary Coleman, Paul Curtis, Aaron Curtis.

Under-13 ladies footballers, 2000: Aishling Keating, Claire McKiernan, Maria Geheran, Elaine Twomey, Sinéad Ní Lanagáin, Emer Walsh, Clare Mullarkey, Emer

Keenan, Lynn Galligan, Anne Marie Flynn, Lorna Walsh, Aine Moore, Alison Hickey, Therese Hickey, Fiona Ryan, Niamh Russell, Ruth Dowdall, Caroline Geraghty, Mary Roche, Therese Hanafin, Lorraine Rea, Ciara Reidy, Karen Kenny, Cliona McDonnell, Orla McKelvey.

Under-14 Division 1 Dublin Féile Peil winners, 2000: Kevin Byrne, Ciarán Russell, Donal McNamara, Philip Corcoran, Peter Callaghan, Paddy Lee, Johnny McCaffrey, Kevin Moran, Darragh McCarthy, Gerry O'Brien, Liam Murphy, Andrew O'Neill, Cormac McBride, Shane O'Brien, Colin O'Donnell, John Keating, Kieran Burke, Richard McAndrew, Richard Price, Barry Aird, Niall Healy, Cathal Casey, Michael Kirwan, Gavin Flynn, Fiachra McGrath.

Under-21 hurling, 2000: Niall Clifford, Alan Barnes, Fintan Clandillon, Barry Corcoran, Seán Corkery, Dara Cunningham, Cronan Dooley, Brian Fagan, Fergus Gordon, Gerard McGarry, Michael Mooney, Tony Molton, Eoin Ó Lanagáin, Shane Russell, Paul Clifford, Tomas Cummins, Emmet Farrelly, Barry Hurson, Brendan McGarry, Pierce O'Leary, Alan O'Neill, Brian Percy, Aidan Glover, Ciarán O'Neill, Ger Power, Seán Quinn, Darragh Reidy, Kevin Roche, Tommy Somers, Darragh Brennan, Andrew Duff, Jerome Twomey, Damien Mitchell.

Under-21 footballers, 2000: Cronan Dooley, Cyril Buggie, Fran O'Hare, Alan Barnes, Paul Casey, Alan Hurson, Thomas Cummins, Shane Russell, David Hickey, Stephen Speight, Kevin Corrigan, Tony Molton, Michael Moore, Michael Mooney, Alan O'Neill, Terence Smith, Kevin McGonigle, Donal Crowley, Niall McKiernan, Fergus Gordan, Maurice Wallace, Evan Kane, Niall Clifford, Eoin Ó Lanagáin, Gerry McGarry, Brian Percy, Darragh Walsh, Anthony Norton, Barry Doherty, Brian Griffin, David Brien, Stephen Shaughnessy, Aidan McKelvey, Emmet Farrilly.

Junior B footballers, 2000: Alan Hurson, Dave Cullen, Tony Molton, Eoin Ó Lanagáin, Alan Mooney, Kevin McCarthy, Fintan McCarthy, Jonathan Brien, Dave Brien, Stephen O'Brien, Andrew Hanley, Paul Gogarty, Ger Griffin, Brian Griffin, Niall McKiernan, Maurice Wallace, Alan Casey, Shane Casey, Mark Behan, Vincent Smith, James Buggle, Fergus Gordon, Stephen Speight, Alan O'Shea, Kevin O'Brien, Michael Moran, John Liddy, Paddy Keogh, Barry Kelly, Paul Horgan, Peter Horgan, J.J. Hegarty, Donal Crowley, Brian Clarke, Eddie Carroll, Donal Buckley, Dara Walsh, Stephen Shaughnessey, Shane Russell.

Junior camogie team, 2000: Lynn Flannery, Aideen Casey, Siobhán Ryan, Julie McGinley, Ailish McGarrigle, Marian Flynn, Edel O'Brien, Caroline Flynn, Patricia McGarrigle, Róisín Hayden, Caitriona Beirne, Marian Freeman, Gillian Flannery, Gráinne Ní Lanagáin, Emer Keenan, Audrey Murtagh, Frankie Andrews, Caitriona Doyle, Ann Ward, Heidi Doyle, Vivienne Ralph, Margaret Ryan.

Under-15 camogie team, 2000: Marian Flynn, Marie Golden, Debbie Corcoran, Fiona Doolin, Niamh Conboy, Carmel Kavanagh, Julie McGinley, Marie Fagan, Laura Kenny, Ciara Sloan, Anita O'Neill, Karen Kenny, Kerri Rapple, Emma Nealon, Louise Long, Emma Byrne, Emer Keenan, Louise Byrne, Aisling Toolin.

Junior A hurlers, 2000: Jerome Twomey, Brendan McGarry, Brian Fagan, Daragh Reidy, Tommy Somers, Fran Kearns, Cathal Corcoran, Daragh Brennan, Kevin Roche, the Cliffords, Ciarán O'Neill, Seán Quinn, Alan Glover, Pearse O'Leary, Alan O'Neill, Joey Byrne, Ger Power, Tomas Sealy, Stephen Murphy, Seán Corkery, Gerry McGarry, Tony Molton, Damien Mitchell.

Junior C hurlers, 2000: Brian Percy, Michael Mooney, Paul Clifford, Niall Clifford, Alan Barnes, Seán Corkery, Tony Molton, Pierce O'Leary, Barry Hurson, Mark Cristal, Seán Murphy, Paul Tobin, Brian Cooper, Gerrard Gregg, Dessie O'Brion, Fergus Gordon, John Clancy, Eoin Mullarkey, Jim Shelly, Thomas Sealy, Vincent O'Connor, Declan Gregg, Ian Fitzgerald, David Hurson, Darren McAuley, Emmet Farrelly, Richie McKenna, Donnie Dowling.

Ladies senior footballers, 2000: Lynn Coffey, Siobhan Donachie, Sinéad Coffey, Nicola Rock, Maeve McGuire, Antoinette O'Shea, Karin Bartelt, Aileen Quinn, Elena Griffin, Gillian Flannery, Yvonne McHugh, Gillian Ryan, Jackie Quinn, Tracey O'Brien, Audrey Murtagh, Trudy Keogh, Siobhan Casey, Patricia Gordon, Louise Heffernan, Lucia Gavin, Caitrin McGrath, Lynn Flannery, Anna McGillicuddy, Linda Tapley, Gillian Mulqueen, Maria McGrath.

Senior hurlers, 2000: V. Shanagher, D. Cunningham, J. Mills, N. Kelly, S. Clandillon, A. Nolan, P. Doyle, C. Dooley, D. Maher, B. Fagan, D. Carr, P. Lanigan, L. Bergin, S. Farrell, T. Clandillon, A. Mockler, D. Kelly, F. Clandillon, E. Ó Lanagáin, D. Lanigan, C. Sunderland, M. Burke, A. O'Neill, B. McGarry, T. Somers, G. McGarry, J. Byrne, J. Twomey, S. Quinn.

Junior B football championship winners, 2001: Dave Cullen, Kevin McCarthy, Alan Hurson, Paddy Kehoe, Shane Russell, Vinny Smith, Fergus Gordon, Alan Casey, Stephen Speight, Paddy Devaney, Donal Crowley, Shane Casey, Brian Griffin, Mark Behan, Maurice Wallace, Tony Moulton, Jimmy Buggle, Andy Hanley, Ger Griffin, Mark Moran, Brian Clarke, Dave Brien, Paul Gogarty, Fintan McCarthy, Alan Mooney, Stephne O'Brien, Tim Griffin, Eddie Carroll, Aidan McKelvey.

Under-10 Football, 2002/03: Michael Hughes, Eoin Hayes, Seán Lynch, Shane Donohue, Jason Yeomans, Shane Ryan, Karl Yeomans, Conn O'Donnagain, Craig Carabini, Gavin Carabini, Kevin Nolan, Mathew O'Byrne, Stephen Donoghue, Shane O'Neill, Jonathan Murray, Seán McLelland, Liam Keenan, Seán Keane, Daragh Byrne, Kevin Coakley, Jake Dunne, Liam Sweetman, David McCarthy, Seán Flynn, Jack Minihan, Carl McDermott.

Under-21A hurling championship finalists, 2002: Ger Gleeson, Johnny McCaffrey, Aidan Glover, Jerome Twomey, Dave Corrigan, Brendan McGarry, Tommy Somers, Kevin Roche, Seán Quinn, Alan O'Neill, Aaron Dunne, Ciarán O'Neill, Daragh Brennan, Dara Reidy, James Mulhern, Ger Twohig, Damien Mitchell, Cian Fleming, Kevin O'Reilly, Ger Power, Brian Bergin, Keith Brennan, Pearse O'Leary, Paddy Mulhern, Andrew Duff and Joe Byrne.

Junior C hurling, 2002/03: Fran Kearns, Tom Sealy, Seán Murphy, Pat Hennessy, Damien Duggan, Jim Shelley, Seán Corkery, Michael Mooney, Mark Regan, Seamus Loughnane, Mark O'Dwyer, Brian Percy, Stephen Murphy, Tony Moulton, Gerard

Twohig, Brian Bergin, Barry Cuff, Trevor McCarr, Barry McCormack, Alan Clarke, John Collins, Peter Nealon, Gerard Cooper.

Under-13 A footballers, 2003/04: Ben Egan, Simon Collins, Raymond Dowling, Kevin Doyle, Rory Kelly, Brian Long, Kieran McHugh, Brian Mullarkey, Niall Smith, Declan Weldon, Stephen Garbutt, Bill Malone, David Courtney, Noel Larkin, Conor Toolin, Barry Torsney, Andrew Malone, Thomas Collender, Robert McNulty, Seán Mulhern, Conor Murphy, Glenn O'Neill.

Junior C hurlers, 2004: Philip Corcoran, Declan Shaughnesy, Donal O'Neill, Enda Tucker, Peter Nealon, Gavin Foley, Fran Kearns, Tom Ronan, Tom Sealy, Marin Burke, Tony Molton, Peter Duff, John Collins, Barry McCormack, Aaron Dunne, Tom Farrell, Ger Cooper, Pierce O'Leary, Mick Farrington, Dave Corrigan, David Mescall, Damien Mitchell, Gavin Reidy, Seán Murphy, Seán Corkery, Mick Mooney, Diarmuid O'Connor, Jim Shelly, Richie Walsh, Martin Foran.

Under-14 hurlers, 2005: Seán Mulhern, Simon O'Keeffe, Niall Smith, Ciarán Byrne, Afees Ilesanmi, Brian Mullarkey, Pavlo Romanachuk, Sujon Amalgir, Stephen Garbutt, Brian Long, Bill Malone, Barry Torsney, Rob McNulty, Ben Egan, Eoin Brennan, James O'Connor, Seán McNicholas, Simon Collins.

Under-14A footballers, 2005: Ben Egan, Eoin Brennan, Thomas Collinder, Simon Collins, Brian Long, Brian Mullarkey, Pavlo Romanachuk, Niall Smith, Ciarán McHugh, Lauranc Alia, Bill Malone, Stephen Garbutt, Sujon Alamgir, Rory Kell, Barry Torsney, David Courtney, Rob McNulty, Conor Murphy, Elvis Kucuk, Callum Sally, Conor Toolin, Glen O'Neill, James O'Connor, Andy Malone.

Under-14B football, 2005: Wayne Nolan, Seán McNicholas Declan Weldon, Simon O'Keeffe, Darragh Kennedy, Colin Byrne, Ian Brogan, Ciarán Byrne, Afees Ilesanmi, Stephen Mahady, Michael Duncan, Dylan Payne, Matthew Tuite, Noel Larkin, Colin Byrne, S. McNicholas, Neal Morrin, Ger Walsh, Eoin Brennan, Kevin McBride.

Minor A hurlers championship winners 2005: Owen Quinn, Gearóid Brennan, Paddy Brennan, Cathal Rochford, Eamonn Comaskey, Peter Callaghan, Peter Carroll, Peter Kelly, Aaron Doonan, Andrew Mockler, Shane O'Neill, John Byrne, Niall Gleeson, Mick May, Alan Whyte, Eoin McCarthy, Johnny McCaffrey, David Quinn, Kevin O'Reilly, Aidan Roche, Naoise Fleming, Gary Coleman, Robert Smith

Under-15 football, 2006: Sujon Alamgir, Laurence Alia, Ian Brogan, Ciarán Byrne, Simon Collins, David Courtney, Bryan Creed, Stephen Garbutt, Shane Hennessy, Afees Ilesanmi, Rory Kelly, Elvis Kucuk, Brian Long, Bill Malone, Kevin Mc Bride, Ciarán McHugh, Rob McNulty, Seán Mulhern, Brian Mullarkey, Conor Murphy, Darra Mylod, Simon O'Keeffe, Barry Torsney, Callum Sally, Niall Smith, Pavlo Romanachuk.

Minor footballers, 2006: Aidan Roche, Mark Beegan, Dan Brady, Adam Byrne, John Byrne, Eoghan Carabini, Peter Carroll, Brian Collopy, Chris Dunne, Conor Downes, Dermot Gallagher, Niall Gleeson, Gareth Hamilton, Alan Hardiman, David Hayes, Dean Hickey, Andrew Hope, Owen Hughes, Brian Kealy, Peter Kelly, Colm Larkin,

Michael May, John McCormack, Keith Moran, Jake Murphy, Gary Norton, Brendan O'Shaughnessy, David Quinn, Robert Smyth, Alan Whyte.

Under-21 A football championship winners, 2006: J. Fahy; D. Quinn, M. Twomey, D. Shaughnessy; D. Gallagher, J. McCaffrey, M. Kirwan; P. Callaghan, A. O'Neill; A. Hope, E. Fitzgerald, B. Gallagher; M. May, P. Kelly, N. Gleeson. D. Gallagher, Fiachra McGrath, M. May.

Under-15 B football championship winners, 2007: David O'Sullivan, Gearóid Markey, Liam McClelland, Alan Parsons, Lorenc Alia, Bryan Creed, Thomas Jackman, Seán Stapleton, Shane Donohue, Matthew McCaffrey, Daragh Harte, Oisin McCabe, Peter McCabe, Seán Clancy, Seán McClelland, Conor Hayes, Emmett Ó Conghaile, Eoin Casey, Eoin Gray, Owen Ennis, Donie Geheran.

Under-16 footballers, 2007: Barry Torsney, Darra Mylod, Bill Malon, David Courtney, Bryan Creed, Elvis Kucuk, Brian Mullarkey, Ian Brogan, Ciarán Byrne, Kevin McBride, Ciarán McHugh, Lawrence Alia, Conor Murphy, Mathew Tuite, Conor Toolin, Niall Smith, Pavlo Romanachuk, Rory Kelly, Seán Mulhern, Seán Newcombe, Shane Hennessy, Simon O'Keeffe, Stephen Garbutt, Sujon Alamgir.

Minor hurlers, 2007: Maurice Ryan, Liam Ruane, Paul Tansey, Keith Masterson, Eoghan Carabini, Peter Kelly, Colm Larkin, Kevin Fitzgerald, Anto Lee, Barry Torsney, David Quinn, Gareth Hamilton, Sujon Alamgir, Alan Whyte, Dermot Gallagher, Darragh Kinsella, Darragh Quinn, Will Garbutt, Rob Lester, Wesley Redmond, Ollie Collins, Neil Ryan, Jimmy Comaskey.

Minor A footballers, 2007: Adam Behan, Dan Brady, Eoghan Carabini, Brian Collopy, David Courtney, Kevin Fitzgerald, Dermot Gallagher, Stephen Garbutt, William Garbutt, Gareth Hamilton, Dean Hickey, Brian Kealy, Peter Kelly, Darragh Kinsella, Andrew Kirwan, Colm Larkin, Anthony Lee, John Mc Cormack, Keith Moran, Conor Murphy, Jake Murphy, David Quinn, Brendan O'Shaughnessy, Barry Torsney, Alan Whyte.

Under-11 camogie, 2008: Charlotte Rooney, Laura O'Mahoney, Sadhbh Byrne, Ciara Casey, Jane Doran, Amy Gorman, Tara Farmer, Eimear Murray, Jenny Ryan, Courtney Clarke, Niamh Murray, Sarah Boland, Gabrielle Sommers, Lorna Reville, Holly Smith, Sharon O'Sullivan, Julie Lang, Orla Carroll.

U-14 camogie, All-Ireland Féile Division 1 champions, Dublin Division 1 league and championship winners, 2008: Ailish O'Grady, Gráinne Rochford, Grace Mulhern, Niamh Williams, Sarah Courtney, Ali Twomey, Tara Keenan, Lucy Mulligan, Siobhan Grimes, Lynsey Jordan, Laura Murtagh, Aoife Dodrill, Sarah Muldoon, Ailbhe Ryan, Kate Whyte, Ciara Sheehan, Ailise Dowling, Rachael Kenny, Claire Rigney, Anne Marie Courtney, Shannon Clarke, Juliette Sejean, Anna Ryan, Lauren Malone, Laura Morrissey, Orla Beagan.

Under-21 A hurling championship winners, 2008: David Quinn, John Byrne, Peter Callaghan, Paul Tansey, Mick May, John McCaffrey, Niall Gleeson, Garry Coleman, Kevin Fitzgerald, Kevin O'Reilly, Peter Carroll, Peter Kelly, Aidan Roche, Alan Whyte,

Paddy Brennan, Eoin Carabini, Dermot Gallagher, Matthew McCaffrey, Colm Larkin, Robert Lester, Aaron Doonan, Anthony Lee.

Junior D ladies football championship winners, 2008: Ann O'Shaughnessy, Tracy Burke, Cliona McDonald, Michelle Kelly, Katie Dillon, Hannah Muldowney, Niamh Malone, Niamh Nolan, Ellen Downes, Lisa Heavey, Siobhan O'Neill, Leanne Behan, Elaine Twomey, Lorraine Moran, Helena O'Toole, Imelda Smith, Aishling O'Farrell, Amy Martin, Laura Murtagh, Deirdre Dee, Emma Cooney.

Under-15 A camogie championship winners, 2009: Sarah Courtney, Siobhan Grimes, Tara Keenan, Grace Mulhern, Ailish O'Grady, Orla Beagan, Anne Marie Courtney, Amber O'Connor, Niamh Byrne, Gráinne Rochford, Ali Twomey, Aoife Dodrill, Lynsey Jordan, Kate Whyte, Claire Rigney, Ailbhe Ryan, Ciara Sheehan, Ailise Dowling, Shannon Clarke, Sarah Galvin, Rachael Kenny, Lauren Malone, Laura Murtagh.

Under 14B camogie Féile Division 3 winners, 2009: Grace O'Shea, Sarah Galvin, Isabelle Fagan, Deirdre Stapleton, Laura Connelly, Emma Flannery, Elaine McClelland, Claire D'Arcy, Rachel Leonard, Orla Whelan, Maura Madigan, Caitríona Ryan, Holly Walsh, Marissa Britton, Cianna Ryan-Lynch, Aisling McHugh, Jenny Foy, Róisín Reid, Aoife Reynolds, Clodagh Flanagan. Manager: Bill Ryan.

Under-15 B camogie, 2009: Bronagh Coakley, Laura Moore, Emer Maloney, Ellen DeSay, Nianh Kelly, Louise Gibson, Rachel Meehan, Isobel Fagan, Aoife McElwee, Rachel Walsh Lilly Wang, Naomi Feighery, Ellen Fahy, Laura Greally, Tega and Anisha.

Junior C Ladies football championship winners, 2009: Maeve Maguire, Imelda Smith, Hannah Muldowney, Amy Martin, Tracey Burke, Laura Murtagh, Niamh Malone, Sarah Maloney, Ellen Downes, Emma Cooney, Lorraine Moran, Leanne Behan, Elaine Twomey, Caoimh Moran, Lisa Heavey, Niamh Nolan, Emer Moloney, Helena O'Toole, Cliona McDonell, Niamh Nolan, Lorna Sexton, Katie McCormack, Emma Moore, Dena Jones, Holly Moore, Emma Day, Cliona Flynn.

Minor A footballers, 2009: Alan Parsons, Barry Torsney, Brian Mullarkey, Bryan Creed, Chris Crummy, Ciarán McHugh, Conor Murphy, Dara Mylod, David Courtney, Emmett Ó Conghaile, James Cavanagh, Kevin McBride, Laurence Alia, Matthew McCaffrey, Matthew Tuite, Niall Smith, Owen Ennis, Robert Dent, Rory Kelly, Seán Newcombe, Shane Donoghue, Shane Hennessy, Simon Collins, Stephen Garbutt.

Under-14B camogie team, 2010: Ayobami Akinse, Dayna Barry, Olwen Dent, Isobel Digby, Fiona Dowler, Rebecca Geraty, Eimear Hayes, Megan Irwin, Jenny Kavanagh, Nadia McDonagh, Hannah Morrin, Aoife O'Brien, Jessica O'Leary, Stephanie Reilly, Caitriona Ryan, Jane Doran, Laura O'Mahony, Eimear Murray, Maebh Dowler.

Under-15A camogie team, 2010: Orla Beagan, Niamh Byrne, Ellen Cavanagh, Aoife Clancy, Shannon Clarke, Anne Marie Courtney, Ailise Dowling, Rachel Kenny, Laura Morrissey, Lauren Malone, Aoife Flynn, Clodagh Flanagan, Amber O'Connor, Sinéad O'Keeffe, Juliette Sejean, Claire Rigney, Ailbhe Ryan, Jenny Ryan, Ciara Sheehan, Kate Whyte.

Under-16 A camogie championship winners, 2010: Laura Murtagh, Ailish O'Grady, Lauren Malone, Kate Whyte, Rachael Kenny, Siobhan Grimes, Lynsey Jordan, Emer Maloney, Niamh Byrne, Ailbhe Ryan, Niamh Berry, Ailise Dowling, Claire Rigney, Ali Twomey, Ciara Sheehan, Sarah Courtney, Tara Keenan, Laura Morrissey, Orla Beagan, Aoife Dodrill, Gráinne Rochford, Amber O'Connor, Shannon Clarke, Anne Marie Courtney.

Under-14 ladies footballers, 2010: Danielle Carroll, Ellen King, Millie Grogan, Fiona Dowler, Sabrina Maloney, Cliodhna Jones (Capt.), Sophie Flanagan, Meadh Dowler, Eimer Murray, Samra Kulijancic, Shauna Kinsella, Orla Moloney, Niamh Farrelly, Kellie Crowe, Clare Allen, Rachel Leonard, Rachel Cosgrove, Jane McDonald, Katie Redmond, Niamh Murray, Rachel O'Neill

Under-9 hurlers, 2010: Niall Murray, Colm Behan, Daragh Reid, Danial Coogan, Luke Gearty, Robert Moloney, Luke Finnerty, Cathal Shanahan, Liam O'Connor, Ben Mullins, Rory Maguire, Finan Breen, Dylan Kelly, Jake Rooney, Nathan Browne, Jamie O'Neill, Brian O'Sullivan, Conor Danials, Luke Neville, Mark Daly, Alex Hanley, Matthew Dunne, Philip Kane, Conor Tighe, Adam McGarry, Cian Buckley, Conal Chambers, Cian Leavy, Daragh Byrne, David Robutu, Eoin Reddan, Jack Lawlor, Jordan Joseph, Kingsley Okarpu, Mark Lavin.

Under-16 hurlers, 2010: Iftakhar Alamhir, Niall Stagg, Larry Jordan, Alan Flanagan, Daire Hassett, Seánie McClelland, Dan Furness, Philip Smith, Rory Fleming, Conor Cuggy, Robbie Madden, Stephen Jones, Ciarán Carbury, James Hallissey, Brian Mahon, Mark Condon, Seán Breen, John Bellew, Cian Torsney, Seán Ryan, Conor Moran.

Under-12A footballers, 2010: Harry Ladd, Michael Robinson, Ciarán Smith, Colum Rogers, Ciarán Dowling, Jack Monahan, Conor Heffernan, Daniel Forde, Declan Kelly, Donal Keane, Evan Lombard, Colm Keenan, Luke Murphy, Luke Maguire, Rory Stapleton, Ross Ward, Seán Copley, Seán Foley, Paul Claffey, Jack Kellighan.

Under-12B football, 2010: Adam Cramp, Adam Finnerty, Aidan O'Driscoll, Caomhan Ó Conghaile, Charlie Rowe, Dean Davis, Dylan Cannon, Eoin Burke, Eoin Byrne, Eoin Tighe, Eric Neville, Evan Rooney, Jack Shannon, James Loftus, Matthew O'Donovan, Paul O'Grady, Rian Daly, Robert Tyrell, Seán Kelly, Seán O'Se Kelly, Seán Townsend, Stephen Dowling, Tom McCauley.

Minor footballers, 2010: Alan Parsons, Brian Creed, Chris Crummy, Daire Harte, Daire Hassett, Dara Mylod, David Bellew, Emmett Ó Conghaile, Eoghan Cregan, Gavin Carabini, Graham Fay, James Cavanagh, Laurence Alia, Mathew McCaffrey, Matthew Connaughton, Oisin McCabe, Owen Ennis, Owen Gray, Rory Downes, Seán Newcombe, Shane Hennessy, Stephen Jones.

Under-21 A football championship winners, 2010: Aidan Elliot, Alan Whyte, Andy Kirwan (captain), Barry Torsney, Brendan O'Shaugnessy, Brian Collopy, Bryan Creed, Chris Crummy, Ciaran McHugh, Colm Larkin, Darragh Kinsella, Darragh Mylod, David Quinn, Dermot Gallagher, Emmett Ó Conghaile, Eoghan Carabini, John McCormack, Keith Moran, Kevin Fitzgerald, Kevin McBride, Laurence Alia,

Matt McCaffrey, Niall Smith, Ollie Collins, Owen Ennis, Peter Kelly, Sean Newcombe, Shane Hennessy, Simon Collins, Stephen Garbutt, Will Garbutt.

Under-14 All-Ireland Féile camogie Division 1 winners, 2010: Emer Murray, Amy Gorman, Ciara Casey, Rachael Leonard, Daena Barry, Tara Farmer, Orla Beagan, Laura Morrissey, Orla Moloney, Niamh Power, Jenny Ryan, Maeve Ward, Sarah Boland, Charlotte Rooney, Ruth Mulligan, Aoife Greene, Cisca Deveroux, Aoife Flynn, Anne Marie Courtney, Rhona Downes, Amy Conroy, Aoife Clancey, Amber O'Connor Niamh Byrne.

Minor A camogie championship winners, 2010: K. Whyte, A. Dowling, S. Grimes, C. Sheehan, E. Downes, R. Kenny, A. Ryan, M. Kelly, C. Rigney, A. Martin, L. Murtagh, T. Keenan, S. Courtney, N. Berry, A. Towmey, A. O'Grady, L. Jordan, C. Flynn, M. Moynihan, L. Sexton, E. Moloney, S. Clarke, L. Malone.

LUCAN TRUE AND TRUE

Verse 1

I'm from the town drenched in football and rain,
That fathered the terrible twins.
Kevin Cummins, our barman, was a footballer/singer,
Retired and spread his wide wings.
Where the Spa once buzzing with shifts and refusals,
Stands silent, dejected and old.
Where we played games of hurlin' for a longer duration
Than anywhere else in the world.

Chorus

Well I'm Lucan true and true,
Lucan I love you.
We've a rock-solid spirit
That'll never be broken.
We've songs to be sung
And we've words to be spoken.
From the town that was built
Where the Liffey just opens.
And no matter where you're from
Everyone's local.
I'm Lucan true and true,
Lucan I love you.

Verse 2

'Tis where we'd spend all our weekends to help pass the winter
In the alley above in the Lock.
Or we'd travel away for a match into Dublin,
Phoenix Park or out in Blackrock.
They'd be calling us culchies, the boys inner-city,
But I didn't care what they called me.
Just blank it I'll rise it again for the New Year,
Chappie still never knew what to call me!

Verse 3

Here in our town Patrick Sarsfield once reigned,
With the wisdom of ages gone by.
We had an old cinema that ran down by the Weir,
It's been dwarfed by apartments in white.
Where the travellers are settling, the settled gone travelling,
The pubs full of gossip and rumour.
You'll never better my people of Lucan
For their power, passion, packets and humour.

Adapted (from 'All the Way From Tuam' by the Saw Doctors) and most notably performed by Cronan Dooley.

CLUB CHAIRMEN

1935 - 1942: Tom Slattery
1954 - 1958: Billy Kelly
1962: Don Dardis
1966 - 1969: Jack O'Brien
1980: Cha O'Connor
1989 - 1992: Paddy Kelly
2000 - 2002: Gerry McAndrew
2008 - 2010: Paul Stapleton

1943 - 1949: Frank Brophy
1959: Jack Collins
1963 - 1964: Jack O'Brien
1970 - 1974: Billy Malone
1981 - 1985: Padraig McGarrigle
1993 - 1998: Billy Gogarty
2003 - 2005: Paul McGann
2011- Sean Ó Conghaile

1950 - 1953: Billy Malone
1960 - 1961: Billy Kelly
1965: Peadar Condron
1975 - 1979: Mick Molloy
1986 - 1988: Billy Gogarty
1998 - 2000: Shay Hurson
2006 - 2007: Mick Roche

CLUB SECRETARY

1943 - 1948: Eamon Moffett
1959: Don Dardis
1980: Una McCaffrey
1991 - 1992: Mick Mulhall
2000 - 2001: Ailish McGarrigle
2008: -Alice Whyte

1949 - 1956: Don Dardis
1960 - 1968: Tom Higgins
1981 - 1985: Billy Gogarty
1993 - 1998: Livinus Smith
2002 - 2004: Mick Roche
2009 - 2011: Derek Quilligan

1957 - 1958: Tom Higgins
1969 - 1979: Billy Gogarty
1986 - 1990: Joan Fitzharris
1998 - 2000: Gillian Ryan
2005 - 2007: Paul Stapleton

CLUB PERSON OF THE YEAR

1982: Paddy Kelly
1985: Billy Gogarty
1988: Tony Strong
1991: Mick Molloy
1994: Anne Carton
1997: Hugh McNulty
2000: Mick Roche
2003: Kathleen Roche
2006: Liam Ryan
2009: Pat O'Keeffe

1983: Seán McCaffrey
1986: Jim Quinn
1989: Liam Carton
1992: Jim McCarthy
1995: Peter Flannery
1998: Gerry McNamara
2001: Willie O'Neill
2004: Ronan O'Flynn
2007: Paul McGann
2010: Eoghan Williams

1984: Joan Fitzharris
1987: Seamus Clandillon
1990: Paul Heneghan
1993: Shay Hurson
1996: Seaghan Ó Lanagáin
1999: Gerry McAndrew
2002: Fergal Walsh
2005: Alice Whyte
2008: Josephine Donohue

HALL OF FAME AWARD

1994: Peadar Condron
1997: Tommy Malone
2000: Mick Mulhall
2003: Padraig McGarrigle
2006: Hugh McNulty
2009: Eddie Waters

1995: Tommy McCormack
1998: Mick Molloy
2001: Sean Walsh
2004: Jim McCarthy
2007: Paul Heneghan
2010: Mick Casey Snr

1996: Don Dardis
1999: Billy Gogarty
2002: Bob Dardis
2005: Seamus Clandillon
2008: Dinny Malone